The Buddha's Radical Psychology: Explorations

The Buddha's path to serenity, wisdom and happiness

Rodger R. Ricketts

Callisto Green

Published in 2016 by
Callisto Green
4 Caprice Close
Swindon
SN5 5TB

www.callistogreen.com

© 2016 Rodger R. Ricketts

A copy of the CIP entry for this book is available from the British Library.

ISBN 978 1 909985 19 3

This book is dedicated to those teachers who have taught me not only the significance of psychology but also the deep teachings of the Buddha, and to the fellow aspirants who have participated with me in searching for and following the path set forth by the Buddha.

Also, thank you to my wife and my family for their support during the writing of this book. My sincere hope is that this work facilitates future discussions concerning the relevance of the radical psychology as set forth in the Buddha's teachings, and also aid in the reduction of suffering in the world.

About the Author

Rodger R. Ricketts, Psy.D. is a clinical psychologist and mindfulness meditation teacher. He has been studying Buddhism for over thirty years, both as part of his own personal quest and also in the application of its principles as a therapeutic tool in psychotherapy. Rodger has given numerous presentations at wellness and professional psychological conferences on the topics of cognitive psychology, mindfulness and  wellbeing. Rodger continues his study of both science and Buddhism, and maintains a regular meditation practice.

Acknowledgements

I want to thank LoveInTranslation PM for their excellent editing, as well as Callisto Green's professional editing and publishing services, and Wolfram Schommers, Mae Wan Ho and Sue Hamilton for their past supportive comments. Also, I thank my old time meditation friend, Steve Bartlett, for giving me insightful suggestions regarding the clarification of text in this book.

Contents

Preface xi

Chapter 1

Introduction.. 1

Chapter 2

Self/No-Self 7

Chapter 3

Self as Construction..23

Chapter 4

The Human Being as a Collective, Unified Unit..................35

Chapter 5

*Awakening and Enlightenment: Psychological Transformation
and Transcendence* 61

Chapter 6

Enlightenment: Reality, Actuality and Transcendence..........73

Chapter 7

Knowing and Not Knowing – What is Possible? 81

Chapter 8

The General Doctrine of the Law of Dependent Co-arising.99

Chapter 9

Kamma.. 109

Chapter 10

Sense of Agency.. 119

Chapter 11

Agency Labelled as Self.. 129

Chapter 12

Dividing Existence – Duality...143

Chapter 13

Language Construction of Duality 163

Chapter 14

Identification... 181

Chapter 15

The Buddha's Compassion 197

Chapter 16

Memory 207

Chapter 17

The Unconscious 227

Chapter 18

Habits 243

Chapter 19

Cognitive Biases 253

Chapter 20

Meta-cognition and Mindfulness 267

Chapter 21

Automatic Influences on our Actions and Perceptions 277

Chapter 22

Organisms as Coherent Embedded Systems 299

Chapter 23

Happiness 379

Chapter 24

The World without a 'Self' 391

Chapter 25

Closing Thoughts.. 405

Appendix A

Explanation of the effects of stress on the different systems of the human body...411

Appendix B

Special experiences 415

'The fundamental teachings of Gautama, as it is now being made plain to us by study of original sources, is clear and simple and in the closest harmony with modern ideas. It is beyond all disputes the achievementof one of the most penetrating intelligences the world has ever known. Buddhism has done more for the advance of world civilization and true culture than any other influence in the chronicles of mankind.'

H. G. Wells

'Why are you unhappy?
Because 99.9 percent
Of everything you think,
And of everything you do,
Is for yourself –
And there isn't one.'

Wei Wu Wei

Preface

The Buddha took his doctrines seriously and hopes we will too.

My aim in writing this book is to explore, from a modern psychological and biological perspective, what the Buddha was telling us. The ancient text and the modern point of view both complement and clarify each other. I see there is much to be learnt through a comparative approach, while at the same time keeping the Buddha's original doctrines at the core of the discussion. This approach unveils a unique and cogent perspective that incorporates the traditional Buddhist teachings with the research and study of modern scholars and scientists. Therefore, this book goes beyond what is usually taught in traditional Buddhist as well as comparative psychology texts.

At this point I want to add a caveat that it is beyond the scope and purpose of this book to delve extensively into the ever-evolving complexities of theory and research in cognitive science and the other scientific disciplines that I quote herein. Nevertheless, what I do present in this book are the current thoughts and research of some of the most respected and contemporary thinkers in their fields. I recommend the reader delve further into the works of the authors cited to explore their fascinating ideas.

In my over 30 years of study, reflection and meditation experience in Buddhism, I have noticed that the teachings of the Buddha are often shrouded in a mystical or esoteric point of view which, I believe, obscures the original intention of the Buddha. This book will show that the Buddha's teachings are best understood as a psychology in which the mind is the prime mover for the transformation and wisdom needed for the culmination of insight development – Awakening or Enlightenment.

Buddha maintained that the experience of Enlightenment was the ultimate phenomenological foundation of both the self and the world, while dening that an authentic self existed. Once we stop focusing on our illusionary virtual reality of a self, an amazingly complex, dynamic and interrelated world appears to us 'as it is'. The Buddha's systematic Eightfold Path is a concise and clear plan showing how to proceed to reach the goal of *Nibbāna*, or Enlightenment, returning us to knowing our 'original mind'. This book will explain in a psychological perspective how we can understand better the Buddha's doctrine and succiently apply it into our contemporary culture.

1

Introduction

'As soon as we cease to regard Buddha's teachings simply intellectually and acquiesce with a certain sympathy in the age-old Eastern concept of unity, if we allow Buddha to speak to us as vision, as image, as the awakened one, the perfect one, we find him as a great prototype of mankind. The intellectual content of Buddha's teaching is only half his work, the other half is his life, his life as lived, as labour accomplished and action carried out. A training, a spiritual self-training of the highest order was accomplished and is taught here, a training about which unthinking people who talk about "quietism" and "Hindu dreaminess" and the like in connection with Buddha have no conception.'

Mahatma Gandhi

'...that first drew me to the world of Buddhist thought but my professional interest as a doctor. My task was to treat psychic suffering and it was this that impelled me to become acquainted with the views and methods of that great teacher of humanity, whose principal theme was the chain of suffering, old age, sickness and death.'

Carl Jung

Over 2500 years ago there was a prince named Siddhartha Gautama, who achieved after an intensive seven-year psychological quest the title Buddha – meaning *Awakened One*. With his awakening, the Buddha discovered the answer to the question of what creates suffering. To be *awakened* means to have been 'woken up to reality', to see reality as it is, not as we want it to be. We understand that our dis-ease and dissatisfaction in life is not created so much by external conditions, but by our cognitive apparatus, which easily creates psychological myopia, misperceptions, obsessions, cravings, anger, bias and prejudices. Through our own mental training we can end the cause of our suffering. This insight, experienced as the Buddha sat under the Bodhi tree on a full-moon night, was a unique psychological epiphany, which forever changed his life, and has continued to change millions of other people's lives. The Buddha's insights and teachings remain radically cogent and inspiring. In fact, the Buddha remains one of the most original and profound thinkers to have graced the earth.

The focus of this book is on exploring the links between Buddhist teachings and modern psychology in a mutually illuminating way. Even though the Buddha taught over 2500 years ago, his insights are being supported by the newest discoveries in psychology, biology and other branches of science. Whilst Western mainstream academia typically understands Buddhism as a religion or a philosophy, the teachings of the Buddha are not in fact, a religious doctrine (religion defined as the belief in or the worship of a god or gods). The Buddha did not endorse a god or external agency that interfered in the lives of living beings, nor did he encourage or endorse the metaphysically sacred or divine. According to the Dona sutta, the Buddha's answer when asked the question, 'Are you a god?' was, 'No, Brahman, I am not a god.'

And after answering several more questions he ended by saying, 'Remember me, Brahman, as *awakened.*'

Whilst the Buddha was alive, his followers never worshipped or made statues of him. Instead, the earliest and most common symbols of Buddhism, like the lotus flower or the dhamma wheel, were used as representations of his teachings. Throughout his teachings, the Buddha attributed all of humankind's attainments, achievements, and foibles to human effort and human understanding, or the lack thereof. He established a method of ethical and psychological training that leads to a complete psychological freedom of the mind.

This book explores how the Buddha's teachings offer to the world of psychology and psychotherapy significant and groundbreaking (yet not unfamiliar) perspectives and solutions to many of the most pressing psychological and social difficulties in the human condition. Although the Buddha never completed a scientific theory of personality (he wasn't a scientist) there are striking similarities, as well as several significant underlying differences, between modern Western psychology's analysis of a human being's personality and the early Buddhist view. In fact, the Buddha's teachings and original suttas are best understood as a sophisticated psychological doctrine with very rich psychological concepts.

In this work, the term 'psychology' is defined as 'the study of mind and behaviour'. Psychological knowledge forms an essential part of the training for experiencing the definitive goal of Buddhism – nibbana (nirvana). Detailed ongoing personal psychological analysis is one of the main purposes of meditation.

Even as the Buddha's teachings have become better known and analysed in Western societies, many academic psychologists still generally perceive the Buddha's fundamental teachings as being irrelevant or inappropriate as a study in psychology. Nevertheless, in the past 50 years some attempts have been made to bridge and integrate clinical psychology, such as psychoanalysis and other schools of psychotherapy, with Buddhism. These attempts, however, have viewed Buddhism through the lens of Western psychology, with much of the significance of the Buddha's original and radical message having been lost or obscured as a consequence.

Therefore, it is not my intent here to use Western psychological and biological concepts to assimilate the Buddha's original perspective into an already preconceived Western psychological theory, but to illuminate both, and thereby enhance the understanding of each. The Buddha's teachings are profound, unique and revolutionary in their understanding of human psychology, and have in many ways foreshadowed modern psychology – this book endeavors to explore these connections.

The Three Universal Truths

In the Buddha's teachings there are three core concepts, often called *The Three Universal Truths:*

Anicca – The law of impermanence asserts that all phenomena are always in a process of existing, in constant flux, co-rising and falling at different complexities.

Dukkha – The law of dukkha states that the unenlightened experience suffering, since the origin of suffering lies in one's egotistical psychological perspective, creating craving (binding, sense-based and selfish), which is in the final analysis insatiable, stressful, insufficient and un-quenchable.

Anatta – The third law states that no fixed essence or no permanent self, ego or soul in phenomena exists. There is no self.

It is evident that these three fundamental concepts are interrelated. Here, I aim to explain how these and other core teachings of the Buddha create a significant radical understanding and perspective for us and our world today. As the Buddha's teachings are psychologically based, they are therefore explained here within that framework. I will highlight this remarkable teaching in relation to many academic disciplines, including the study of psychology, psychobiology, biology, ecopsychology, evolutionary psychology and wellbeing.

The Buddha's teachings directly challenge the very notion of an independent, inherently existent self and therefore offers a groundbreaking perspective for the understanding of human nature, our motivation, and how we create our own pain and suffering as well as our own happiness. Of course, due to the multi-dimensionality of the teachings, these vital insights offered here are not the only that are possible, but I believe that any insights which are gained to be well worth any effort.

Extensive translation, discussions or excerpts from the original texts will not be found here – instead, the reader will be presented with selective and appropriately well-thought-out translations and suttas, based on scholars interpretations, for ease of reading and clarity of the presentation of the Buddha's teachings. This interpretation breaks new ground in the application of the Buddha's teachings in psychology and I sincerely hope that through this reading, a new, relevant understanding of how human beings can suffer less and be happier will continue to emerge.

2

Self/No-Self

'We are but whirlpools in a river of ever-flowing water. We are not stuff that abides, but patterns that perpetuate themselves.'

Norbert Wiener

'Body is not self, feelings are not self, perception is not self, mental constructs are not self and consciousness is not self...When one sees this one becomes detached from these things, being detached the passions fade, when the passions have faded one is free, and being free one knows one is free.'

Samyutta Nikaya 3.66

After many intense years of study and bhavana, or mental development, the Buddha, sitting under the Bodhi tree on the night of a full moon, experienced a remarkable insight. He realised that all observable phenomena are dynamic, subject to constant change, to co-rising and ceasing, and that there are no permanent beginnings or end states, physical or mental. Everything changes; there is no fixed *essence* or ultimate nature, only a process of becoming (Anicca). Likewise, there is no static, permanent self or soul, only a continuously evolving pattern.

This seemingly simple perspective has profound implications. According to the Buddha's teachings, when we draw arbitrary distinctions between a self and the environments in which we live, our actions become distorted by self-centeredness. Frustration and suffering (dukkha) are the inevitable consequences. By contrast, when the self is correctly understood to be a cognitive construction – a representation, many of the (supposedly essential) *problems* of life lose their urgency and emotional strain. But, by taking the Buddha's perspective, we can revolutionise our understanding of what we call our *self*, and our interpretation of the world around us.

Our journey towards developing a comprehension of the Buddha's teachings begins with an examination of the definition of the *self*. Western conceptions of the self and their historical roots will be discussed and contrasted against the Buddha's doctrine of non-self (anatta).

Contemporary Western Self

In Western cultures, the word *self* is usually taken to refer to a unique, inherent, core identity at the centre of each person. The Western belief in the sense of self is deeply entrenched in popular, scientific and philosophical traditions. In Western culture, the reality of an authentic self is normally taken entirely for granted. From when we first begin to understand and use language as infants, and continuing throughout one's life, the use of words such as 'I', 'me', and 'mine' reinforces the ideas of individuality and independence. This in turn shapes how we explain the world and our place within it.

To better understand how we typically think about the self, it may be helpful to begin with some current definitions of self, which reflect the prevailing Western cultural view.

- The total, essential, or particular being of a person.[1]
- '...when we describe a "self" usual core conceptions include: an individualistic self that is very aware of itself, its uniqueness, sense of purpose, will it is at the center of an individual's psychological world.'[2]
- 'The self is always on center stage, and the world is judged and evaluated by and through it. Also, the self and other are sharply demarcated: the self is a distinct entity and has an identity unique from other selves and all other things. The self "belongs" to the individual who is its sole owner and who has a sense of personal control of it which is thought essential to maintaining a strong, healthy self. It is believed that in a healthy state, the self is stable, it is coherent and integrated. Rooted in individualism, the Western self is, in short, the measure of all things.'[3]
- The self includes, 'Specific psychological boundaries, an internal locus of control, and a wish to manipulate the external world for its own personal ends.'[4]
- Underlying Western self-conceptions are presuppositions asserting: (a) a subject–object distinction; (b) a self–other demarcation and individual identity; and (c) the centrality and sovereignty of selfhood. *Sampson* (1988)

From these definitions, it is clear that the self includes being essential, bounded, sovereign, the measure of all things, and distinct. An understanding of the elemental nature of the concept of the inherent static self, or I, in our modern Western culture can begin to be developed. To further illustrate this, here are a few famous quotes from an almost endless list of sources by modern writers extolling the individualistic self:

- 'I care for myself. The more solitary, the more friendless, the more un-sustained I am, the more I will respect myself.' *Charlotte Brontë*

- 'From where I'm sitting, I AM the centre of the Universe!' *Sebastyne Young*

- 'And now I see the face of God, and I raise this God over the earth, this God whom men have sought since men came into being, this God who will grant them joy and peace and pride. This God, this one word: "I".' *Ayn Rand*

Reflecting the modern fascination and enchantment with the self, one of the few words recently added to the English dictionary is *selfie,* which is defined as, 'A complimentary self-portrait photograph, typically taken with a hand-held digital camera or camera phone and is displayed on social media'. The Oxford Dictionary even declared 'selfie' as word of the year. As an endorsement of this modern self-absorption, some writers have even promoted selfies as an appropriate tool of self-love, stating the practice can be equivalent to staring at your reflection in the mirror. Truly, the selfie may be taken to represent the apex of modern misunderstanding about the nature of the self and, correspondingly, the search for happiness and equanimity through pride and self -admiration.

The centrality of the self in Western thought can be traced back through antiquity and perhaps even pre-history. Archeological evidence from ancient cave paintings in France suggests to some observers that prehistoric human beings already pondered the existence of a non-physical, psychological self. Werner Herzog, who produced a recent film documentary about France's famous Chauvet Cave, described viewing the pre-historic paintings found therein as akin to witnessing, '*The origin of the modern human soul'*.

In Western culture, the existence of a self has long been established on the basis of a wide variety of soul theories.

For example, Greek philosophers such as Socrates, Plato, and Aristotle posited that an individual's essence consisted of an immaterial and spiritual substance, named spirit, psyche, or soul, which is separate from the body, and thus survives death. Similar ideas were continued by theologians of the Middle Ages such as Thomas Aquinas who, in the 1200s, emphasised the immortality and superiority of the soul to the body in which it dwelled. This conception of an individual's psyche or self as a spiritual entity separate from the physical, led to subsequent conceptions of mind and body duality. Famously, in the 1600s, beginning with his *Cogito, ergo sum* (I think, therefore I am), René Descartes proposed Cartesian rationalism, which emphasised a mind and body duality. Even though careful analysis shows that to somehow separate the physical (body) from the non-physical (mind) is nonsense, Cartesian dualism, what the English philosopher Gilbert Ryle said characterised the human mind as, 'the ghost in the machine', has continued to dominate Western thinking until today.

Descartes's notion of the soul was given a degree of respectability when the word *mind* was introduced to replace the religious concept of *soul*. Raymond Martin, Professor of Philosophy at Union College, has written extensively about the intellectual transformation that occurred in the eighteenth century, when the religious soul was replaced first by a philosophical self, and then by a scientific mind. In fact, many supposedly new and contemporary theories of the self were first discussed in the eighteenth century.[5]

Naturally, as a reflection of the culture in which it is embedded, Western psychology has also become dominated by a worldview whereby the individual self plays a central role as an explanatory construct. As Girishwar

Misra and Kenneth J. Gergen recently wrote, on the place of culture in psychological science:

> 'Mainstream psychology has been vigorously engaged in characterizing human lives in terms of mechanistic and individualistic constructions, with the aim of predicting and controlling the behaviour of a cultural and decontextualised others. Committed to a belief in psychological universals, this enterprise is directed at verifying a peculiarly Western intelligibility.'[6]

Although no longer identified as being a *soul*, the self as a common construct permeates contemporary psychology. There is a surfeit of models of the self applied in psychotherapy and self-help literature, and according to Edward G. Muzika, there are at present over 200 varieties of psychotherapy, and since few, if any, assert that self is an illusion, most work at strengthening the self and making it more able to bear pain and create pleasure.[5] All of these theories aim towards lessening distressing symptoms and agitation, to result in greater self-acceptance and adjustment. They seek to strengthen the self so that it can feel and express more feelings, attain a deeper, clearer articulation, and the confidence to able to overcome difficulties and achieve success in the world.

The assumption of the existence of the self has been a major preoccupation of psychologists from the earliest days of the field. The father of American psychology, William James, who wrote his classic text *Principles of Psychology* in 1890, offered a broad definition of the self as a topic for scientific study:

> 'In its widest sense a man's Self is the sum total of all that he can call his, not only his body and his psychic powers (normal cognitive activity), but his clothes and his wife and children, his ancestors

and friends, his reputation and works, his lands and
horses, and yacht and bank-account.[7]

Many other psychologists of the late nineteenth and
early twentieth century had creative and influential ideas
about the nature of the self, including significant figures
such as the originator of psychoanalysis Sigmund Freud,
and psychologist Carl Jung. For example, psychoanalytic
therapy is predicated on expanding the self-as-knower:
to render more of the unconscious conscious. Freud
developed a structural model of the psyche comprising the
entities id, ego and superego while Jung wrote extensively
about the collective unconscious (or transpersonal)
memories of humankind stemming from our ancestral
past as universal predispositions. Psychoanalyst Karen
Horney, later attributed individuals with an *ideal self* to
be representing the type of person that they wish to
be, whereas psychoanaylst Heinz Kohut expanded the
doctrines of psychoanalysis by conceiving the modern
school of Self Psychology, which posits the self as the
central agency of the human psyche. The import of
ideas of these early personality theorists to the field of
psychology (in general), and to psychoanalysis in particular,
was significant. And, whilst much has changed since the
days of Freud and Jung, contemporary psychological
theory still does not address the standing of the more
fundamental issue, that is, the validity of an authentic,
bounded, and individualistic self.

Few of the ideas of the early personality theorists
were formulated as empirically testable hypotheses. In
response, in the early-to-mid twentieth century, B. F.
Skinner and the Behaviorist School of Psychology sought
to redefine psychology as an empirical science by focusing
exclusively on observable behaviours and foregoing
unobservable inner states. Although the Behaviorists made
many useful discoveries, their denial of internal mental

states was not conducive to a greater understanding of cognitive abstractions including notions like the self. In the mid-20th century there was an enthusiastic resurgence of interest concerning the dynamics of the self and personal identity with the Humanistic psychology of Carl Rogers, Abraham Maslow, and Clark Moustakas, to name but a few. Psychologists began to emphasise the importance of the self-concept and positive self-regard, and to reconsider mental constructs as valid objects of scientific investigation.

The term 'cognitive psychology' was put forward in the late 1960s by American psychologist Ulric Neisser. Cognitive psychology can be described as the study of mental processes such as attention, language use, memory, perception, problem solving, creativity and thinking. According to Neisser, cognition involves all processes by which the sensory input is transformed, reduced, elaborated, stored, recovered, and used. In other words, every psychological phenomenon is a cognitive phenomenon. Other significant figures in the field of Cognitive Psychology include Albert Bandura, Aaron Beck, Antonio Damasio, Albert Ellis, Michael Gazzaniga, George Kelly and Lev Vygotsky.

Whilst comparisons between the Buddha's teachings and Western psychology are not uncommon, most have only compared the techniques and applications of the two. Although this can be informative and useful for both traditions, it is only through accepting the primary doctrines of the Buddha that one can truly understand the similarities and profound differences. These differences are at the heart of a very different world view, which Western psychology is not at present willing to assimilate.

The Doctrine of Anatta

In contrast to traditional Western views, the Buddha discovered through his mental training and final Awakening, or Enlightenment, that the self is, indeed, a fiction. It is an abstraction of the mind, which we continue to construct over the course of a lifetime. The Buddha taught that one can observe and understand mental processes without any need for an innate *I* at the centre of the experience. There is thinking, there is feeling, and there is perception, but these activities do not require a substantial self as an authority except as a linguistic convention. In actuality, there is nothing authentic about the self except our belief in it. This realisation is at the heart of the Buddha's Truth of Anatta, or no-self.

The doctrine of Anatta is the Buddha's most unique and radical teaching. Mark Epstein, psychiatrist and author, has said that, *'This emphasis on the lack of a particular, substantive agent is the most distinctive aspect of traditional Buddhist psychological thought.'*[8] Even though most people will commonly agree that our body, thoughts, feelings, and experiences change over time, they also believe that underneath the change is a unique and consistent self. Indeed, a majority of people still believe in the self's continuation after physical death.

As the philosopher, René Descartes, famously concluded, *'I think therefore I am,'* it is normal to identify what we do, think, and feel with our self – our I, me, and mine. For example, I am happy, this is me, and the car is mine. For the Buddha, the roots of dukkha, or suffering, are found in such identifications. These identifications, although they are only conventional labels, once believed in, become psychologically established and propagate a view of the world in which we feel separate and alienated from our inner and outer experiences. Believing in the separateness of you and I, and attempting to maintain, nourish, and propagate this identification of I (often at the expense of the other), we cause ourselves, and others, much grief and suffering through our self-deception. It has been said that the Buddha wanted to destroy the *self*, or the *I*. But this is incorrect simply because there is no permanent and substantial basis of personal identity called *self* to destroy.

The teaching of anatta is in no way a denial of the empirical reality of the individual personality. The Buddha taught that the individual personality is a functional, unified and interconnected integrity operating on many levels. Personality factors have a constancy, yet are also ever-changing. Whilst recognising that the *I*, or self, is a fluid cognitive fiction, the Buddha also understood that it is a convenient and helpful functionality. The Buddha himself used such terms as 'I', 'you', 'he', 'she', and 'person', but he did so only to facilitate communication in conventional speech with conventional understandings. The Buddha teaches not in order to destroy, but to transcend, or surpass, the ignorance which comes from attributing a substantial reality to the self. As David J. Kalupahana explains: *'In the context of the five aggregates (khandhas), the Buddha was not reluctant to speak of "I" or "myself" or even of the "self". Without admitting to a "ghost in the machine" or a transcendental apperception, the Buddha was willing to recognize the feeling of individuality, of self. It is a feeling that can contract and expand depending on the context. It does not represent a static entity to which everything belongs. [...] There seems to be no justification for assuming the Buddha encouraged the annihilation of this feeling of self. Indeed, the reality of feelings and emotions that occur in the stream of experience are relevant to an explanation of harmonious life. [...] Thus the Buddha spoke of "I" or "myself" and "mine" but avoided*

*and discouraged "I-making" or "mine-making", both terms
imply egoism.'*

We can see that as much as the Buddha emphasised
the elimination of egotism, he did not intend the
annihilation or depersonalisation of what modern
psychology labels the empirical self or the individual
experiences. The terms 'I', or 'self' are pragmatic linguistic
conventions that reflect the living experience that all
conscious living beings have. The idea of no-self doesn't
mean that we don't exist, or that we are robots with no
volition to act in the world. Instead, we are constantly
changing beings, always in flux. Giving it a fixed name and
identity is just a convention that humans came up with
that enables us to talk about it. The whole idea of self is
a fiction or narrative. The problem is that as soon as we
attach labels and concepts to something, our egos start
objectifying it, conclusively establish, and create fantastic
stories to make something static and permanent out of it.
And that's where begins our point of illusion and suffering.
Actually, *I* refers to an illusory epiphenomenon, a useful
abbreviation that can represent a myriad of identifications,
schemas and the numerous chemical/electronic
transactions taking place among them, every single
second. We regard our *I* as real. This is the reference
that culture and society gives to the level of complexity
in the physical system underlying it. And as the Buddha
discovered, we are conditioned to construct notions using
high level abstractions.

If, as in the Buddha's psychology, the intrusion of
the self into the field of sense perception begins with
the construction of the notions of I (subject), and mine
(object), the self originates at the stage of sensation, and
this duality is maintained until it is fully crystallised and
sustained at the conceptual level. We don't recognise it

as abnormal because the subject-object relationship is the foundation of cognition. So, what starts as a complex, conditionally arisen physiological process, develops into a conceptualisation between the subject and object, a duality. This concept of *I* serves as the matrix of our complex cognitive processes, and as such, becomes a convenient symbolic device. In fact, the self-concept is a cognitive construction.

As Kalupahana states, *'...This selectivity in consciousness accounts for the possibility and, therefore, the ability on the part of the human being to choose, think and act, and these represent the core of selfhood or personality in the Buddha's doctrine.'*[9] The abstracted cognitive embellishments serve as relative, convenient designations or identifications, which construct a virtual presence of the self illusion. It is based in ignorance, and through steadfast identifications and identity, creates craving and suffering. Only now are we beginning to empirically support the Buddha's insights of anatta, which he gained through the introspective practice of bhavana, or meditation.

The accomplishment of a transcendent state of equanimity, void of an illusion in owning one's self, is the aim of the psychological training, or bhavana in Buddhism. The belief and fascination with the self, and the futile clinging to personal identities that it engenders, is understood to be a basis of personal and societal suffering. Specific negative manifestations of this ignorance by the individual include lust, hatred and delusion. At the societal level, some of recognisable symptoms may comprise quarrel, strife, petty disagreements, conceit, dogma, slander and jealousy. What the Buddha discovered upon awakening, was that contrary to a static, inherent self, there '*was only a changing stream of becoming...constantly fed by perceptions, which does not represent a static entity to which everything belongs.'*[10]

To understand the consequential change in psychology when moving from the Western to the Buddha's views of selfhood, it is instructive to consider an analogy from the field of immunology. Philosopher Alfred I. Tauber has argued that the traditional view of the self in Western culture is analogous to an individual-based biology. In such a framework, the biological entity (the self) requires defence against threats or pathogens (the other).

Immunology is often described as the science of discrimination between self and non-self by following a reductive exercise: defining the components of immunity and their regulation as a self-contained system. Since the end of the nineteenth century, immunologists have generally adopted this insular perspective, and the standard description has evolved as a military metaphor, whereby an entity, or self, is defended by an army of immune factors fighting to protect the organism. Accordingly, in this formulation, the self, as a distinctly defined entity, is separated from (and even hostile towards) the environment.

Alternatively, Tauber describes biological functions, and the immune system in particular, from an ecological standpoint, which emphasises the interaction between an organism and its environment as a series of exchanges, with the regulation of biologicial systems arising in response to this. When the self/no-self discrimination recedes as a governing principle, the self is recognised as an archaic formulation and ecologic controls arise from the larger organisation in which the immune system is fully integrated.

'In other words, as applied to the problem of self/non-self discrimination, from this ecological perspective, there can be no circumscribed, self-defined entity that is designated the Self, but rather there is an organism that is under constant challenge to respond along a continuum of behaviors, and it adapts and changes accordingly. In the case of the immune system, reactivity may vary from a fully-fledged immune response to mild irritation to quiescence.'[11]

Terry Marks-Tarlow offers an alternative, organically-based description of how we cannot separate ourselves from our experience, which takes place through the body:

'Most of us take for granted the ability to distinguish between ourselves as observers and what we observe in the world. Outwardly our skin seems visible proof of a clear boundary that encases and protects our organs. Inwardly our sense of self, when intact, also feels like a relatively clear boundary, at times even to the point of isolation from others. Yet whether we consider our bodies or minds, the subjective experience of closed boundaries rests precisely on the opposite state of affairs – wide-open portals that continually allow transaction between inside and outside, body and world, self and not-self. Cycles of re-entry continually oscillate between creating and erasing the seam where observer and observed, perceiver and perceived, inner and outer, self and other, intersect and self-cross paradoxically. At this seam, self and world appear mutually co-determining.'[12]

These perspectives are analogous to Buddhist psychology, which seeks to transcend the distinct self/no-self distinction.

Bibliography

1. Morris, W. (1969). American heritage dictionary of the English language. American heritage.

2. Deaux, K., & Snyder, M. (Eds.). (2012). The Oxford handbook of personality and social psychology. Oxford University Press.

3. Ho, D. Y. (1995). Selfhood and identity in Confucianism, Taoism, Buddhism, and Hinduism: contrasts with the West. Journal for the Theory of Social Behaviour,25(2), 115-139.

4. Cushman, P. (1990). Why the self is empty: Toward a historically situated psychology. American psychologist, 45(5), 599.

5. Barresi, J., & Martin, R. (2012). Naturalization of the soul: self and personal identity in the Eighteenth century (Vol. 1). Routledge.

6. Misra, G., & Gergen, K. J. (1993). On the place of culture in psychological science. International Journal of Psychology, 28(2), 225-243.

7. James, W. (2013). The principles of psychology. Read Books Ltd.

8. Epstein, M. (2004). Thoughts without a thinker: Psychotherapy from a Buddhist perspective. Basic Books.

9. Kalupahana, D. J. (1987). The principles of Buddhist psychology. State University of New York Press.

10. Ibidem

11. Tauber, Alfred, "The Biological Notion of Self and Non-self", The Stanford Encyclopedia of Philosophy (Winter 2012 Edition), Edward N. Zalta (ed.).

12. Marks-Tarlow, T. (2004). Semiotic seams: Fractal dynamics of re-entry.Cybernetics & Human Knowing, 11(1), 49-62.

3

Self as Construction

'The truth is that all things are impermanent and there is nothing that can be characterised as the self!'

The Buddha

'Man, to the extent that he is able to construe his circumstances, can find for himself freedom from their domination. It implies that man enslaves himself with his own ideas and then wins freedom again by reconstruing his life'

George Kelly[1]

What is the self, and how do we know it?

Of all the categories and concepts in Western psychology's mental lexicon, none are as well known, or deemed so central to psychological wellbeing, as the concept of I and me. Yet despite this centrality, or perhaps because of it, grasping the true character of our inner nature is a daunting task. Many theories have been proposed to explain the development of personality and to account for differences between individuals. The question has understandably preoccupied philosophers and psychologists for a long time, and most readers probably have their own ideas about the subject as well.

The concept of the self often conjures up thoughts of an immaterial soul or essence of a person, a non-physical entity that generates mental activity. However, both traditional Buddhist thought and much of modern science reject this idea. In fact, a more nuanced, objective view of the self is emerging in Western science; that it is a biologically–based, organising principle expressed as an abstraction through meaning, constructing psychological processes.

Although the Buddha emphasised the impermanence and process-nature of the human personality, he also admitted to a functional unity, which is in reality what contemporary psychologists often refer to as *personality*. In the Buddhist definition a personality is something more, but not independent of, the body, the perceptual function, nor feelings, but is the very special combination of all of them.

We will explore the idea of self as being a dynamic process, drawing comparisons between the Buddha's teachings and a selection of theories developed by psychologists working in the Western empirical tradition.

Self-knowledge

Since the *self* construct is so pervasive in Western society, it raises the question of how people construct their story of a *self*. One possibility is that people have direct introspective access to all of their mental states. This however, cannot be the case, as much of the cognitive apparatus operates in the non-conscious mode, and even conscious awareness is often based on self-deception. Alternatively, people may develop stories about their self in accordance with the Self-Perception Theory (SPT). Developed by psychologist Daryl Bem in the late 1960s, SPT is an account of how individuals gain insight into their attitude through observing their own behavioural responses to environmental stimuli, in much the same way as a third party observer would do.[2] For example, a person could be unaware that they hold biased attitudes towards certain groups of people until they 'observe' themselves performing an obviously biased action. The way in which people often adjust their own opinions of themselves based other people's reactions to their behaviour and actions is another, perhaps more familiar way, in which we gain insight into our self.

In 1902, Charles Cooley coined the term 'the looking glass self',[3] and theorised that a person's self grows in response to their social interactions with others. In this case, our view of ourselves grows out of reflection on others' reactions to us. Therefore, our construction of our view of ourselves does not come directly from actual characteristics, but rather from how we believe others see us. As an extension of this, the social psychologist Leon Festinger proposed in 1954 the Social Comparison theory, in which he hypothesised how we may formulate accurate self-evaluations by comparing ourselves with others in order to learn what characteristics make our selves unique.

People also evaluate themselves by comparing their lives with the lives of others. Naturally, these social comparisons have the potential to make us feel either superior or inferior. While cognitive biases (which will be explored later in more detail) may offer some protection to our self-esteem, it is often defensive and at the expense of more accurate self-knowledge. For example, people tend to attribute other people's behaviour to enduring traits ('Joe was late for the meeting because he is lazy') whilst believing that their own behaviours are primarily the results of external contingencies ('I was late for the meeting because of a terrible traffic jam'). This is known in social psychology as the 'fundamental attribution error'. Psychologists have identified many related self-enhancing strategies that individuals often use to help cope with perceived negative self-relevant information. The way in which information about the self is organised in memory also plays an important part is shaping self-esteem.

The notion of the narrative self is another influential perspective on how we 'know' or define our self. The narrative self can be thought of as the story of the self, a sort of autobiographical narrative by which we make sense of our lives. In his collection of neurological case-histories, *The Man Who Mistook His Wife for a Hat and Other Clinical Tales*, neurologist Oliver Sacks describes the narrative self:

> *'To be ourselves we must have ourselves – possess, in need be, re-possess – our life-stories. We must "recollect" ourselves, recollect the inner drama, the narrative, of ourselves. A man needs such a narrative, a continuous inner narrative, to maintain his identify, his self.'*[4]

Neuroscientist Michael Gazzaniga proposed on the basis of his clinical observations of split-brain patients (patients whose left and right hemispheres were surgically separated), that the left hemisphere of the brain may contain an 'interpreter' whose function is to generate a narrative that makes sense of all the events in an individual's life, even if it has to distort stories in order to do so.[5]

The concept of the narrative self is closely related to autobiographical memory and therefore to our sense of possessing a continuous identity over time. With its close ties to memory, the narrative self is a dynamic process. Through the process of recalling and constructing narratives to explain our lives, we can update our self-image, bringing the re-constructive nature of memory to the fore.

Although memories are ostensibly records of past events, recalling of past events often involves something more than simply bringing up an old record. When we remember past events, we also re-interpret and alter our memories in light of our present-day knowledge. In this way, we are each both the author and editor of a continuously unfolding story called the *self*. The narrative self (not to be confused with the Gazzaniga's proposed interpreter), is notably abstract, and may not correspond to any particular neurological process. In a sense, the narrative self may be viewed as a useful fiction as a personal narrative, which over time helps us to organise our lives and predict human behaviour. This practical perspective is entirely consistent with the Buddha's psychology.

Paradoxically, although many of the psychological theories discussed in this chapter acknowledge that the self is a dynamic, evolving abstraction, most psychologists have no compunction in discussing how to go about protecting and promoting a healthy self as if it were a substantial presence. This approach reinforces the underlying acceptance and belief in an authentic self. By contrast, Buddhist practices encourage people to bring their feelings in line with the intellectual realisation that there is no real permanent *me*, so that with time and practice the psychological belief of an innate sense of self greatly diminishes, and, perhaps, is completely transcended, allowing equanimity to prevail.

The dynamic character of personality

A common psychological construct of personality assumes that individuals are characterised by traits that are relatively consistent across situations and over time. Indeed, consistency is part of what defines a trait. More or less stable personality traits such as how outgoing or introverted, a person normally behaves, have some utility in describing social interactions. Although there are regularities in the characteristic thoughts and patterns that define a personality, recent research demonstrates that individuals' features show considerable variability across situations, and personality continues to evolve over the lifetime.

Psychologists have also begun to pay closer attention to more 'situational' personality characteristics.[7] They have found that just as personality changes over time, it also highly situational. For some, personality is assumed to have a genetic basis, and for this reason, prominent personality theories like the Five-factor model postulate that traits should develop through childhood and stabilise following maturation.[9] However, a more recent large-sample study of personality (N = 132,515) in adults (aged 21-60) contradicted the hypothesis that personalities are set by genetics. Instead, researchers found that certain defined characteristics, such as conscientious and agreeableness, would increase or decrease with age.[10]

By conceptualising personality as a learned, adaptable system, it becomes possible to account for both the consistency and the flexibility of personality. The Cognitive-Affective Personality System (CAPS) theory offers a comprehensive unifying view similar to that of the Buddha's. It accounts for both the variability in the behavioural expressions of personality and the stability in the personality system that generates them.[11] According to

CAPS theory, behaviour does not result directly from global personality traits, but rather from an interaction between a person and a situation. Personality is conceptualised as an organisation of cognitive-affective processing structures that become activated when the individual encounters relevant stimulus features.

Mischel and Shoda identified five cognitive-affective units that enable people to interact with their environments in fairly stable, yet dynamic ways. They comprise encoding strategies, competencies, expectations, goals and emotional responses. Each of these components can vary across individuals and situations, but the system can generate situation-specific regularities. Regularities within individuals can be represented as an if/then profile. However, the system is also dynamic: individuals' behaviours generate consequences, which in turn affect the psychological responses to situations that are subsequently encountered. For example, strategies for encoding or retaining information can be influenced by the outcomes of past behaviours.

Developmentally, the organisation of the cognitive-affective units reflects the individual's learning history in interaction with environmental and biochemical factors. The cognitive system is activated in reaction to situations as they are experienced, whilst continuously receiving information via internal feedback. This may include processes such as reactivation of old memories, long-term planning related to sustained goal pursuit, and mental imagery or daydreaming. This type of internal stimulation can influence how we react to future situations just as surely as external stimulation. In this way, continuous internal and external feedback helps to shape and stabilise the personality system over time.

A particularly interesting feature of CAPS theory (from a Buddhist perspective) is the realisation that personality cannot be understood by studying the individual in isolation from the environment. Instead, the personality, or self, is best understood as an emergent property of an organised system of interacting parts. The description of processes which produce changes in cognitive-affective structure, and hence one's intended actions (kamma), is largely compatible with Buddhist teachings. Verses 1 and 2 of the Dhammapada scriptures claim that all the mental phenomena are an outcome of the quality or state of the mind. Each thought or action not only influences the environment, but reverberates in the individual's cognitive structures, and therefore has the potential to influence their future actions. If the mind is occupied with angry, negative thoughts, then that mind experiences suffering and sorrow; any unguarded actions will reflect the mindset. This idea is reflected in the CAPS theory, in that reactivated memories and judgments influence how we may perceive and hence act in future situations.

To view the self as a static entity is precarious and inaccurate. Rather, the self may best be understood as a dynamic, cognitive construction. Although the self is insubstantial, the concept of self is useful. Its cognitive structure allows us to make sense of our experiences and to generate predictions regarding our own, as well as other people's, behaviours. We can gain understanding of the empirical self by mindful observation of our internal physical and cognitive processes as well as by mindfully observing our responding to other people and situations. Whilst an individual's personality can be defined as regularities in that individual's thought and behaviour, it is not strictly a matter of global dispositions. Personality is also situation-specific and learns and adapts over time.

Buddhist psychology is in agreement with many contemporary cognitive approaches to the study of the self with respect to its dynamic structure. Indeed, a central pillar of Buddhist teaching is that the personality does change, and with a specific goal-oriented programme (the Eightfold Path), we can develop more wholesome and skilful habits of thought and action. Where Buddhist practices diverge from the Western tradition is in terms of the goals of expanded self-awareness. Western culture (and many psychologists) seek to promote a stronger, healthier, more positive and adaptive sense of self, whereas Buddhist practices prescribe the transformative, 'seeing through the ignorance of believing in the normal worldly invention and expansion of the self'.

By 'seeing through' the relative and unsubstantial nature of the self, we are able to detach, disenenage and disentangle from our egotistical clinging to our narrative and anecdotal personal story.

Buddhism teaches us to purposefully direct the mind to gain control over one's thoughts, attitudes and desires, via mindfulness, meditation and other enlightening practices. With correct effort and perseverance, these practices lead to positive changes not only in monitoring and altering conscious thoughts, but also in unconscious processes, which are ultimately the platforms from which our thoughts and behaviours are influenced. The end point of this process is Awakening, the release from craving, desire, judgment and dis-ease. At this point the self becomes explicitly known as insubstantial and fictional. And with that insight, a great burden is lifted from our psychic shoulders. Or, as the Buddha is reported to have joyfully exclaimed immediately after Awakening:

*'O house-builder(self), you are seen! You will not
build this house again. For your rafters are broken
and your ridgepole shattered. My mind has reached
the Unconditioned; I have attained the destruction
of craving.'*

Bibliography

1.   Kelly, G. A. (1955). The psychology of personal constructs. Volume 1: A theory of personality. WW Norton and Company.

2.   Bem, D. J. (1967). Self-perception: An alternative interpretation of cognitive dissonance phenomena. *Psychological review, 74*(3), 183.

3.   Cooley, C. H. (1902). The looking-glass self. *O'Brien*, 126-128.

4.   Sacks, O. (1998). The man who mistook his wife for a hat: And other clinical tales. Simon and Schuster.

5.   Gazzaniga, M. S. (1998). The split brain revisited. *Scientific American, 279*(1), 50-55.

6.   Kammrath, L. K., Mendoza-Denton, R., Mischel, W. (2005). Incorporating if... then... personality signatures in person perception: beyond the person-situation dichotomy. *Journal of personality and social psychology, 88*(4), 605.

7.   Friesen, C. A. & Kammrath, L. K. (2011). What It Pays to Know About a Close Other The Value of If-Then Personality Knowledge in Close Relationships. *Psychological science, 22*(5), 567-571.

8.   McCrae, R. R. & Costa Jr, P. T. (1999). A five-factor theory of personality. *Handbook of personality: Theory and research, 2*, 139-153.

9.   Srivasta, S., John, O.P., Gosling, S.D., Potter, J. (2003). Development of personality in early and middle adulthood: set like plaster or persistent change? *Journal of personality and social psychology, 84*(5), 1041.

10. Mischel, W. & Shoda, Y. (1995). A cognitive-affective system theory of personality: reconceptualizing situations, dispositions, dynamics, and invariance in personality structure. *Psychological review, 102*(2), 246.

4

The Human Being as a Collective, Unified Unit

'The 'world' of experience is not given in experience: it is constructed by thought from the data of sense.'

C. I. Lewis[1]

'Why do you take the "self" for granted, Mara? Your opinion is false. Here is nothing but a multitude of activities, and no "self" can be found. For just as a combination of parts is called "carriage", just so do we use the word "self", when all khandha (factors) are there.'

Sister VajirZi (S I 135)

The Khandhas

To understand the Buddha's psychology, it is fundamental to examine the khandhas (Pali) (Sanskrit: skandhas), or in English, the Five Aggregates. The khandhas describe how we represent and create our inner world, as well as the outer world in which we live. Before the Buddha's use of the word, khandha usually meant a pile, a bundle, a heap or a mass. Since his first sermon, however, the Buddha always referred to the khandhas as a collective, a unit. It is exactly this perspective of unified unit that allows a clear understanding of the khandhas's function.

As a collective, the khandhas refer to the body as a living organism that provides the basis for our ability to know anything. In early Buddhist texts, this schema of the five aggregates was not meant to be a complete classification of the sentient being. Rather, it describes the various aspects of the way in which an individual establishes his or herself.

The five khandhas are commonly defined as matter, sensations, perception, volitional and consciousness activities:

1. **Matter or form** (rupa) – External and internal matter. Externally, rupa is the physical world. Internally, it is the body as the world of a living organism.

2. **Sensation or feeling** (vedana) – The bare, affective quality of an experience in reception of sensations as input from the world around us and within us.

3. **Perception and/or cognition** (sanna) – The cognitive function of distinguishing and naming appearances; the ability to perceive what one is experiencing as some-thing; it involves language and memory.

4. **Volition or mental formation** (sankara) – The cognitive process by which an individual decides on and commits to a particular course of action. Volitional processes can be applied consciously or they can be the habitual dispositions that motivate a person to act, or react, to events or objects within one's experience and they cause the arising of future conditioned intentional actions.

5. **Consciousness** (vinnana) – The functional conditioned faculty of awareness or conscious processes that accompanies the operation of the whole living organism. The function of consciousness is being aware. Consciousness cannot emerge in the absence of conditions; it is dependent on causal process.

Modern formulation

The Buddha conceived the five khandhas to function as an integrated, organic whole. Together, they represent how we experience our existence. It is not possible to know anything other than through the khandhas, nor can we separate our body from our experience. The khandhas therefore must be understood not as five separate 'bundles' of bodily material, but as a cohesive, living, physical apparatus, the main operating processes being centred on the survival of the organism and the functioning of its cognitions. The Buddha's innovative and crucial interpretation of the khandhas as a unified, organic unit is far removed from the point of view of organisms having five individual senses functioning independently.

The Buddha's analysis is similar to the enactive cognitive thesis of the scientist Marek McGann.[2] He notes that whilst individual sensory organs are vital, no perception depends on, or can be explained by, the input of a specific organ alone. All perception is inherently unified and multi-modal. The modalities do not operate separately; rather, they are a dynamic process which involves an embodied agent (with goals and sensitivities) and an interacting world. In other words, our coherent body is a dynamic, self-sustaining, living organism, an organisation of interacting modalities through which we construct our world and its meaning, as perceived through our cognitive apparatus (eyes and ears, optic and auditory nerves, sensory nervous system, brain). The human ability to conceptualise relies on the sensory data that are filtered through the collective unit of khandhas. Our modern understanding of physiology indicates that our senses are indeed filters, not clear windows to the world, and what we see isn't truly what is out there, but instead is our subjective, informed guess, which we call our reality.

Our bodies are crucial

The first khandha is the body (rupa), which is significant not simply as a 'pile' of matter, but as the living organism – the matrix of one's experience. As neuroscientists J. A. Scott Kelso and David Engstrom affirm:

> 'The body is crucial to our experience of the world because it provides the sense organs through which we access the objective world and it has the organizing capacity of the mind that processes and constructs data understanding. Organisms are not just pieces of matter; they are matter in motion – animate forms. [...] Coordination dynamics (the study of how human beings and human brains – singly and together – coordinate behaviour) has stressed the co-evolution of real organisms coupled to and acting in real environments, a view captured in the term "embodied cognition".'[3]

In the Buddha's analysis there are six senses of the body: seeing, hearing, smelling, tasting, touching, and the mind. Whereas the first five are familiar to us, we do not typically consider mind as a sixth sense. As Sue Hamilton states, '[...] in the early Buddhist teachings, 'mind' is the faculty, or sense, which filters and collates all sensory data so it can actually make sense to us'.[4] In the Buddha's teachings, 'mind' has a physical correlation to brain processes, designated to mediating the information gathered by other senses. It organises and confers a meaning to the huge volume of information arising from the interaction between the other senses and their stimuli.

The mind should not be viewed as a separate entity, but as part of the whole with its physical counterparts, the brain, and the body. Furthermore, the mind cannot be static. Rather, it is constantly collecting, filtering, labelling and updating information of every type. Fundamentally, the mind is the dynamic ongoing process of conceptualisation and emotion.

In Pali, citta means both heart and mind, with emphasis placed on the emotive and intellectual facets of the mind. In fact, citta primarily represents one's mindset or state of mind, and therefore, refers to the quality of mental processes as a whole. Modern research is confirming the inter-relationship of the heart and brain. David Paterson, PhD, a professor at Oxford University, research indicates that the brain is not the sole source of emotions, but indeed, the heart and brain work together in producing emotions:

> 'The heart actually contains neurons, similar to those in the brain, and the heart and brain are intimately connected, creating a complex symbiotic emotional whole because the heart also contains thousands of specialized neurons, predominantly located around the right ventricle surface, forming a complex network. With neurons the brain forms thoughts. While much about the neurons in the heart is still unknown, they communicate back and forth with the brain - it's a two-way street. It's the neurons in your heart that decide how the heart will behave, not the neurons in your brain. The heart responds when the brain with each dependent on the other.'[5]

The body however, is also crucial to our experience of the world. It provides not only the sense organs through which we access the 'objective world', but also the cognitive apparatus with which we can organise the information. The most basic physical response to changes in the environment is called a reflex action. They are extra-rapid responses to stimuli that result in an immediate physical reaction and are not dependent on consciousness. An example of a reflex action is the constant adjustments the iris in our eye makes to alter the size of the pupil in response to changes in light levels.

Normally, when a sense receptor is energised, it sends a signal to the central nervous system, where the brain co-ordinates a response. Even before we concentrate our attention onto something, the incoming information has already been filtered of a lot of the background noise and the appropriate cognitive network selected to process the data. There are many stages of processing, and the results of processing are modulated by attention repeatedly. In fact, it has been demonstrated that with the series of processing, our conscious awareness lags 80 milliseconds behind actual events as our brains seek to create a cohesive picture of the world from stimuli that arrive at a range of times Because there is time lag in our perceptions, then the response to stimuli is not a direct confrontation, but a process. The object of experience is always internal.

Our senses pay attention and send an input to our brain only if our surroundings change in a significant way; we don't always have to notice the background noises. The brain uses a 'spotlight' to highlight the relevant information. If you are standing in the forest and a bird begins to sing loudly in a nearby tree, you hear it and see it. You know instantly that what you are hearing and seeing has to do with the bird. Each organ has receptors sensitive to particular kinds of stimuli. This information about the outside world is transformed by our sensory organs into a code made of series of electrical impulses that travel along the nerve cells (neurons) from the receptors to the brain. It is believed that a part of the parietal cortex of our brain allows us to focus the attention on a single aspect (the bird and its song), and puts together the relevant information from all our senses (bird singing in a tree).

New research indicates that different neurons in the brain respond to different parts of the information. The onset and the intensity of a stimulus is indicated by the timing and frequency of the electrical impulses. Some nerve cells are responsive to the first impulse that arrives, whilst others respond to multiple electrical impulses arriving at certain frequencies. As Scanziani, an Assistant Professor of Biology explains:

> 'Our work shows that deciphering the enormous amount of information that is conveyed to the brain at any time-point is a matter of division of labour between specialized neurons. Each neuron literally "picks" the type information it is supposed to process, that it is competent for. Very much like each musician in an orchestra only reads that part of the score of a symphony that was written for his or her own instrument.'[6]

At any moment, any of the specialised brain neurons could receive numerous messages from multiple sources and they selectively respond to the timing or frequency information of the impulses it is receiving, allowing the neurons to respond selectively to specific patterns of incoming electrical signals. It is possible, for example, for us to perceive someone's lip movements before hearing the words being spoken. Since stimulus intensity influences the response, the brain also needs to know its intensity. Possibly there may even be an 'alarm neuron' in the brain that responds to high frequency electrical impulses by triggering the appropriate muscle response to escape the stimulus. *'[...] the brain reads a code made of identical electrical impulses, in order to produce a coherent perception of the world,'* Scanziani says. *'Deciphering the language of the brain will help us understand the neuronal basis for sensation and cognition and their associated disorders.'*[7] How information is sorted by the brain has been an open question, but the research team discovered that different neurons in the brain are dedicated to respond to specific portions of the information.

The input through our sense organs is then processed by our sophisticated and complex mental activities to form what becomes our experience, or knowledge of the world. We tend to see what we are looking for, or are ready for, or what we want or don't want. Personal needs or desires decide to a great extent what is perceived and how it is interpreted. The world therefore becomes personal and self-related; attention is determined by interest. We play tricks with perception depending on the strength and type of interest. If frightened, a sound becomes a danger, a rope becomes a snake; objects are loaded with feelings and meanings. We are continually creating a world of our own reality, and we are attracted to others who reinforce our perceptions. We join through a perceived common agreement on a common reality, but in the abstracted, propagated realm, there is seldom agreement.

Experience, then, is not simply a sensation or a perception but is also embodied, unified, and interpreted through the mind's operation of organizing, processing, and constructing our meaning of the world. Whilst we cannot directly comprehend the things that make up the real world, we do sense and measure them, and construct an internalised model of them. Scholar Alfred Korzybski argued a similar point of view when he asserted that no one can have direct access to reality, given that the assimilated knowledge of the world is filtered through the brain's responses to reality. Therefore it is limited both by the human nervous system and the languages humans have developed. His dictum was, *'The map is not the territory.'*[8] So, human beings know the world through their abstractions, not facts or base data.

Figure 4.1 illustrates this point, For the Buddha, however, 'mind' is not strictly associated with brain processes. The illustration denotes the indeterminacy of the constructed subjective reality, or 'world', for each person.

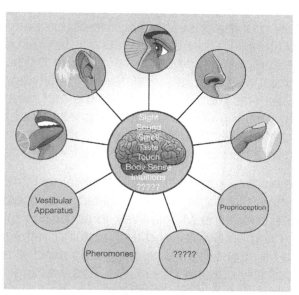

Figure 4.1   *Illustration depicting the various external elements interacting within the mind/brain and cooperating to the construction of meaning from external stimuli.*

The importance of how the body operates is emphasised in the Buddha's psychology. It places a different perspective on what one may find in some Buddhist meditation practices and teachings regarding the body. Sometimes, the body is taught in a negative light, as cumbersome, a heap of unwanted bile, pus and cells; a burden.

An example of this attitude, as Sue Hamilton writes in *Identity and Experience*, can be found in an oft-cited text by the 5th century AD Indian Buddhist scholar, Buddhaghosa. It has been translated as, 'Wherefore, monks, be ye disgusted with this body.' However, in Hamilton's opinion, a more appropriate translation (both in this specific text and the wider context of the Buddha's teachings) is, '*So monks, be indifferent towards or disenchanted with your body.*' She posits that this second interpretation of the passage, and the accompanying general attitude – rather than encouraging bhikkus to feel disgust and repulsion towards their 'impure' bodies – is simply meant to discourage them from identifying with their bodies. This may be correct, as the early Buddhist attitude toward the body was neither positive nor negative but neutrally analytical. In fact, the Buddha repeatedly encouraged a healthy lifestyle and care for the body.

Before his Awakening, the Buddha realised that strict asceticism would not lead him to fulfilling his quest, so instead, he chose the Middle Way. In accepting milk-rice from a girl named Sujata, and then bathing in the river Neranjara he strengthened his body and mind to allow him to optimally continue his quest. This was the lesson learned which the Buddha is reported to have said, '*To keep the body in good health is a duty...otherwise we shall not be able to keep our mind strong and clear.*'

This perspective is reaffirmed by Dr. Pinit Ratanakul:

'In the Buddhist perspective the unique body of

each of us, both in appearance and structure, is a result of our past kamma. The human body is at the same time the means by which we contact the world and the physical manifestation of our mind. Being such an important instrument, the body must be duly attended to, i.e. one must not abuse it through unwholesome food, alcohol, drugs, or by taxing it with over-indulgence and deprivation. Even enlightenment, the highest goal of Buddhism, cannot be attained by the mortification of the body, as witnessed in the personal experience of the Buddha. This is due to the interdependency of the mind and the body (mind and the body are also labelled name and form). Intellectual illumination can be attained only when the body is not deprived of anything necessary for the healthy and efficient functioning of all bodily organs.'⁹

Henceforth, the Buddha taught an analytic and pragmatic Middle Way as the Right Attitude to have toward our bodies.

Consciousness

Consciousness is essential for living and therefore for all of the activity of the khandhas. A succinct definition of consciousness (viññāna) as applied by the Buddha, is cognitive awareness. A temporal event that co-arises at the interface of a sense-organ and its correlative stimuli, cognitive awareness is simply the event that arises when requisite conditions come together – when the sun rises, and temperature and light intensity increase. The stimuli need not necessarily be objects *per se*, for consciousness depends upon distinctions, or discernments, within the sense field, whatever catches the attention. In the suttas, however, the examples are often based on the sense organs and their corresponding stimuli. For example, *'Dependent on eye and forms, eye-consciousness arises, the concurrence of the three is contact.'* (Samyutta Nikāya 35) Or, in other words, one needs more than the eye and forms in order to see, but also conscious engagement.

That moment of meeting or sense impression (phassa) follows after the object has arisen in one's awareness, forming the subjective sense of contacting the object. Consciousness is said to cling to, or be absorbed by, an apperceived object and become enmeshed with it. Then vitakka, or a placing or hovering of the mind, is applied, which allows for the discrimination of skilful or unskilful affective processes of experience. The inevitable result of this is feeling (vedanā), or an emotive aspect (like/dislike/ neutral). We can see, therefore, that consciousness is empirical and dependently and dualistically arisen. It is through the interactions between external ayatanna (six sense objects: sight, sound, taste, smell, touch, thought) and internal ayatanna (six sense bases: eye, ear, tongue, nose, tissues and mind) that viññāna and response results.

According to the Buddha's psychology, the cognition that arises begins with focusing or directing one's attention. As an aware living being we are continually sensing. We not only sense the outer environment on a broad scale, but also the inner. Consciousness follows after the awakening of attention. I am conscious of what my attention picks up. Even though I have in front of me so many apparently visible objects, until my attention is focused, eye-consciousness does not occur. It is only after the eye has become aware, that the other necessary factors for sense perception proceed. The basic function of this type of consciousness is to discriminate between the eye and the object seen. When something arises that interests the cognitive apparatus in some way, attention directs the mind to that object, and upon meeting, consciousness (awareness, cognition) arises.

With the continual shifting of our attention and hence our awareness, nothing remains continuously in our consciousness. Therefore, the necessary condition for all of the activities of the khandhas is consciousness.

In psychology and neuroscience, the nature of consciousness continues to be hotly debated. The Buddha meant it as the activity of being conscious or aware, and dependent on the organic integrated operation of the khandhas. For the Buddha, consciousness refers to a relationship of actual awareness between an organism and external or internal stimuli. Cognitive awareness however, cannot cognise everything – it is simply the awareness that arises when the requisite conditions come together. Consciousness is an act rather than an event, as watching is to seeing. Upon awakening, the Buddha found consciousness to be an unburdened, pure experience. Awareness is not in itself an intentional act, but rather an event that occurs. Ultimately, there is no residence in consciousness for an active agent or a substantive self.

Rupa (physical phenomena or sensations) represents either one's physical body or material objects. It refers to the practical way in which these affect an individual. Unless there is an actual physical basis of an experience, it is considered a fantasy. Nama represents the union of mental phenomena or mind. Interactions are nama/rupa pairs and they are complementary. Similarly, John F. Kihlstrom suggests that, at the psychological level of analysis, consciousness requires a link between an activated mental representation of an event, and an activated mental representation of oneself as the agent, or participant of that event.[10] Therefore, for him, the search for the Neural Correlates of Consciousness (NCC) should focus on the neural representation of the self and the neural systems responsible for self-reference.

The final three khandhas

Research shows that the whole physical process of object recognition is quite complex. The Buddha's simplified model of object recognition, however, is accurate in its representation of this process. The final three khandhas – sensation, perception, and volition – explain how incoming sensory data is filtered through the mind, and awareness becomes our knowledge, or what we know. We need to remember that we do not attend to our raw sensations one after the other, and therefore this process is non-linear. Rather, many inputs constantly course through the various sense organs, which the cognitive apparatus then filters and specific inputs are given first unconscious and then conscious priority and attention.

McGann states that:

> 'Cognition is not added to perception after the fact, because it is inherent in the process of perception itself, it is part of what continually initiates, drives and structures the act of perceiving. An enactive approach to perception thus maintains a strong distinction between sensation and perception. Perception, wrapped up as it is in cognition, action, sense-making, is an activity embedded within, contextualized by, value driven intentional action. Sensation is an aspect of an embodied agent's interaction with the world, an important part certainly, but not one with any veto or absolute authority as the character of experience.'[11]

So whilst in everyday language, the terms 'sensation' and 'perception' are often used interchangeably, they are very distinct, yet complementary processes.

Sensation

Vedanā – Sensations are the energy absorbed from physical stimuli in the environment that we initially experience through the five senses of sight, hearing, smell, taste, or touch. They are the bare, affective processes of bringing information from an outside reality into our body. The process is passive because we are not consciously engaged in the sensing process. While the sensory receptors convert this energy of the impinging sensory data into electrical physical impulses, we are mostly unaware of the pure sensation and experience. In this pre-reflective stage, experience is direct, immediate, and intuitive. Subject and object, inner and outer, are unified. This is the khandha of sensation.

Perception

To follow are discrimination and identification, which are associated with the khandha of perception (sañña). Recognising individual objects is only part of perception. Perception is the active process of selecting, organizing, and interpreting the information brought to our awareness by the senses, and translating it into something meaningful. All aspects of perception (recognition of the object, interpretation of the event) involve some form of cognitive operation, which often is inferential, or like a map. In modern terms, this equates to cognitive functioning – a conscious process of understanding or perceiving, in terms of a person's previous knowledge, experiences, emotions and memories.

One becomes perceptually aware and identifies what was previously only a sensation when it reaches a certain threshold to trigger impulses that register in the various mediating processes. This is how we identify things individually by contrasting and distinguishing them from their surrounding contexts, independently from us, and giving them a separate continuity. 'Ideas' about the object mingle with the awareness of its sense presence – we name it, categorise it, and compare it to other things. Importantly, the independent status of objects is purely an attributed state. Objects are typically embedded in context with other objects or with the general layout of a scene, also known as the 'gist'. They are distinguished contrastively, and they no longer correspond to an original 'pure' sensation, because they are now labelled as the result of a complex, constructive, cognitive process.

To distinguish what characterises the stage of sensation (vedanā), or immediate awareness, from that of perception (sañña), or ascertaining single features of an object, take, for example, the act of looking at a flower. In the first instant of experience, based on a directed attention, the flower and the observer are one. The stimulus is impinging on the sense outlet, but it hasn't yet reached the threshold that triggers registration in the cortex. The flower seen and the seeing of it are one indivisible act, which is the datum, or the 'pure sensation' experience. Sensation is therefore defined as the contact between sense organ and sensory input. After the direct experience, sensory receptors transmit the information as neural impulses to the brain, where the information is translated into something meaningful, thereby establishing significance. At this point we are able to declare that the flower is a flower or, more specifically, a yellow rose. Out of such perceptions arises the conventional reality, the basis of our categorised 'world'. As Hamilton writes:

> 'One sees, hears, tastes, something. As such, thoug one refers separately to sense organs, sense objects and what is sensed – nose, cheese, smell, for example – this separation is in fact an abstraction from the experience 'smelling cheese-smell.'[12]

It is in this reflective phase of perception and conceptualisation that experience becomes a constructive process and sensations are interpreted in light of past experiences. This is a biological process through which the stimuli of the external world are transformed into our internal reality, or 'maps'. What reaches our cognitive apparatus is not directly what is out there in its totality, although what is perceived may be more or less patterned by external reality, or comprise aspects or facets of realities. As geneticist R. C. Lewontin wrote:

> *'First, there is no "environment" in some independent and abstract sense. Just as there is no environment without an organism. Organisms do not experience environment. They create them. They construct their own environment out of bits and pieces of the physical and biological world and they do so by their own activities.'*[13]

Volition

The fifth khandha, volition, (saṅkhāra) is a very complex aspect of our cognitive processes. John Holder defines saṅkhāra as, *'The features of the human mind that motivate a person to act, or react, to events or objects within one's experience.'*[14]

> *'We have affective responses to whatever we experience; these can be pleasant, unpleasant, or neutral. Although cognitions drive emotions, those emotions in turn, inform the thoughts of the person. Accordingly, there is a functional role for emotions in that they, 'establish our position vis-à-vis our environment, pulling us toward certain people, objects, actions, and ideas, and pushing us away from others.'*[15]

A neutral response is merely registered as a sensation and we become aware of it only in a non-attached, factual sense. If we consider an experience to be pleasant, we bond to it and we want to continue or repeat this event. If, on the other hand, we consider an experience to be aversive, we avoid it. These become learned and familiar as preferred choices. They can range from minor preferences in the positive domain and mild aversion in the realm of the negative to very profound affective states in both. These affective states respond not only to bodily sensations, but also to abstract concepts and beliefs and can be established on, among other things, one's beliefs, desire to live, identifications, traditions and customs. They can be general desires, such as to be loved, successful, accepted, happy or wealthy. These biases and inclinations make up our psychological orientation and represent our affective world.

According to the Buddha, our affective volitional characteristics fuel the kammic process and continue to until these states are extinguished upon achieving Enlightenment. Their continued functioning is conditioned (dependently originated) by the level of insight on which we are operating. As we better understand how to see things 'as they are', the degree of our ignorance, and therefore our volitions, becomes differently conditioned. David J. Kalupahana states:

> *'The Buddha insisted that desire is not identical with the variegated objects in the world. It is the thought of lust which is generated by wrong ideas or misconception, primarily the metaphysical conceptions of self and object. As such it is possible to maintain that on occasions of sense experience, which are represented by the coming together of the subject and object, the subject does come to be affected in a certain way and this is conditioned by views it holds regarding its own nature as well as the object.'[16]*

It is to understand the operation of the khandhas that is the focus of insight meditation. We can see that dukkha, or our dis-ease, is intimately linked with our cognitive evaluation and reaction to our ongoing experiences. As our affective-volitional apparatus is cognitively based, our dukkha is also. The cessation of suffering, or Enlightenment, is therefore a radical cognitive re-orientation. The Buddha taught that our cognitive experiences are dependently originated, dynamic, ever-changing and impermanent. This is the Truth of experience.

The Buddha's model of perceptual process

The Buddha's theory of this perceptual process comprises the six stages:

1.   **Sense-consciousness** – For example, visual consciousness arises with the eye and visual object as its conditions. At this point, the detection probability is the likelihood when a given stimulus is detected against background noise and there is a threshold that is defined as the intensity occurring approximately 50% of the time. It is the bare sensation before the object is fully recognised.

2.   **Sensory impression** – Defined as the impression, or contact of the sense-organ, the sense-object and sense-consciousness. Cognitive awareness occurs at the interface, the concurrence, of a sense-organ and its correlative stimuli; it is transactional as well as temporal. The reaction time is the amount of time that it takes an observer to respond to the onset of a given stimulus. Though the stimulus may leave a lasting impression on the human nervous system through memory, attention is always transient.

Attention only focuses on the system of transitory processes which guide behaviour.

3. **Sensation** – Refers to the output of sensory systems, to the passive process of bringing information into the body and to the cognitive apparatus by stimulation of a sense organ or from an internal bodily change. It is passive in the sense that we do not have to be consciously engaged. A simplified way to state it is that the sensory organs absorb energy from a physical stimulus in the environment. Then sensory receptors convert this energy into neural impulses and send them to the brain. It has also an affective component.

4. **Perception** – In contrast, perception is centrally determined. It comes from activity of the brain using information from the senses. Perception is a large-scale synthesis or act of construction. It can be influenced by ideas and memories as well as sensory inputs. It refers to the active process of selecting, organising and interpreting the information brought to the mind by the senses. The mind organises the information and translates it into something meaningful. At this stage of stimulus recognition, discrimination occurs where a person responds differently to a variety of stimuli, either through learned associations or through innate predispositions. It is not a simple phenomenon, and involves psychological processes such as stimulus recognition, learning and generalisation.

5. **The initial application of thought** – The fifth stage is the point at which the perceived object is interpreted. This is called discrimination learning, and is the process by which a person distinguishes between recognisable stimuli. Compound stimuli that differ in two dimensions are more easily

discriminated than those that differ in only one. An important phenomenon associated with discrimination learning is generalisation. When one learns about a rewarded stimulus and an aversive stimulus along a given dimension, a gradient of excitatory and inhibitory responses becomes evident around each stimulus. These gradients are known as generalisation curves, and are predictable because humans respond to similar stimuli, either in an adaptive fashion or mistakenly confusing them to varying degrees with the original stimulus.

6.   Finally, **mental proliferation** (papañca) – Refers to the tendency of the individual's imagination to proliferate. This is a complex level of experience that is tainted and filtered by our desires and biases.

Five Sense - Data	The First Five Conscious- nesses	The 6th	The 7th	The 8th
1. Form 2. Sound 3. Smell 4. Taste 5. Tangible	1. Visual con- sciousness 2. Auditory consciousness 3. Olfactory consciousness 4. Gustatory consciousness 5. Tactile con- sciousness	Mental con- sciousness	Ego con- sciousness	Storehouse consciousness
The physical world	Sense percep- tions	Integrator of sense percep- tions	Creator of the idea of I, mine and myself	Receptacle of residual force of experiences (memory)

Figure 4.2   *Resuming scheme of the entities involved in the processing of data from external world.*

The following sutta passage outlines the progression to papañca. To begin is the impression the sense makes on the sense organ, with consciousness being the connecting awareness of that contact; next there is the resulting sensation, which may be pleasant, painful or neutral; then is the perception of that sensation, which causes reasoning about it; before finally, there is conceptualisation, categorising through cognition that which we take to be a crystallised fact or inherent reality.

> 'Brethren, because of the sensitive surface of the eye as the support and the four originating material elements as the object, there arises "eye consciousness", by the meeting of those three arises "contact". Because of that contact arises sensation, with contact as its condition by way of co-nascence etc. Whatever object is sensed by that sensation, that, "perception" perceives; whatever perception perceives, "reasoning" reasons about that very object; whatever reasoning reasons about, "papañca" transforms into papañca (conceptual proliferation) that very object with these factors such as the eye and visible object. Papañca overwhelm that man who is ignorant of those facts; that is, they exist for him.' (M. A. II 75)

We can understand that from the Buddha's perspective, in each moment consciousness arises dependent on sensory conditions, and then fades away. Consciousness is not an individual functional unit, but part of a process. Normal consciousness is not a tabula rasa, rather it is influenced by the immediate contact, or coming together, of the sense and the corresponding object, as well as filtering of the conditioning and conditioned unconscious schemata or dispositions that are components of the psychophysical personality. The gateway to experience requires both sense organ and sensory data. With the addition of associated feelings, the dispositions increase in power and produce attachments of pleasant, aversion of unpleasant or ignoring the neutral. As these dispositions solidify, the self individuates and develops an inherent, authentic sense of identification, and a self. Yet, whilst emotions, feelings and sensations are an inevitable response to living, they can always be restrained or eclipsed. The Enlightened interact with the processing of this series with the non-attachment of equanimity, whereas for the unenlightened, when feeling/sensation occurs they become emotionally and intellectually entangled and often obsessed and driven.

The mind has a specific function: it is able to survey the objects of all the other senses and at the same time is a form of reflection, which also becomes the source of a sense of personal identity or conception of self, a feeling of self, an empirical self. It is important to highlight that it is a feeling like all other feelings produced by the senses. The mind functions are perceived as consciousness. Our consciousness is an internal process of observing, remembering and constructing an autobiographical self. As Damasio states, *'Consciousness offers a direct experience of mind, but the broker of the experience is a self, which is an internal and imperfectly constructed informer rather than an external, reliable observer.'*[18]

The Buddha referred to dukkha not as the simple occurrence of the sensation of inputs alone, but as the secondary processing which then identifies, contrasts, classifies and responds with pleasure or discomfort (and then desires or craves or rejects as a consequence of preferences). In the Second Noble Truth, the Buddha clearly teaches that the sources of our suffering are our volitions based on our cognitive preferences and their accompanying cravings or aversions. With Enlightenment, through equanimity, one ceases to grasp at the craving, aversion or even neutrality, created by the ignorance of adherence to the static duality of an object and subject of experience. Enlightenment results from gaining insight into, and transcendence of, the thoughts and conceptual constructions, identifications and projections that provide the foundation for our pre-enlightened cognitions, with their attending cravings and desires or aversions. This transcendence of Awakening (pure experience, defined as non-conceptual and devoid of interpretive overlay) along with the letting go of attachments to our affective-cognitive cravings, transforms our basic and mundane mode of existence.

Bibliography

1. Lewis, C. I. (1990). Mind and the world-order: Outline of a theory of knowledge. Courier Corporation.

2. McGann, M., De Jaegher, H., Di Paolo, E. (2013). Enaction and psychology. *Review of General Psychology, 17(2), 203.*

3. Kelso, J. A. & Engstrøm, D. A. (2006). The complementary nature. The MIT Press.

4. Hamilton, S. (2001). Identity and Experience: The Constitution of the Human Being According to Early Buddhism. Oxford: Luzac Oriental, 181.

5. Musialek, P., Lei, M., Brown, H. F., Paterson, D. J., Casadei, B. (1997). *Circulation Research, 81(1), 60-68.*

6. Pouille, F., & Scanziani, M. (2004). Routing of spike series by dynamic circuits in the hippocampus. Nature, 429(6993), 717-723.

7. Pouille, F. & Scanziani, M. (2004). Routing of spike series by dynamic circuits in the hippocampus. *Nature, 429(6993), 717-723.*

8. Korzybski, A. (1958). Science and sanity: An introduction to non-Aristotelian systems and general semantics. Institute of GS.

9. Ratanakul, P. (2004). Buddhism, health and disease. *Eubios Journal of Asian and International Bioethics, 15, 162-164.*

10. Kihlstrom, J. F. (1993). The psychological unconscious and the self. *Experimental and theoretical studies of consciousness, 10, 147-67.*

11. McGann, M. (2010). Perceptual modalities: modes of presentation or modes of interaction? *Journal of Consciousness Studies, 17(1-2), 72-94.*

12. Hamilton, S. (2000). Early Buddhism: A new approach: The I of the beholder (Vol. 16).

Psychology Press.

13. Lewontin, R. C. (1994). Inside and outside: Gene, environment, and organism. Clark Univ Pr.

14. Holder, J. (2006). Early Buddhist discourses. Hackett Publishing Company. p. 33.

15. Levenson, R .W. (1994). Human emotion: A functional view. In Ekman, P. & Davidson, R. J. (Eds.) The nature of emotion: Fundamental questions, 123–126. New York: Oxford University Press.

16. Kalupahana, D. J. (1987). The principles of Buddhist psychology. State University of New York Press.

17. Damasio, A. (2010). Self comes to mind. New York: Pantheon, 64.

5

Awakening and Enlightenment: Psychological Transformation and Transcendence

'The monk Ānanda, Buddha's attendant asked, "It is said that the world is empty, the world is empty, lord. In what respect is it said that the world is empty?" The Buddha replied, "Insofar as it is empty of a self or of anything pertaining to a self: Thus it is said, Ānanda, that the world is empty."'

Suñña Sutta

'It has been said that when the Buddha started to wander around India shortly after his enlightenment, he encountered several men who recognised him to be a very extraordinary being. They asked him: "Are you a god?" "No," he replied. "Are you a reincarnation of god?" "No," he replied. "Are you a wizard, then?" "No." "Well, are you a man?" "No." "So what are you?" They asked, being very perplexed. Buddha simply replied: "I am awake."'

Dona-sutta

Buddha's Awakening

The Buddha's profound insight resulted in him reaching an understanding about the truth of No-Self and impermanence, which led him to develop his doctrines and teachings of the Eightfold Path. For most people, this experience – which is the foundation of the Buddha's Awakening – is very difficult to appreciate from our everyday point of view.

The Buddha's teachings about transcending the ignorance of a belief in the validity of an authentic, static and representational (identity) self is most clearly understood by us today in a psychological sense. Buddhist psychology recognises a perpetuation of a personality, that there is a continuation of influences and a causal connection between one moment and the next, but there is no unconditioned, substantial entity. 'Enlightenment', which is the Western translation of the term bodhi, has mistakenly become synonymous with Self-realisation, and the True Self, as a substantial essence being covered over by social conditioning. But the Buddha did not intend or believe in transcendence in a metaphysical or ontological way.

As Buddhist scholar David J. Kalupahana states:

'When metaphysical beliefs in the self and ultimately real objects are relinquished, the influxes (asava, or mental biases), such as desire, becoming, views, and ignorance cease. The constant thirsting for this and that causing worry and frustration ceases along with it. With the waning of influxes, the constraints (nirarana) or hindrances relating to perception and conception are removed. Yet the removal of the hindrances does not mean that the perceptions and conceptions are themselves eliminated. Only that one is not strictly confined or constrained

*by any of the perceptions and conceptions [...]
Elimination of hindrances represents freedom. This
elimination of hindrances would definitely bring
about a transformation of the human personality.
The transformation would be both physical and
psychological.'*[1]

Laid down in traditional Buddhist history, Siddhartha
Gautama, is the story of a person's journey through a
psychological crisis which occupied his mind for many
years. The solution to his crisis was the psychological
insight, or resolution, which completely changed both his
life and, ultimately, the lives of millions of people around the
world who have affirmed his answer to similar questions
and experiences in their lives. This insight is called his
Awakening, or Enlightenment. Whether the story of the
Buddha's life is an archetypal journey or in fact represents
an accurate rendition is not important here, for the subject
is universal. The questions are, and continue to be, 'What
creates dis-ease?' and 'Is it possible to end the distress
we experience in this life?'

The Buddha's Awakening was the culmination of a
long psychological journey of transcendence. After six
years of strict asceticism, he realised that none of the
ascetic practices had provided him with the answer to his
question. So he took food and drink to regain his health,
and sitting under the Bodhi Tree, entered into a deep,
contemplative state. Here, the Buddha gained his final
insight into the significant extent to which our total world
of experience is dependent on our cognitive apparatus
(eyes and ears, optic and auditory nerves, sensory
nervous system, brain), which we use to make 'sense'
of, or construct, our experience. In short, our 'world' as
we understand it, as well as our 'self', is relationally and
subjectively constructed.

The Awakening experience created a state of freedom for the Buddha which led him to the cessation of craving, identification, and suffering. The bhavana, or meditation processes that led to the achievement of Enlightenment were incremental, and during this phase the Buddha gained progressive insights into the ignorance created by his multiple cognitive constructions.

Historically, only the Buddha would point out that one cannot win release from the duality of form and formlessness without transcending them. Release from both can only be achieved through the cessation of the consciousness (state of awareness) that discriminates between form and formlessness. The Buddha's Awakening provided a superior criterion of certainty rooted in actual experiential knowledge; his unique and ground-breaking perspective created a revolution in our understanding of 'self' and personal identity, as well as our understanding of our perceptions and comprehension of the world around us. Buddhist scholar Susan Hamilton argues that this, 'is completely different' from the then contemporary teachings of the Upanishads, in that the Buddha's focus:

> '...on understanding the workings of one's cognitive apparatus [...] is entirely epistemic. And further, it is clear that it is here that a key aspect of impermanence, the intrinsic characteristic of existence, lies. There is nothing about the process of experiencing qua that is in any sense permanent: it is, rather, at all times dynamically in process. Nothing that is epistemic can be anything other than impermanent.'[2]

The Buddha's Enlightenment was a life-altering experience, which gave him a radically new perspective. A correct understanding of the Buddha's Enlightenment centres not only on the concept of impermanence (even though this is a complementary insight), but on his

Pure Experience of Emptiness, or sunyata. The Buddha understood that our cognitive manifestations are relative, constructed, and impermanent. The Sanskrit word, *śūnyatā*, is most often translated as the English word 'emptiness', which means, according to Thanissaro Bhikku:

> *'[...] Emptiness as a mental state, in the early canons, means a mode of perception in which one neither adds anything to nor takes anything away from what is present, noting simply, "There is this." There is the 'emancipation of the mind by emptiness' which is caused by the realisation that "this world is empty of self or anything pertaining to self."'* [3]

This direct knowing is non-conceptual; it has no interpretive overlay. Having this insight transforms the basic mode of cognition from conscious discernment into direct knowing, or pure experience. Consequently, the insight of Emptiness undercuts any adherence to attachments.

Pure experience of emptiness

Kitaro Nishida, perhaps the most significant and influential Japanese philosopher of the twentieth century, defined pure experience as follows:

> *'To experience is to know facts just as they are, to know in accordance with facts by completely relinquishing one's own fabrications. What we usually refer to as experience is adulterated with some sort of thought, so by pure I am referring to the state of experience just as it is without the least addition of deliberative discrimination. The moment of seeing a colour or hearing a sound, for example, is prior not only to the thought that the colour or sound is the activity of an external object or that one is sensing it, but also to the judgment*

of what colour or sound might be. In this regard, pure experience is identical with direct experience. When one directly experiences one's own state of consciousness, there is not yet a subject or an object, and knowing and its object are completely unified. This is the most refined type of experience. In pure experience there is not the slightest interval between the intention and the act. Every action is a unity indivisible into temporal stages [...] there is no prior or posterior, no inner or outer; no witness precedes or generates experience.'[4]

On which, Nishida's student Keiji Nishitani explicates further:

'To speak of a mind that sees things, a self within that views what is on the outside, does not refer to experience in its pure form but only in a later explanation of experience. In direct experience there is no self, no-thing, nothing separate or individual at all. [...] We cannot think in terms of things existing on the outside and a mind existing on the inside. This is a later standpoint; the prior standpoint is that of pure experience where subject and object is one and undifferentiated. The ultimate integrity of experience is in its indivisibility into "experience" and "content."'[5]

Pure experience, as Nishida and Nishitani describe it, unveiled for the Buddha how we cognitively (relating to the mental processes of perception, memory, judgment and reasoning) construct a complementary dualistic subjective-objective world. It boils down to understanding that what one has conceived and constructed as the so-called object (or other) and the so-called subject (or 'I'), is a misconception, or something illusory, without substance.

As Hamilton writes:

> 'This is what pure experience is: neither the world nor 'I' in it other than experience.'[2] Hence, the realm of pure experience is the ordinary world of phenomena experienced directly, with no intervening conceptualisation.'[6]

As Bhikkhu Dhammapala explains:

> 'With emptying the mind, delusion ends when the mind empties itself of all conditioning, of all desires, hopes and fears, in which the mind does not concentrate on a pre-chosen object or state, but just watches with direct awareness of what is. By direct perception of what is one is without judgment, there is an emptying of the mind of all conditioning, of all distortion, delusion, conflict, of all 'self' deception and hypocrisy. It is just all and complete, with tenderness and subtleness, always fresh and new, without memory and without clinging, without hope and without fear, without projection in time and space and without craving for continuance. There is no 'I,' it does not embrace the 'I,' it does not absorb the 'I'. There is just stillness, peace, release, freedom.'[7]

Joanna Macy furthers this idea:

> 'Bare attention (in its purest, freest form) as another term describing pure experience, yields no experiencer separable from experience, and the Buddha's teaching about the self becomes more than a theory. The absence of a permanent, separable self erupts as a reality that changes the face of life.'[8]

So when my awareness is pure, I do not attend to any objects or contents of mind. My only awareness is awareness itself. There is no object of attention to focus on in pure awareness. Pure awareness cannot be an object; rather, it is an absence of mental representation of objects, or emptiness. I am aware of my existence, but don't abstract or conceptualise who, or what, I am. There is the gestalt foreground of possible activity, and in the background, a void. Just as silence is the absence of sound, the distant gong is an object witnessed in the field of sound. In silence you are aware of the absence of sound; of emptiness, you can know this nothingness, it has a value. But once I objectify my experience, then it is no longer a pure experience. The appearance of objects presupposes the existence of a subject to which they appear. When I, the 'subject', acknowledge that I consist of objects, the result is that I divide the universe into two parts – one consisting of myself, and the other consisting of everything else. Hence, I believe my 'self' to be a separate being. It is then that the human predicament of alienation and dis-ease becomes possible.

My pure awareness, once realised, is a more obvious reality than anything that may appear to me, because any form I attend to already presupposes the background. The awareness itself does not appear as an object of attention. This means, then, that the experience of pure consciousness is prior to any particular concept of a 'self', or any opinion about the nature of my self. My access to a pure experience is immediate and non-observational (that is, it doesn't involve a perceptual or reflective act of consciousness).

The true nature of experience is the awareness of my being. This awareness of our own experience – our pure awareness – is shared by all, and is the most intimate and obvious fact of experience. This is also called 'original mind'. In this regard, the awareness of pure experience is the pre-reflective point of origin for action, experience, and thought. Any further reflection by me, as to who or what I am, implies that I have already realised my existing.

We are certain of our pure experience. It is an experience in which the two fundamental qualities of our self – *being* and *knowing* – are recognised as one. I can be aware of thoughts, sensations, and perceptions and their creative influence, but, at the same time, I recognise that I am not inherently made out of a thought, sensation or perception – the label 'I' can never actually become a substantial person or object. Knowing this inherent absence of abstraction is the experience of bliss; this imperturbability is peace. Happiness and peace are always present in pure experience.

Contentment and peace are, in essence, our true nature – our 'original mind'. The separate self is only the illusory point of view created from dualism. In pure awareness, there is no separation, no objectification, and no alienation. When we veil our true nature, the peace and the happiness that are the natural condition of pure experience are obscured. It is for this reason that the dis-ease of the separated self – the ignorance and angst of separate experience – evolves. Yet, the separate self continually seeks what it can never fully achieve: lasting peace, happiness, and gratification. This is the nature of suffering. Many people's lives are spent trying to ease or numb the pain of this alienation through substances, objects, activities and relationships. The separate self however, cannot find what it wants because there is nothing certain or enduring in existence.

All ignorance, suffering, and alienation are attributable to the belief of a separation, a static, inherent, subject/object duality that is found in pre-enlightened cognition. It is because of this manner of cognition that grasping and craving occur, and by transcending this misconception, the Awakened are those who are free from grasping and craving. The Awakened have seen through the bondage of dualism, the presumption of a separation that causes a tension and alienation between two opposing systems – the 'I' and the 'world', or the 'self' and 'other'; discovered is our ignorance and its by-products of suffering, hollowness, and essenceless-ness.

The purified, non-deluded awareness is the goal of Buddhist practice. Many of the sutta discourses deal with the subject of the non-manifest consciousness in regarding nibbana. Some commentators have misinterpreted this perspective because of a lack of understanding that transcendence has to be understood in a psychological sense, not an ontological one. For the Buddha, there is the fundamental comprehension in the unfettered awareness, or the non-manifest, purified consciousness, of the emptiness experience – all is dynamic and flows so there is no substantiality, and therefore no clinging to concepts or fixations. Since the label 'self' is merely a concept, there is no self or personal identity to cling to. 'Self' and identity are understood only as constructions of the cognitive apparatus. To illustrate this, I again cite how the Buddha used the following simile (where the **house builder is the cognitive habit of conceptually constructing a 'self'**) of his insight upon Awakening:

> 'House builder, you're seen!
>
> You will not build a house again.
>
> All your rafters broken, the ridge pole destroyed, gone to the Unformed, the mind has attained the end of craving.'

(Dhp 154)

Bibliography

1. Kalupahana, D.J. (1987) The Principles of Buddhist Psychology, Albany, NY: State University of New York Press.

2. Hamilton, S. (2000). Early Buddhism: A new approach: The I of the beholder(Vol. 16). Psychology Press.

3. Bhikkhu, T. (1994). The Buddhist Monastic Code. In USA: Library of Congress Cataloging.

4. Nishida, K., Abe, M., & Ives, C. (1992). An inquiry into the good. Yale University Press.

5. Keiji, N. (1982). Religion and nothingness. University of California Press.

6. See Reference 2.

7. Van Zeyst, H. (Bhikkhu Dhammapala) (1986). Touching the Essence, Six Lectures on Buddhism. The Wheel Publication No. 132/133/134.

8. Macy, J. R. (1976). Systems philosophy as a hermeneutic for Buddhist teachings. Philosophy East and West, 21-32.

6

Enlightenment: Reality, Actuality and Transcendence

'So habitual is the trance of ordinary life that one could say that human beings are a race that sleeps and awakens, but does not awaken fully. Because half-awake is sufficient for the task we customarily do, few of us are aware of the dysfunction of our condition.'[1]

Arthur J. Deikman

'The fermentations by which I would go to a deva-state, or become a gandhabba in the sky, or go to a yakkha-state & human-state:

Those have been destroyed by me, ruined, their stems removed.

Like a blue lotus, rising up, unsmeared by water, unsmeared am I by the world,

and so, brahman, I'm awake.'

Buddha AN 4.36 Dona Sutta

One definition of transcendence, in the sense of Enlightenment is: 'Transcendence, the fact of transcending, means a state of interpretation which goes beyond typical comprehension or experience.'

The Buddha's transcendence is defined by the radical comprehension, or pure experience, of the relativity and impermance of our cognitive-based world. We now understand that pure experience illuminates the difference between reality and actuality. Emptiness, or what is also called 'actuality', is what Buddhists use to denote an accurate expression of the way things are. The removal of the obscuring cognitive constructions is called 'the radical reorientation to actuality'. This truth is the actual beyond the representation; the antecedent behind the referent.

Removed from actuality is the addition of interpretative factors that create our reality. Reality is our cognitively conceived world based on a subject-object dichotomy, for, as we have seen, it is our cognitive apparatus that organises and creates this world. As psychiatrist Daniel N. Stern explains, '*We all agree that the subjective world is a mental construction that emerges from the interaction between Actuality and fashions it into a subjective psychic reality.*'[2]

In other words, what we mean as 'reality' is that which is perceived with a subjective consciousness and interpretation, meaning, or value, including all the self and identity constructs of who we believe we are. Our reality is based on how we understand and organise all the complexities of existence. We make a model of life, create our world, and operate using that blueprint. This blueprint determines what we perceive, and what it means; it serves as a means to process and filter incoming information. Due to the very fact that this reality is embraced, it is binding. Therefore, when such terms as 'I' and 'mine', or a 'self' are normally used, they are not merely expressions, they signify a level of reality that corresponds to a person's extent of insight regarding the true subjective nature of reality.

Knowing the subjectivity of reality *versus* the truth of actuality, it is easy to understand why the same event can be witnessed and interpreted in many different ways. Even though 'actuality' is that what *is* – reality is the model we normally cognisize, which is an approximation, or an interpretation of that existence. This external existence can never be truly conceptually understood by us, but individuals can transcend their subjective constructs and experience actuality, or emptiness.

Buddhist insights to Transcendence

The variously described experience of emptiness, suchness, the way things really are, bare attention or original mind, is the ultimate goal of Buddhist meditative practice. Buddhist meditation asserts that people can transcend the ways in which they normally experience reality to attain enlightenment. Through a gradual mental transformation programme as taught by the Buddha – the Eightfold Path – a practitioner is able to transcend the ordinary cognitive state of experiencing the world through the filter of their reality to attain tathata or actuality.

The focus of this Buddhist method is the mind – understanding, shaping or development, and liberation of the mind. Buddhist practices weaken and eventually transcend conceptual attachment and identifications. Interestingly, some psychoanalytic ideas deeply resonant with Buddhism, particularly the principle that, *'Knowledge leads to transformation, that theory and practice must not be separated, that in the every act of knowing oneself, one transforms oneself.'*[3]

One significant difference however, between Buddhist philosophy and Western ideas of psychology, is that physcotherapy aims to maintain and strengthen the self, whereas the Buddha transcended this belief in the substantial self. Buddhist psychology understands the imposition of static constructs and concepts onto experience, maintaining the notion of a 'self', and applying dichotomous constructs as interpretations of reality, a means to creating suffering and distress.

Buddhist insights go against the grain of what is commonly accepted as 'real' in everyday, Westernised experiences. As a result of Awakening, the 'self' is revealed as fiction and it exposes the 'I' as *'a self-representation as agent, as an image, abstraction, or simulacrum'*.[4] Such insights necessitate an understanding that our ordinary representation of self and personal identity is fundamentally a fiction and, therefore, illusory in nature, which we mistakenly take to be authentic. In his conversation with a student named Vaccha, the Buddha recognised and reflected on the difficulty of comprehending his teachings. The Buddha said:

> *'[...] Deep, Vaccha, is this phenomenon, hard to see, hard to realie, tranquil, refined, beyond the scope of conjecture, subtle, to-be-experienced by the wise. For those with other views, other practices, other satisfactions, other aims, other teachers, it is difficult to know.'*[5]

A common misconception of 'no-self' is that it is equated with the loss of personhood, or the denigration of psychological functions. Buddhism, however, does not negate mental functioning, denigrate the agency function of the individual, nor eradicate functional life-skills. Any such simplistic interpretation of Buddhist teachings commits a grave error. Throughout the suttas, the Buddha encourages skillful living by warning against associating with reckless or immature people, and instead encourages the adoption of what in modern psychology would be called ego strengths: realism, emotional control, responsibility, reflection, open-mindedness and empathy.

Instead, what is given up is the erroneous concept of an inherently existing ontological static self. Buddhist practice does not resort to repression, denial or fantasy. In other words, the empirical, functional and psychological 'ego' does not disappear with a realisation of selflessness, and a person still uses the term 'I', has a name, and a unique historical identity, but they are no longer fixed, obsessed or overinvested in representations, identities or habitual reactions.

Mental training in Buddhism is based on an empirical perspective. Experience is the ultimate criterion of truth. With the penetrative insight of enlightenment, Arahant (worthy, or noble one) is a title given to someone who has attained Enlightenment as a result of listening to,and practicing, the teachings of a Buddha, and who now sees through the usual proposed ultimate validity of concepts. For the Arahant, all concepts are transparent and not grasped at dogmatically. They are not regarded as ultimate categories. Concepts are, *'merely worldly conventions in common use, which an Arahant makes use of, without clinging to them.'* (D. N. I. 202)

One's entire conceptual blueprint has to be released, though gradually, and in the final awareness, even those concepts that have given us the greatest help in our practice are given up. To illustrate this point, the Buddha used a raft simile:

> *'In the same way, monks, I have taught the Dhamma compared to a raft, for the purpose of crossing over, not for the purpose of holding onto. Understanding the Dhamma as taught compared to a raft, you should let go even of Dhammas, to say nothing of non-Dhammas.'[6]*

The result is that the Arahant is under no illusion of worldly concepts through transcending them, rather than destroying them. Although the difference between the relatively true and false (in theory); between the precise and the vague (in terminology); and between concepts more conducive to the attainment of enlightenment than those which aren't can still be distinguished, it should always be remembered that none are regarded as absolute and inviolable categories. This revelation is gradual and collateral with rewarding personal experiences. Hence, the three significant terms in Buddhist ethics – gradual training, gradual doing, gradual practice – are applied. Use can be made therefore, without inhibition, of the conceptual tools that the Bhavana meditation employs, only they must be sharpened, and continued to be sharpened, until they are worn out in the process. So even Arahants will continue to use concepts as worldly conventions, in spite of all their flaws and contradictions, because concepts, with their ability to delude us, are not to be blamed *per se,* for they are merely objectifications or representations.

So, our perceptions and conceptualisations are our unique reality. We perceive and cognitively construct the world in which we live, and we often assume that everyone else interprets the world in the same way. But perception and cognitive construction is *our* 'reality', not actuality. Our perception and schemata are the basis of our ordinary decisions. We believe what we perceive to be true, and we base our decisions on that assumption. We decide what to do based on what we believe will best satisfy our lives. Our mistakes can show us – if we choose to acknowledge them – that our reality is tentative and relative, and that we can change. With change and insight, our reality can ultimately be transformed to transcend to actuality. These transformations mark our acquisition of wisdom.

The Middle Path (living between the polarity of sensual hedonism and extreme asceticism) of the Buddha's teachings is a pragmatic approach of choosing and using what is essential for the purpose, without attachment, and based on empirical evidence or the fact of experience. The principles of empiricism, relativity and pragmatism are the guide. In a famous quote, Zen Master Ch'ing-yuan Wei-hsin wrote of how his 'knowing' transformed and transcended with his Bhavana practice, resulting in his own Awakening:

> *'Thirty years ago, before I began the study of Zen, I said, "Mountains are mountains, waters are waters. "After I got an insight into the truth of Zen through the instruction of a good master, I said, "Mountains are not mountains, waters are not waters." But now, having attained the abode of final rest [Awakening], I say, "Mountains are really mountains, waters are really waters."'[7]*

Bibliography

1. Deikman, A. J. (1983). The observing self: Mysticism and psychotherapy. Beacon Press.

2. Stern, D. N. (1988). The dialectic between the "interpersonal" and the "intrapsychic": With particular emphasis on the role of memory and representation. Psychoanalytic Inquiry, 8(4), 505-512.

3. Fromm, E., Suzuki, D. T., & De Martino, R. (1960). Zen Buddhism and psychoanalysis. Oxford, England: Harper.

4. Epstein, M. (2008). Psychotherapy without the self: A Buddhist perspective. Yale University Press.

5. Aggi-Vacchagotta Sutta: To Vacchagotta on Fire (MN 72). Translated from the Pali by Thanissaro Bhikkhu. Access to Insight (Legacy Edition), 30 November 2013.

6. Majjhima Nikaya: The Middle-length Discourses. Edited by Access to Insight. Access to Insight (Legacy Edition), 21 December 2013.

7. Gaskins, R. W. (1999). " Adding legs to a snake": A reanalysis of motivation and the pursuit of happiness from a Zen Buddhist perspective. Journal of Educational Psychology, 91(2), 204.

7

Knowing and Not Knowing – What is Possible?

'Human thinking can only imagine reality, just as a portrait represents a person. And as a portrait is not 'the person' it represents, likewise any theory is not 'the reality' it describes. We then must humbly recognize that our minds' coherence and logic do not necessarily match the consistency of reality. And that also entails that reality does 'occur' and that we cannot conclude it is an 'illusion of our minds' simply because we cannot make sense of it.'

Henri Salles[1]

'The universe is not only stranger than we suppose, but stranger than we can suppose.'

J.B.S. Haldane[2]

'Much exists and evolves in this world which is not accessible to our comprehension, since our cerebral organization is primarily devised so that it secures survival of the individual in natural surroundings. Over and above this, modest silence is the appropriate attitude.'

Walter Hess[3]

*'Behind anything that can be experienced there is
something that the mind cannot grasp and whose
beauty and sublimity reaches us only indirectly and
as a feeble reflection.'*

Albert Einstein

*'What we observe is not nature itself, but nature
exposed to our method of questioning.'*

Werner Heisenberg[4]

There is an intrinsic impossibility of comprehending
actuality through the means of our cognitive
abilities. Actuality is the backdrop and physical source
from what we ultimately base our subjective and
conjectual interpretation of reality. This is the fruit of a
conceptualisation processes. The Buddha, understanding
all of the flaws inherent in conceptualising, would not
have thought to put a label on his teachings and, in fact,
there are many texts in which he discourages speculation
about the ontology of the external world. His message
was that we should focus our awareness on our cognitive
experience of life here and now. So, although describing
aspects of the 'doctrine' of the Buddha is a form of
conceptualising with which we are cautious, it nevertheless
helps us to better grasp a Right View and to develop
confidence in what the Buddha wanted us to understand.

Construction of Reality

The Buddha emphasised the crucial role of our
construction of reality using our cognitive apparatus.
His teachings can be best described as a form of
transcendental idealism, not, as sometimes said, a
model of metaphysical idealism. The crucial feature of
transcendental idealism is its assertion that, while our
world of experience is subjectively created, and the 'real'

lies beyond most of the ordinary range of our perception and conceptualisation of what can be experienced, we *have* our experience only *because* there is the transcendentally real or the actual.

The Buddha taught that, through the khandhas, a vital and clear link between the sense organs and the sense data can be found. This was not an idealistic assertion. There is a substantial 'environment' with which we interact, and to which we respond. So, for the Buddha, there was no denial of the existence of an external world as there is in Idealism. Rather, the Buddha taught that our ignorance is the ordinary, pre-enlightened, representational, cognitive understanding and experience of our world. We process what we sense and then create subjective representations at the reflective phase of experience; we mistake our interpretations of the world for the world itself – we take our mental constructions to be the world. Ignorance is 'seeing' and believing the world as consisting of discrete, static entities, both internal and external.

Professor of Philosophy Thomas Metzinger, in his book, *The Ego Tunnel,*[5] uses a metaphor to explain how our conscious experience is like a tunnel, and indeed, modern neuroscience has demonstrated that the content of our conscious experience is not only an internal representation but also an extremely selective way of representing information. What we see, hear, feel, smell and taste is only a very small sampling of what actually 'exists', because our sensory organs are necessarily limited and embedded as they evolved to promote the organism's survival. Our conscious model of reality is an inadequate projection of the inconceivably richer actuality surrounding and sustaining us. Therefore, the ongoing process of conscious experience is not an actual image of 'reality'.

Transcendental Idealism

In transcendental idealism, that which we call the 'external' world – the world we inhabit – is actually only a representation, or interpretation that we create with our cognitive apparatus, not the actual reality itself. We can never truly know or sense Reality because not only are we limited by the input of our khandhas, but our cognitive apparatus has evolved to only accommodate and service that input. The fanciful and inaccessible nature of sense data is such that as soon as one thinks in terms of them, one is estranged from reality. Our entire framework of conceptual categories is only representations, or pictures, of reality. The input through our sense organs is only possible because of an integral relationship between aspects of 'reality' and our sense organs.

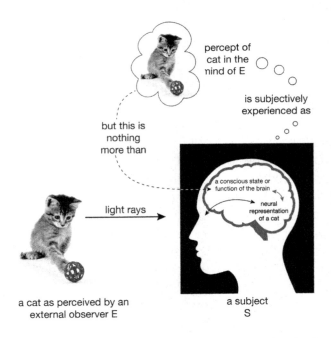

Figure 7.1 *Simplified view of a cat representation in the mind.*

Or, as Hamilton explains:

'[...] the reality of experience is experiential. And the reality of Reality is unknowable in (normal) experiential terms. The aim for the Buddhist is to understand the nature and limits of experience by means of understanding the nature and extent of one's subjective cognitive apparatus. In Buddhist terms, this subjectively and objectively correlated insight is knowing and seeing how things really are.'[6]

The Buddha was not trying to answer ontological or metaphysical questions, because they are misleading and ultimately unanswerable. However, given our pre-enlightened way of how we see things, we assume that the world is as real as we cognitively construct it. We think of the 'self' – the abstracted experiencer – as an individual, independent, and continuing being in a world of other such discrete entities. However, as the Buddha taught that all things existing in samsara are cognitively dependently originated, a subject-object dualism is ultimately a miscomprehension, 'Reality' is not conceptually graspable or verbally articulable. When the experiencer finally sees through the illusion of the projected dualisms and understands the non-substantialist nature of her cognitive world, she experiences nibbana; that is, bliss, serenity, and liberation.

Freedom from pre-enlightened conceptuality arises when representations are understood to be creations or projections of both the sense of 'self 'and the experience of a world where the 'self' and the things of the world together form the entanglement of desire. The 'self' is what desires, the things of the world are what are desired, and grasping with intention occurs when the two meet in the vortical interplay with consciousness. This is the crux of suffering.

Support of modern science

Modern science supports the Buddha's understandings about our relationship with 'reality'. In his attempts to define and explain the nature of a living system, the biologist H.R. Maturana came to a conclusion similar to that of the Buddha's with regards to the limits of our understanding of the nature of experience: 'The observer as an observer necessarily always remains in a descriptive domain, that is, in a relative cognitive domain. No description of an absolute reality is possible. Such a description would require an interaction with the absolute to be described, but the representation which would arise from such an interaction would necessarily be determined by the autopoietic (the natural process which includes the potential for transformation, the creation of novelty, from within the organization itself) organisation of the observer, not by the deforming agent; hence, the cognitive reality that it would generate would unavoidably be relative to the knower.'[7]

Some consider these paradigms, including the Buddha's, to represent a form of Solipsism; that is, that the whole of reality, meaning the external world and other people, are merely representations of the individual self, having no independent existence of their own, and that they may in fact, not even exist. Clearly this is a conclusion (or teaching) that has not been proffered by either the Buddha or the modern authors cited here. Rather, in all of their writings these thinkers advise of an existing separate world; they do recognise that other human beings and creatures share our environment and that it is possible to empathise and interact with them. The Buddha taught the Four Noble Truths specifically so that other sentient beings could awaken from their ignorance and cease their suffering. What all the thinkers cited here are claiming is that the outer environment is only partially accessible through the specialised doors of our sense organs, and that the rest of 'Reality' is beyond the abilities of our input mechanisms to absorb, leaving us with a very limited cognitive construction of Reality.

Scientific evidence has defined the limiters of the human body in its ability to sense the larger environment. So it is clear that there are significant limitations to our senses, and that there are an incredible number of things we can neither perceive nor even detect. For example, the vibration frequencies to which the human ear is sensitive are in the range of approximately 20 to 20,000 hertz (Hz; cycles per second), and this band is just a narrow slit in the total spectrum of sound and vibration. Some dolphins and bats, for example, can hear frequencies up to 100 kHz. Elephants can hear sounds at 14-16hz, while some whales can hear subsonic sounds as low as 7hz (in water).

There are many types of environmental factors (such as radio waves, magnetic fields, inert gases) to which our bodies are completely insensitive, and that we cannot detect at all. So it is clear that there are significant limitations to our senses, and that there are an incredible number of things we can neither perceive nor even detect. The theoretical physicist Wolfram Schommers also postulates that only some information of the possible external reality flows into the body of the observer through his/her sense organs and that the brain 'forms' a picture of that reality. This process is a transformation of representation of the objects in the outside world. On the one hand, we have the 'Reality', whilst on the other, we create a picture of reality, and the structures in the pictures are different from the external 'Reality' they are created to represent. Echoing the Buddha's reluctance to search for and answer metaphysical questions, Schommers writes, 'Furthermore, we can say quite generally that there is no picture-independent point of view conceivable, i.e. there is no external point of view which would enable a direct observation of basic reality. Thus, questions like, "How is basic reality built up and what kind of processes take place in it?" makes no sense.'[8]

In his later book, Schommers expands this idea:

> '*Events occurring in the cosmos are presented inside a biological system only as symbols in a picture. The picture (mental manifestations) in the mind contains aspects of reality only in symbolic form, i.e. the elements in reality are not identical with the pertinent elements in the picture. Therefore, 'basic reality,' i.e. reality which exists independently of the observer, is in principle not accessible in any DIRECT WAY. Rather, it is observable or describable by means of pictures on different levels, i.e. levels of reality [...] Everything is located in the head, not only the products of fantasy and scientific laws, but those things which we understand as 'hard' objects.*'[9]

Although some might disagree with the specific language Schommers uses to represent this process of representation, the basic stance of the difference between the outside environment and the internal creation of usable and comprehensible cognitive models is not disputed by most neurologists. Schommers argues, from the perspective of a modern physicist, a viewpoint that is very similar to the Buddha's and to Transcendental Idealism.[10]

Theoretical physicist Bernard d'Espagnat, also argues that we cannot directly know the Transcendental Reality, because:

> '*When, in its spirit, quantum theory and Bell's theorem are used as touchstones, the two main traditional philosophical approaches, realism and*

*idealism, are found wanting. A more suitable
conception seems to be an intermediate one, in
which the mere postulated existence of a holistic
and hardly knowable Mind – Independent Reality
is found to have explaining power. [...] This model
considers Reality as not lying in space and time,
indeed being a prior to both, and it involves the view
that the great mathematical laws of physics may
only let us catch some glimpses on the structures of
the Mind-Independent Reality.'[11]*

Veiled Reality

D'Espagnat calls this model Veiled Reality to suggest
that the Mind-Independent Reality, so similar to what
we are calling Transcendental Idealism, is for the most
part inconceivable. Veiled Reality refers to a 'world' that is
independent from humans and veiled by perception, brain
structure, and the language of our minds' participation
in knowledge. Furthermore, d'Espagnat believes that we
are involved in this actuality because it is not separated
from us by the dualistic chasm of object *versus* subject.
Rather, we exist in it. We are an integral part of the actual.
We are 'swimming' in it. Reality is not a specific area of
the universe that exists separate from our senses, our
limitation is that we only have the capacity to be involved in
an *exceedingly* small aspect of it.

D'Espagnat maintains that as the Buddha taught,
sense impressions and sensations are real, as are our
sense organs. In sight and colour, the photons (or waves),
along with the retinal cones are real, and their interactions
create our vision. The same is true of our other senses.
This is the middle way of understanding our place in
reality. We don't have to seek our participation in it; we
are a part of it. However, in our ignorance we take our
cognitive representations or pictures of reality, to be Reality

itself. But under certain meditative conditions, we can understand how our subject-object dualistic substantialism creates this illusion – the illusion that it is ignorance that creates our suffering.

As the Buddha explained in a descriptive explanation of the doctrine of kamma and dependent origination, life has a certain level of predictability – certain conditions have their origins in certain other conditions. Life is not total randomness, but it is also not total determinism. This approach is not dissimilar to d'Espagnat's idea of Veiled Reality. We know that we are involved in reality when we obtain approximately the same results regardless of our methods of investigating a phenomenon or replicating behaviours. Stability is a reliable criterion of reality. Or in other words, a reasonable or practical attitude towards life is needed, one that recognises that an event is created when a certain cause or causes originate it. When my hungry cat comes into the kitchen, under most circumstances she will go to her food plate and eat. I don't know if she will walk or run, eat quickly or slowly, or if after entering the kitchen she'll choose not to eat because a loud noise will startle her or because she does not feel well. But under most circumstances, quite reliably, she will eat the food on her plate. In the affective/cognitive realm, when I am thirsty, if I think of a drink that I enjoy a lot, cognitive feedback will generate physical responses such as salivation, and my desire or craving for that drink will increase. If my physical-affective-cognitive experience repeats itself in a replicable way, I can assume that this stability of phenomena demonstrates an indication of Reality.

Space and time

*'The relationship between space and time in
the human mind has long been the subject
of philosophical inquiry and psychological
experimentation. There is now no doubt that space
and time are intimately linked in our minds, yet the
nature of this relationship remains scientifically and
neurologically unclear.*

Lera Boroditsky[12]

*'There is no first beginning, no first beginning is
knowablecBuddha.'*

SamyuttaNikaya 15.1-2

The Buddha's teachings suggest that how we
experience (and interpret) time and space has important
implications. As Sue Hamilton notes:

*'[...] if the structure of the world of experience is
correlated with the cognitive process, then it is not
just that we name objects, concrete and abstract,
and superimpose secondary characteristics
according to the senses. It is also that all the
structural features of the world of experience are
cognitively correlated. In particular, space and time
are not external to the structure but are part of it.'[6]
Therefore, everything that is knowable in temporal
and spatial terms is dependent on our subjective
cognitive processes.[6]*

Hamilton continues:

*'If the entirety of the structure of the world as we
know it is subjectively dependent, including space
and time, it follows that the very concept of there
being origins, beginnings, ends, extents, limits,
boundaries and so on, is subject-dependent. The
entirety of temporality and of special extension are*

concepts which do not operate independently of subjective cognitive processes.'[6]

When Hamilton turns to the 'the classic unanswered or undetermined questions' of the Buddha, such as, 'Is the world eternal or finite?', she points to an important difference of the Transcendental Reality model regarding time and space as we understand the implications of the Buddha's teachings today. Inherent in these questions about eternity is the assumption that time and space:

> *'...are transcendentally real – that is, that they operate externally to subjective cognitive process. As with the questions on the self, they seek to find a permanence or immortality. However, if space and time are part of the structural characteristics of the experiential world, and that is cognitively dependent, then one can see that the presupposition of the transcendental reality of time and space is false, and that the fundamental premises on which the questions rest are therefore also false and unanswerable.'[6]*

The Transcendental Idealism model assumes that 'Reality' is embedded in space and time, whereas the Buddha teaches that space and time don't exist outside of us but are a part of our cognitive constructions of 'Reality'. D'Espagnat, from the perspective of a physicist, takes a similar position and argues that our experience of space-time is subjective to our cognitive constructions of phenomena:

> *'I am therefore inclined to think that 'the Real – alias human independent reality – is not embedded in space-time. And indeed, I go as far as speculating that, quite the contrary, the nature of space-time is [...] not "nominal but phenomenal," that space-time is a "reality – for-us."'[13]*

Space-time and reality are a cognitive construction. The experimental physicist Manoj Thulasidas, builds on, an insight from cognitive neuroscience about the nature of Reality:

'Reality is a convenient representation that our brain creates out of our sensory inputs. This representation, though convenient, is an incredibly distant experiential mapping of the actual physical causes that make up the input to our senses. [...] Reality is nothing but a cognitive model created in our brain starting from our sense inputs, visual inputs being the most significant. Space itself is part of this cognitive model. [...] Once we identify the manifestations of the limitations of our perceptions and cognitive representations, we can understand the consequent constraints on our space and time.'[14]

Schommers takes a similar stance on the issue of space-time:

'We normally assume that our sensations produced by the brain are identical with reality itself, but this should not be the case as we have argued that space-time cannot be outside the brain because space-time has to be considered as an auxiliary element for the representation of physically real processes. In other words, the outside world, the material bodies, cannot be embedded in space-time. That in particular means that not only the things in front of us (cars, houses, trees, etc.) are in our head but also space-time, where all these things are positioned. We have only impressions that all these 'hard objects', together with space-time, are located outside us. Space and time are obviously elements of the brain; they come into existence due to specific brain functions.'[10]

To support this perspective, Schommers also relates the position of the important philosopher Immanuel Kant: *'Space and Time are exclusively features of our brain and the world outside is projected on it.'*[15] As reported in Schommers's Quantum Processes, *'Kant argues that Space Time (and the Causal Motion of Matter in Space) are our constructions of our own mind.'*[10]

So this model asserts that even space and time are intimately linked in our cognitive experience, resulting in a construction of a reality constructed by our cognitive representations.

Actuality

Actuality is not fully accessible to us because of the sense/input relationship inherent in the khandhas. This can absorb (from the larger transcendent reality) only a small amount of information, which can then be cognitively processed. Actuality is not accessible in a direct way, and the subjectively independent point of view is cognitively constructed. In actual reality, space and time as we experience them do not exist. Although cognitive constructs can be formed on the basis of the different types of space-time structures, there will be no similarity between our corresponding cognitive constructs and the corresponding structures or characteristics of the 'Veiled Reality'.

To put it another way, a transcendental reality does exist. The human mind and ideas that are dependent on human bodies and brains do exist. There is a necessary connection between the matter of our brain, our body and other matter of the universe, which enables us to see it, function, move around. Our representation of Reality (including space and time) does not come directly from our senses, but is constructed by the mind, and so is limited to sensing only a tiny fraction of what exists in Actuality.

So we have the assertion that space-time is a part of our cognitive modelling of the external world, a modelling that is severely limited by input of information picked up by our senses that then creates our cognitive constructions is selective and narrow. The conclusion, as the Buddha explained, is that we cannot know the absolute reality; chasing after this knowledge is a part of the pre-enlightened ignorance that creates frustration and suffering.

Modern science continues to expand our knowledge of the selective knowable reality because it continues to create more sophisticated sense-dependent measuring instruments (such as the electron microscope, positron emission tomography (PET) scanner, telescope, and X-ray astronomy detector) that allow us to investigate previously unknown aspects of the known universe. This does not change the fact, however, that what is being expanded upon is only such knowledge as is available through the khandhas and cognitive apparatus. Basic Reality, the reality which exists independently of us, remains inaccessible in any direct way. As Karl Mannheim states,

> *'[…] The world as 'world' exists only with reference to the knowing mind, and the mental activity of the subject determines the form in which it appears. […] This is the first stage in the dissolution of an ontological dogmatism which regarded the 'world' as existing independently of us, in a fixed and definitive form.'*[16]

For the Buddha, questions concerning the existence of the world in time and space are unanswerable because they are formulated on false premise, and therefore can never really be answered.

Speculating about these questions is not the way to end our suffering, find peace, to release, to nibbana. Buddhism is very pragmatic and empirical: the practice of mental culture or development along the Eight-factor Path is aimed at that direct understanding of how our cognitive apparatus works and, therefore, at showing us that our lived experience is truly neither an inherent 'I' nor 'world'.

Bibliography

1. Salles, H. (http://gravimotion.info/coherence_consistency.htm) Retrieved 7 June 2013.

2. Haldane, J. B. S. (1927). Possible Worlds and Other Papers. Piscataway, New Jersey: Transaction Publishers.

3. Hess, W. R., & Fischer, H. (1973). Brain and Consciousness: A Discussion about the Function of the Brain. Perspectives in Biology and Medicine, 17(1), 109-118.

4. Heisenberg, W. (1971). Physics and Philosophy: The Revolution in Modern Science (3rd imprint). George Allen & Unwin Ltd. p. 58.

5. Metzinger, T. (2009). The Ego Tunnel: The Science of the Mind and the Myth of the Self. Basic Books.

6. Hamilton, S. (2000). Early Buddhism: A New Approach: The I of the Beholder (Vol. 16). Psychology Press.

7. Maturana, H. R., & Varela, F. J. (1980). Autopoiesis and Cognition: The Realization of the Living (No. 42). Springer Science & Business Media.

8. Schommers, W. (1994). Space and time, matter and mind: The Relationship between Reality and Space-time. London: World Scientific.

9. Schommers, W. (1998). The visible and the Invisible: Matter and Mind in Physics (Vol. 3). London: World Scientific.

10. Schommers, W. (2010). Quantum processes. World Scientific Books.

11. d'Espagnat, B. (1998). Quantum theory: A pointer to an Independent Reality. arXiv preprint quant-ph/9802046.

12. Casasanto, D., Fotakopoulou, O., & Boroditsky, L. (2010). Space and time in the child's mind: Evidence for a cross-dimensional asymmetry. Cognitive science, 34(3), 387-405.

13. d'Espagnat, B. (2006). On Physics and Philosophy (Vol. 41). Princeton: Princeton University Press.

14. Thulasidas, M. (2008). Constraints of Perception and Cognition in Relativistic Physics. Galilean Electrodynamics 6, 103-117.

15. Haselhurst, G., "Kant", (http://www. spaceandmotion.com). Retrieved 7 June 2013.

16. Mannheim, K. (2013). Ideology and Utopia. London: Routledge.

8

The General Doctrine of the Law of Dependent Co-arising

'That comes to be when there is this; that arises with the arising of this.'

MN 38

'All the entities of reality, be they of the within or the without, come into existence in interrelation.'

Herbert Guenther[1]

'Things come together in this world to make things happen, that's all you can say. They come together.'

Graham Swift[2]

'... all physical and mental manifestations which constitute individual appearances are interdependent and condition or affect one another, in a constant process of arising and ceasing.'

John Bowker[3]

'Paticca-Samuppada, The Teaching of Dependent Co-arising or Origination', is a critical text of the Buddha's teaching and is at the core of all schools of Buddhism. When the Buddha expressed his own experience of Enlightenment, or explained

*more generally how one could attain Awakening,
he referred frequently not only to the importance of
understanding the Four Noble Truths, but also to
the understanding of dependent origination. The
Buddha said, 'Whoever sees Dependent Co-arising
sees the Dhamma; whoever sees the Dhamma sees
Dependent Co-arising.'*

Mahjima Nikaya 1. 191

There are often two perspectives accompanying any topic: the descriptive and the explanatory. The same holds true for dependent origination. The Buddha taught that everything in existence is dependently originated and they are, therefore, always dynamic, interrelated and impermanent. We exist interdependently in the embedded interaction of the niche and organism. A descriptive interpretation of this is to understand that everything arises as the result of conditions and ceases when those conditions change: it is not so much that x will cause y; a better approach is if there is a y, then there must have been an x.

This descriptive way understanding the concept of co-arising means that when a phenomenon arises, it also causes its effect to arise simultaneously. The fact that nothing exists independently of conditioning factors is, with a little observation, not difficult to grasp. For example, when the sun rises, heat and light arise with it. Sounds eminate from a violin only when the violin-bow moves across its strings. Whether a plant seed grows is dependent on various factors such as the necessary amounts of earth, water, air and sunlight. Similarly, as particular thoughts arise in the mind, so too do the emotions and actions associated with it. The five senses awaken only when the appropriate sense objects make contact with the correct sense base.

People often believe the misconception that they are inherently isolated and self-contained organisms enclosed within their own circle of private interests perhaps including family and friends, and the outer world is only regarded as and when it may help or hinder what comes within the purview of their selfish interests. But all things, including people, are parts of a whole and do not exist independently from an interrelated process of change. As professor Timothy Morton explains:

> *'All forms of life are connected in a vast, entangling mesh. This interconnectedness penetrates all dimensions of life. No being, construct, or object can exist independently from the ecological entanglement, nor does 'Nature' exist as an entity separate from the uglier or more synthetic elements of life. Realizing this interconnectedness is the ecological thought.'[4]*

As everything evolves is the result of co-arising conditions, the Buddha taught that there is no first cause. No single event in the world, or perhaps the universe, is ever isolated or stands alone. Because everything is in constant flux, there are no unchanging or permanent entities or identity, such as an individual self. While this descriptive explanation of being in the world is accurate and clear, there is also the understanding of the doctrine of dependent origination on an explanatory level, which emphasises experience as our cognitive system.

Knowing originates in our cognition

In studying the physiology of mind/body interactions with the environment, we remember that in accordance with cognitive psychology, cognition involves all processes by which the sensory input is transformed, reduced, elaborated, stored, recovered and used. In other words, every psychological phenomenon is a cognitive phenomenon. Therefore, everything we 'know' actually originates in our mind, and in that way we make sense of our experiences. How we cognitate things, the forms in which we know them, the names we give them as well as our reactions to them – all of these are dependent on our physiological 'mind' system, current and previous cognitations. It is our cognitive apparatus that is the home of our dependent origination.

The Buddha taught that suffering refers to our psychological experience of unsatisfactoriness, distress and despair prior to Enlightenment. Ignorance grows from our concept of ourselves as a static, autonomous being, which causes us to be biased and self-absorbed, resulting in a narrow, subjective focus of mind. As Bhikkhu Buddhadasa reports:

'The Buddha's doctrine states instead that what is designated as the 'self' in fact constitutes an uninterrupted and interconnected process of psycho-physical forces not separated from an external socio-material environment.'[5]

The Buddha taught, through the doctrine of dependent co-arisng, that all things in our conceptual framework are conditioned by other things, even though they seem individually separate. Therefore, 'how' we know everything is through the functioning of our cognitive apparatus as the nexus of our experience. Hamilton explains:

'[...] at a more explanatory level one can see that all things are actually dependently originated in our cognitive apparatus. It is in the processing of all incoming experiential data that the identity of any of the factors of our experience is acquired: in making sense of those data, it is we who give them names. Put differently, what the existence of any of the factors of our experience in the form in which

we know them is dependent on is our cognitive apparatus.'[6]

According to the Buddha, our total world of experience is dependent on our systematic cognitive organisation, with which we make 'sense' of and make 'real' the world of our experience.

The Buddha stated that, *'All mental states (dhammā) are preceded by mind (manopubbaṅgamā), having mind as their master (manoseṭṭhā) created by mind (manomayā).'* (Dhammapada 1) The essential message is that the states of our mind determine whether or not we suffer. The law of dukkha states that the unenlightened experience suffering because the origin of suffering lies in one's egotistical psychological perspective, creating craving (binding, sense-based and selfish), which is in the final analysis insatiable, stressful, infatuating, insufficient and unquenchable.

In Buddhism however, our world is sometimes referred to as a 'fabrication,' meaning that the external world does not exist in the way we cognitively construct it, and that the physical environment does not actually exist in the way we commonly imagine it. Our structuring and representation of the world is dependent on our cognitive processes. For the unenlightened, what their cognitive apparatus creates and imagines involves dualism, most notably of polarities – a subject-object split. This is a significant insight. We are accustomed to, and thoroughly believe, that the external world which we construct through our cognitive apparatus is the fruit available for our taking; the perspectives, beliefs or virtual realities we have developed during our lifetimes are as certain and real as the objects we experience in living. This is a form of ignorance which promotes and fosters our unenlightened ways of thinking and behaving.

Professor L. K. Tong wrote:

*'And so you opted for the substantialist's art of self
making, cutting off all umbilical cords to the Mother of
Field-Being. You first dignify yourself in the kingly robes
of an independent entity, enthroning yourself in the lonely
kingdom of ego-substance. Then with the projective magic
of your subjective substantiality, you objectify everything
on your way to Godlike rigidity. And with the pointing of
the substantialising wand, a bond was broken; a shade
of mutuality has withered and waned. Now everything
becomes merely external and separate from everything
else. External is your objective world, you objectified a
God, and your objectified self. Anything you cannot safely
possess and control you relegate to the dark side of
the Other, the Hell, the objective pole, and condemned
it as ugly, or evil. Oh, in carrying your Godlike rigidity to
all eternity (as if you were in fact rigidly eternal), you, a
virtuoso in dualisation, have created the most unhappy
situation.'*[7]

Therefore, we have become a most unhappy, suffering
creature.

The Gestalt Field theory

The Gestalt phenomenological perspective – or Field
theory – is an example of a Western way of thinking
that is sympathetic to the dynamic nature of human
behaviour, and takes a perspective similar that found in the
Buddha's dependent-origination doctrine.

In the terms of Field Theory, 'Field' is defined as a
dynamic, interrelated system where one part influences
other parts in the system. Instead of the belief of static,
inherent dualism, in which a self is isolated from its
situation, the individual is seen in context. Yontef explains

this life principle as: '*A totality of mutually influencing forces that together form a unified interactive whole.*'[8] 'Field' replaces the notion of discrete, isolated particles and instead, individuals always exist regarding relationships, even if it entails avoidance or denial. Existing on many levels, the 'Field' is a whole in which the parts are in an immediate relationship with, and are responsive to each other; no part is unaffected by what goes on elsewhere in the 'Field'. So according to Gestalt psychology, Field Theory assumes that behaviour and cognitive processes are part of a 'Field' that affect each other. These processes may include memories, beliefs, perceptions and physiology. Any change in one process changes the whole pattern. For example, the world looks different when we are feeling ill or remembering a sad memory. All the conscious/unconscious psychological facts that make our private world continuously change. Some inputs exert a positive influence on us, whilst others have a negative effect. It is believed that it is the interaction between these beliefs which determines human behaviour.

Regulation of the boundary

Seen from the Gestalt Field perspective, the boundary between 'agent' and 'environment' must remain permeable to exchanges, but autonomous enough for homeostatic functioning. Since metabolic processes are governed by the laws of homeostasis, even choice of environmental nourishment needs to be prioritised in accordance with the dominance in a hierarchy of needs. Ideally, the most urgent need energises the organism until it is met or is superseded by another more vital need. Living is a progression of needs – met and unmet – achieving homeostatic balance before going on to the next moment and the new need. The continual transformation and co-arising of all states is the hallmark of existence.

To maintain the flow of life and good boundary functioning, people transition between connecting and separating, being in contact with the current aspects of the physical environment before withdrawal of attention and moving on to the next, and so on. The flow, or contact boundary, is lost in either confluence (fusion) or isolation with unwholesome consequences. In wholesome, organistic self-regulation, choosing and learning happen holistically, with a natural integration of mind and body, thought and feeling, spontaneity and deliberateness.

The Buddha conceived of the idea of the mind-body-environment as a single experiencing system. Our experience is the awareness of the autopoietic system rooted in the psychophysical cognitive apparatus embedded in the external world. Therefore, in order for us to understand how we experience life, we do not by focus on the subjective or objective separately, but through insight meditation, which enables us to gain understanding into the nature of knowledge, or 'seeing things as they are'. This understanding (or solution), while in itself not affecting Reality, helps us to better know how limited we are in terms of our understanding of it and that our Reality is completely cognitively constructed. Sue Hamilton sums it up well when she says:

'If all things are dependently originated, then it follows that nothing has independent self-hood. The way in which human beings occur is therefore not as dependent selves... its relevance lies not in the question of whether or not a (human) self exists but in how whatever there is exists... it is stating that in seeking to know what you are, or even whether or not you are, you are missing the solution to the problem of cyclic continuity... you need to forget even the issue of self-hood and understand

instead how you work in a dependently originated world of experience.'[9]

This 'how' is the focus of a Buddhist-based psychology.

Bibliography

1. Guenther, Herbert V. (1971) Buddhist Philosophy in Theory and Practice. Penguin, London.

2. Swift, G. (1996). Last Orders. Picador.

3. Bowker, J. (1997). "Paticca-samuppāda." The Concise Oxford Dictionary of World Religions. Retrieved from http://www.encyclopedia.com/doc/1O101-Paticcasamuppda.html

4. Morton, T. The Ecological Thought, Harvard University Press, Cambridge, MA, 2010.

5. Bhikkhu, Buddhadasa. (2011). Paticcasamuppada: Dependent Origination in Everyday Life. Thammasapa.

6. Hamilton-Blyth, S. Early Buddhism: A New Approach: The I of the Beholder, 2000, Routledge, p.92.

7. Tong, L.K. Poem, The Third Eye of Field Being. Cited in . Metaphysics, Theology, and Self: Relational Essays Harold H. Oliver 2006 Mercer University Press, p.16.

8. Yontef, G. (1993). Awareness, Dialogue & Process. The Gestalt Journal Press. New York. p.295.

9. Hamilton-Blyth, S. Early Buddhism: A New Approach: The I of the Beholder, 2000, Routledge, p.22.

9

Kamma

'Intention I tell you, is kamma.

Intending, one does kamma by way of body, speech, and mind.'

~ A N 6.621

'It is choice that I call action; it is in choosing that a man acts by body, speech and mind....Actions ripen in three ways: they can ripen here and now, on reappearance or in some life-process beyond that.'

~ A N 6:63

In Buddhist texts, the term kamma (or karma), is used to indicate volition – an action that occurs because of intention (the mind is bent towards that action), created through one's perceptions and cognitive processes and acted on by certain behaviours. Kamma has also been defined as purposive, or willed striving. An important point to remember is that the teaching about kamma isn't about predestination or divining about the futue. Just as how we proceed on the path to awakening isn't influenced by previous lives (you can't practise with that). Instead, the psychologically based workings of kamma equate to the cognitive processes by which we consciously choose actions. The actions we choose leave results of memories and eventually habits. That is, our thoughts, to intentions, to actions have a psychological, emotional and physiological result that shapes our minds.

The moral or ethical nature of people's kamma can vary greatly, depending on an individual's learning, habits of thought and clarity of mind. The moral nature of one's conscious actions determines the quality of life for an individual, as well as for others. As one proceeds in bhavana-citta, or mind development, the mind is conditioned and purified through the cognitions that establish wholesome, ethical choices. If we are consciously motivated by wholesome (compassion), or unwholesome (aversion, fear) choices, then those qualities get established in our cognitive apparatus. As you act, so you become.

The term vipāka (literally meaning fruit), refers to the outcomes of those cognitions, particularly their psychological and emotional consequences – 'the fruit of our kamma'. Wise or skillful thoughts create beneficial kamma, characterised by good will and wholesome cognitive, as well as external, outcomes. Conversely, unwise or unskillful thoughts that lead to actions which create harmful kamma, characterised by unwholesome emotions and negative cognitive and external outcomes. Therefore:

> *'If one speaks or acts with an impure mind, pain*
> *follows one as the wheel, the hoof of draught-ox.*
> *If one speaks or acts with a pure mind, happiness*
> *follows one as the shadow that never departs.'*
> *(Dhammapada, V. 1)*

There is also neutral kamma, or volition, strictly tied to the autopoietic, or maintainance of the functions of the living system, such as eating when hungry or sleeping when tired. This type of volition does not have any kammic influence.

The Buddha's teaching of kamma is a doctrine emphasising the conscious application of will to initiate personal psychological transformation, and is fundamental to his prescription of psychological purification. The nature of an individual's kamma has its origins in the learned, conditioned and habituated thought patterns with accompanying behavioural tendencies applied over time. A key aspect of these teachings is that, although our interaction with environments do influence us, through proper mental training and effort, using the Buddha's Eightfold Path, we are ultimately responsible for the content and expression of our cognitive apparatus. As is discussed in an article by J. Kevin O'Regan and Alva Noë, the transformation of raw sensations into a world of representations imbued with salience, meaning, and value, only occurs through the filtering and sense-making activities of our cognitive apparatus. Our choices of what we attend to and encourage, significantly influences the outcomes of these processes.[1]

Rather than promoting a strict determinism with resignation and powerlessness, the early Buddhist notion of kamma focused on the importance of monitoring and being aware of what the conscious mind is doing in every moment (mindfulness), with the necessity of directing and maintaining our thoughts and reactions to the ethically beneficial, and away from the harmful. The shift created by such possibility is evident: the aware subject stops being confused and can begin to be the organiser of their own thoughts. The cultivation of metacognition capabilities develops the governing skills which makes cognitive transformation possible.

This perspective of having the ability to enjoy a freedom of thinking that enables a person to develop desired mindsets is well known to modern psychologists, who also advocate and observe the possibility of beneficial strategic cognitive structural change among their clients.

The conscious cognitive choices we make can lead to either greater psychic happiness or greater misery, depending on their kammic roots. We can cultivate beneficial kamma by practicing mindfulness and benevolence until it becomes an ego-syntonic habitual characteristic of our cognition and behaviour. The performance of morally or ethically 'beneficial' or 'harmful' actions can also be taken as external indicators of one's progress (or lack thereof) toward Enlightenment. However, whilst the development of purified mental states is reliant on wholesome kamma, the Buddha taught that, ultimately, all intentional perspectives and actions, even relatively benign ones, are misguided, as they contribute to a false dualistic view of the universe:

> 'For the final cessation of suffering, all kamma, wholesome and unwholesome, must be transcended, must be abandoned. Putting aside good and evil, one attains nibbana. There is no other way.' (Dhammapada, V. 1)

According to Buddhist teachings, Enlightenment brings an end to intentionally 'self'-based views, hence volitions, and instead, confers lasting liberation from the cycle of death and rebirth. An *Awakened One*, or person who has reached Enlightenment, lacks volitions based on the ignorance of dualistic concepts, such as 'I want'. Instead, the actions of an Arahant are pragmatic and neutral; he or she has gone beyond thinking in terms of good and evil, and beyond actions rooted in selfish desire and grasping – all duality is overcome. Enlightenment can be described as a deeply felt realisation of the essential unity and impermanence of all reality, which by its nature transcends the distinction between the controller and the world that he or she is attempting to control. This is accomplished by entering a state of pure experience, a kind of non-conceptual sensory awareness, devoid of the usual labels and judgments that motivates so much of our goal-directed behavior. Upon Enlightenment, one transcends the illusionary perspective of dualism that asserts a meaningful separation between 'thou' and 'that', 'self'and 'other'; and ceases to strive for the desired objects found in the pre-enlightened experience. 'Destroyed are their (germinal) seeds (khina-bija); selfish desires no longer grow,' as it is stated in the Ratana Sutta. By letting go of the convictions and dogma that drive our usual egotistical and self-serving actions, one is finally freed from the futile circularity of pursuing selfish desires and suffering that follows.

The liberation found upon Enlightenment does not imply the destruction of one's personality or cognitive apparutas. The earlier unwholesome schemas and habits have been abandoned, and the new, insight-based cognitive processes are retained. In addition, during moments of meditation, one may experience a complete transformation of the boundaries that normally define the individual 'self', which leads to the insight of 'non-self', or Emptiness. However, the previously developed purified thought patterns and memories that led up to the realisation or insight of pure experience, are the platform and support for all future perceptions, thoughts, judgments and actions. The Arahant still tastes sugar as sweet, comprehends a house as a structure for living in, and a gong as making a particular sound. The point is that the Arahant is no longer attached to these objects in an enduring way. When a person achieves nibbana, he or she is no longer deceived by the seemingly true nature of representative, dualistic thinking. Whereas the unenlightened person normally believes they have self agency, 'I make a decision', in more lucid meditative states, it's possible instead to observe how the different actions and reactions which we usually assigned to 'the self' are precipitated only when certain conditions are present; how ego-syntonic habituated responses create actions to those conditions, and how, even in moments of choice, our thought processes are caused by the mix of our cognitive history and present environment. There is no inherent, immanent 'self' as a conductor controlling the orchestra – rather, the improvisional orchestra is the experience we label the 'self'. It's an emergent phenomenon of the vast number of causes and conditions that are happening all the time. Although some may mistakenly understand this state of coherence as an example of determinism, it isn't. It is the seamless, coherent response of the whole person to the physical environment. Therefore, the intention expressed is without conflict or hestitation (which normally creates the illusion of free will as choice).

Understanding this, the Buddha emphasised the transformation of the dispositions, rather than their elimination, through the persevering psychological effort of cultivation refinement and purification. The transformation is created through personal verification, not supposition. In the Kalama Sutta, the Buddha instructed it this way:

> "So, as I said, Kalamas: "Don't go by reports,
> by legends, by traditions, by scripture, by logical
> conjecture, by inference, by analogies, by
> agreement through pondering views, by probability,
> or by the thought." This contemplative is our
> teacher. "When you know for yourselves that,
> "These qualities are unskillful; these qualities are
> blameworthy; these qualities are criticized by the

wise; these qualities, when adopted and carried out, lead to harm and to suffering," – then you should abandon them.' Thus was it said.'

And in reference to this was it said:

"Now, Kalamas, don't go by reports, by legends, by traditions, by scripture, by logical conjecture, by inference, by analogies, by agreement through pondering views, by probability, or by the thought." This contemplative is our teacher. When you know for yourselves that, "These qualities are skillful; these qualities are blameless; these qualities are praised by the wise; these qualities, when adopted and carried out, lead to welfare and to happiness," – then you should enter and remain in them.'[2]

Therefore, the method of personal verification of the teachings creates the ego-syntonic incorporation of the doctrine. Step by step through the learning and verification of the Eightfold Path, the student comes to clearly see and accept and, therefore, incorporate the doctrine points into their schemas, or worldview.

As we saw in the memory section, it is always easier to learn a new habit than to unlearn an old one. So the process of metamorphosis is completed when the mindstate of 'emptiness' is finally created showing the 'original mind'. For the Arahant, the basis of ignorance is completely eliminated, yet the fully discriminating cognitive apparatus still remains. One does not lose one's self-sufficient state of mind. Even in the case of complete liberation, existence continues with existential goals until one dies. But for the Enlightened one, there is no longer a mind affected with ignorance. There is no longer papañca or 'diffusion' of egoistically-based intentionality of one's experience with its tendency to grow and expand. The arahant is nippapañca – without diversifications, free from any attachments, free from habitual burdens accumulatedin the past.

A good example of nippapañca are the Zen Buddhist **proverbs**: *'Before Enlightenment chop wood, carry water...after Enlightenment chop wood, carry water.'* And, *'When hungry eat, when tired sleep.'*

The essence of these quotes is that upon achieving an Enlightened mind, the most important thing is not to be dualistic, leave behind biased (like/dislike), intentionally based actions, and instead, stay with ease and equanimity in the non-volitional (neutral) simplicity of the present moment. Unenlightened human beings do not psychologically live in the present moment with bare attention, but remain attached to their past-based biases, see the present through the darkened lenses of unwholesome mindsets and crave for preferential ideals in the future. All self-centered thoughts limit our 'original mind'. Focusing unbiasedly, simply and openly on the present moment removes and trains the mind from constantly drifting to wants, desires, avoidances... all driven by a mind obsessed with seeking attachments to lasting pleasures and avoiding anything deemed unpleasant.

As the Buddha taught, with craving, clinging attachment and perseverative obsession, comes suffering. But, in the mindset of, *'When hungry eat, when tired sleep,'* one is totally present to life as it is unfolding; fully present to the simple necessities that one's organism needs to survive. There is no abstracted separation or alienation to the process of living. The difference between before and after Awakening is the perspective (hence insight) created through experiencing the 'pure awareness' of non-separateness and non-duality. So, as Kalupahana stated, Enlightenment is not the destruction of the mind, for, *'The elimination of dispositions is epistemological suicide,*' as dispositions determine our perspectives.[3] The importance is the development of one's mindsets in the direction of transformation to purity, which rests with the very dispositions we can improve and purify. In this way, every individual's journey will be unique.

Bibliography

1. O'Regan, K.J., & Noë, A. (2001). A Sensorimotor Account of Vision and Visual Consciousness. Behavioral and Brain Sciences, 24, 939–1031.

2. Bhikkhu, T. (Trans). (2013). Kalama Sutta: To the Kalamas (AN 3.65). Access to Insight (Legacy Edition).

3. Kalupahana, D. J. (1992). A History of Buddhist Philosophy: Continuities and Discontinuities University of Hawaii Press, Honolulu. p. 90.

10

Sense of Agency

'What people think, believe, and feel affects how they behave. The natural and extrinsic effects of their actions, in turn, partly determine their thought patterns and affective reactions.'

Albert Bandura

'...one of the many things the Buddha discovered in the course of his awakening was that causality is not linear. The experience of the present is shaped both by actions in the present and by actions in the past. Actions in the present shape both the present and the future. The results of past and present actions continually interact. Thus there is always room for new input into the system, which gives scope for free will.'

Bhikkhu Thanissaro

'[...] in Buddhism the foundation [of the path] is the understanding that we can learn from contemplating and considering our direct experience. [..] Through noticing the results of our thoughts, attitudes, and actions, we learn what gives the best results — hence a path gets established beneath our own feet.'

Ajahn Sucitto

In Western psychology, the topic of free will gives rise to the interesting discussion of Sense of Agency (SoA), or the impression that we consciously control our cognitive and bodily actions. With the doctrine of kamma and dependent origination, the question of free will, while not figuring as prominently as it does in Western theology, philosophy and psychology, is a topic that was addressed by the Buddha's teachings. According to the suttas, for pragmatic and ethical reasons, the Buddha proponded the Middle Way and rejected both determinism and indeterminism as they were understood at that time. In pragmatic terms, unenlightened beings do not have free choice to achieve any value within their range of circumstances, conditioned and limited as they are by their minds that are dominated by ignorance and its corresponding subordinate mental and emotional dis-ease. As we purify our cognitive apparatus through learning and cultivating wholesome and skillful mindsets, we are more able to have a necessary flexibility of approach to choose between wholesome or unwholesome kamma.

One of the most distinctive features of the Buddha's teaching on kamma, is that a person's current experience of happiness or dis-ease is a combined result of both past and present thoughts. Under those circumstances, we are more or less free to make wise decisions that contribute to our own and others' genuine happiness or not. The cultivation of such inner freedom is a central function of Buddhist meditation:

> *'The Buddha's teachings on karma are interesting because it's a combination of causality and free-will. If things were totally caused there would be no way you could develop a skill – your actions would be totally predetermined. If there was no causality at all skills would be useless because things would be constantly changing without any kind of rhyme or*

*reason to them. But it's because there is an element
of causality and because there is this element of
free-will you can develop skills in life."*

In everyday life, we commonly draw a distinction
between voluntary actions and involuntary actions or
accidents. A 'doer' typically has both some sort of
immediate awareness of his or her physical activity and the
goals that the activity is aimed at realising. In 'goal-directed
action', an agent is aware of the implemention of direct
control or guidance over her own behaviour.[1] For example,
when you deliberately write your name on a piece of paper,
and you believe there is a causal relationship between your
writing and the appearance of the words, you experience
a sense of agency; but when someone pushes your hand
off the paper, you do not. Since the Buddha proposed that
humans have free will – following the Eightfold Path leads
one to Awakening – he accepted the theory that we feel a
sense of agency because we constantly make predictions
about our actions. When these predictions are fulfilled,
we perceive that our volitions created the consequences
of our actions. If I predict that writing is going to make
words appear, and it does, I have the sense of agency
that I caused them to appear. However, the Buddha also
accepted that motor actions often happen subconsciously,
are habitually predetermined, and we only feel that we
consciously willed them as a result of the effects. This
we see in his doctrine of latent tendencies, or non-
conscious impetus to act. For the Buddha, these were not
contradictory, but only expressions of different levels of
volitional action, for even habitual non-conscious actions
are based on the personality schematic structure.

---

* More details from the Stanford Encyclopedia of Philosophy: http://plato.stanford.edu/entries/action/

From a Buddhist perspective, humans mistakenly abstract the sense of agency and create the substantial and pervasive 'self' as the initiator of volitional actions, rather than understand that the ultimate basis of our agency (the ability to think and act deliberately) is biological, and a function of our status as an autopoietic living system.[1] Every living organism must have a degree of independent freedom of action over its own body in response to its surrounding environment in order to maintain physiological homeostasis. These actions often involve control-feedback mechanisms which reduce the discrepancy between the organism's current state (e.g. hunger) and a goal state (e.g. satiation). Some of these functions, such as the processes controlling digestion and heart rate, are highly autonomous and unconscious. While these most basic survival functions are not usually associated with a sense of agenc, higher-level actions, such as writing, require conscious attention to what we are doing.

Intentional behaviour is distinguished from automatic or involuntary behaviour by a number of specific characteristics. Intentional behaviour begins with the conscious recognition of a goal – 'I want x to happen'. Goal formation is followed by the development of a plan to achieve the goal. The organism then executes its plan, possibly overcoming internal and/or external hindrances along the way. The awareness and monitoring of agency also serves the important executive function of providing feedback on the efficacy of the plan to control the internal and/or external environment in a specific way.

How does this all relate to the Buddha's teachings? Well, we can see that for the successful pursuit and completion of the Eightfold Path, it is necessary to set the goal and monitor (both internally and externally) any 'roadblocks' that hinder the progression to achieving that end result.

Acquiring a sense of intentionality as infants

As adults, we often take it for granted that we have control of many internally- and externally-oriented skills. We first acquire and develop these ideas and abilities related to agency and intentionality early in life. As infants we are bombarded by many novel sensory experiences, which as homeostatic living systems, we are well able to process and, eventually, make effective use of such stimuli. Although infants at first have relatively poor control of their bodies, basic orienting responses toward attracting or repelling sights and sounds are present almost from birth, indicating innate preferences and sensitivities.[2, 3] These innate responses provide the initial context for learning and remembering relationships between specific movements and sensory feedback from caregivers and the physical environment. The infant's earliest lessons concern their body, and how to move themselves to facilitate basic survival needs (e.g. grasping, suckling, crying, and later, crawling and walking). The jerky, seemingly random limb movements of infants actually serve the vital purpose of teaching the child how to predict and control the sensory consequences of movement.[4, 5] Similarly, when infants babble and cry, caregivers often respond in predictable ways, thereby teaching the infant how to use vocalised sounds to obtain a measure of control over their environment.

For their part, adult observers usually attribute limited agency to infants as soon as the baby's actions seem to be explainable in terms of intentions and desires. When the infant grabs at a toy or turns his head to refuse a food-filled spoon, adults perceive it as a meaningful goal-directed action, and infer a measure of agency. The infant therefore attains status as a limited agent because he or she is beginning to influence their own sensory experiences. Children increasingly gain better control over their bodies, interact with the world by moving intentionally and develop a growing capacity to learn and remember. In the course of gaining better control over their bodies, children develop a repertoire of motor programmes that have proven successful at achieving certain goals in the past, outcomes that can be thought of as a list of, 'I cans' (as in, 'I can do this,' and, 'I can do that'). Of course, failures are inevitable, so the child also develops a corresponding list of 'I can'ts'.

Most of us spend much of our time and energy doing things that have been successful and pleasing in the past, and avoiding things that have had unpleasant consequences. In this way, effective, meaningful movements and expressions become habitual and no longer require monitoring with direct attention. Ironically, once a task is mastered, the sense of agency that was originally evoked by the action may dissipate. For example, when an experienced driver navigates a highly familiar route, the required actions may be so familiar and automatic that the driver arrives at his destination with little memory of how he got there. The same thing may happen with other daily actions, such as eating. Feeding ourselves is the conscious satisfaction of a need, but it becomes so familiar and routine in everyday life that it is often completed without full awareness. This suggests that feelings of agency may be stronger when individuals consciously monitor their actions.

Agency as a product of both biology and cognition

The sense of agency may ultimately be grounded in the memory of low-level sensorimotor processes, which confers a sense of agency for more protracted goals. One can, for example, feel various degrees of agency or control over long-term projects such as the publication of a book, or the design and construction of a house. And indeed, because these types of events are far removed from basic immediate biological processes, we are also apt to explain them in terms of 'self', or 'I' states, such as, 'wants', 'beliefs', and 'desires'. As the famous personality theorist Abraham Maslow observed, *'We are complex living organisms embodied in our environment.'*[6] Therefore our survival needs as humans go beyond simple homeostasis; we also have significant holistic needs that include physical security, stability, affiliations, as well as affection, learning, abstracting, familiarity and relationship. According to Maslow, our wellbeing as fully developed human beings depends on realising our needs through a lifelong dynamic process of growth, interrelatedness and discovery, a process he called 'actualisation'. Agency is critical to actualisation, because it is usually the internally generated, transformative insights and life-style changes that contribute most to the learned contingencies that comprise our internal and external worlds. Psychological research seems to bear this out. There is considerable variation between individuals in the degree to which their lives represent personal actualisation. Higher levels of personal control and actualisation have been associated with a variety of positive outcomes in both health and occupational performance.[7, 8, 9]

Overall, we see that a complete understanding of human agency must account not only for the basic biological processes needed for monitoring our physical bodies and environment, but also for more complex cognitive abilities shaped by learned, cultural factors. In fact, human functioning is always a product of a reciprocal interplay of internal forces and environmental determinants.[10] We cannot operate independently of the context in which we live. We create social systems and, in turn, these systems direct the organisation of our lives. We are contributors to our life circumstances, not just their product. For both simple movements and higher level goals, human agency entails the control of cognitive processes and to perform certain goal-oriented action in the present.

As psychologist Marek McGann states:

> 'There is a clear, fundamental, and irreducible circularity of the relationship between perception and action. [...] Perception, cognition and action, rather than being separable or clearly distinguishable processes, are more like different aspects of the one process of adaptive coping, in which a goal-directed agent is continually involved. The embodied interaction with the world makes it mandatory for us as living systems to seek or intend endogenously driven activities [...] which are valued and goal-oriented actions.'[11]

Or, to put it another way, we are inherently driven to interact with and through our physical environments in ways that require further perceptions, updated schemas, and new choices. Life is a dynamic process, and we are all simultaneously shapers of, and shaped by, our environments.

The sense of agency seems ultimately to originate from feedback and control mechanisms which evolved to facilitate survival by promoting satisfying, life-enhancing interactions with the environment. From such building blocks, the human ability to consciously monitor, adapt and execute goals and behaviours has enhanced the sense of efficacy that underlies so much of our personal satisfaction. Becoming a skillful agent is closely intertwined with the many subtle ramifications of a sense of personal competence.

Further considerations on the basis of agency

Many have wondered how is it possible to stay in the present moment, acting only as in accordance with the Zen saying, '*When hungry eat, when tired sleep*'. While this question often reflects the pragmatic constraints inherent to living in today's fast-paced, technological world, it also reflects the intrinsic difficulties of maintaining a calm and receptive mind in times of stress and reflexively judging, seeking or rejecting the life that confronts us. When psychologists talk about agency, it is usually only in descriptive terms – 'Agency is the capacity to act intentionally and make free choices.' A fuller understanding of agency is needed, one that can also explain how if there is 'no-self' as an innate entity to be the agent, what actually is the instigating operation that gives the organism the freedom to choose and act. For example, an Arahant continues to interact in life without intentional or kamma-based agency. The concept of 'no-self', so fundamental to Buddhist psychology, needs a plausible explanation of the basis of the awareness of agency, often described as the feeling that 'I am'. To understand this perspective, let us seek answers based on the notion that our agency is rooted in biological processes.

Bibliography

1. Maturana, H. R., & Varela, F. J. (1980). Autopoiesis and Cognition: The Realization of the Living (No. 42). Springer Science & Business Media.

2. Kessen, W., Salapatek, P., & Haith, M. (1972). The Visual Response of the Human Newborn to Linear Contour. Journal of Experimental Child Psychology, 13(1), 9-20.

3. Muir, D., & Field, J. (1979). Newborn infants orient to sounds. Child Development, 431-436.

4. Piek, J. P. (2002). The Role of Variability in Early Motor Development. Infant Behavior and Development, 25(4), 452-465.

5. Thelen, E. (1995). Motor Development: A New Synthesis. American Psychologist, 50(2), 79.

6. Maslow, A. H. (1943). A Theory of Human Motivation. Psychological Review, 50(4), 370.

7. Rotter, J. B. (1966). Generalized Expectancies for Internal versus External Control of Reinforcement. Psychological monographs: General and Applied, 80(1), 1.

8. Chen, J. C., & Silverthorne, C. (2008). The Impact of Locus Control on Job Stress, Job Performance and Job Satisfaction in Taiwan. Leadership & Organization Development Journal, 29(7), 572-582.

9. Shojaee, M., & French, C. (2014). The Relationship between Mental Health Components and Locus of Control in Youth. Psychology.

10. Bandura, A. (1997). Self-efficacy: The Exercise of Control. New York: Freeman.

11. McGann, M. (2010). Perceptual Modalities: Modes of Presentation or Modes of Interaction? Journal of Consciousness Studies, 17(1-2), 72-94.

11

Agency Labelled as Self

A basic premise of the Buddha's psychology is that to be alive requires an organism to not only have the capacity to be continuously aware of itself, but also to monitor and respond to internal and external environmental changes. Humans, perhaps some primates and (to a lesser degree) dolphins have the capacity of meta-cognition, defined as, *'the monitoring and control of one's thought.'*[1]

To do this requires of us the ability to stand back from the process of thinking, and with the use of language, to represent and objectify it. In doing so, we create the subject-object split, and one particular representational object we create is a 'self'. A major consequence of this dualism is our believing in a separation of an innate 'self' from both our objectified internal and external worlds.

As cognitive scientist and philosopher Thomas Metzinger has said, *'We mentally represent ourselves as representational systems in phenomenological real time.'*[2] Metzinger calls the process of self construction as the Phenomenal Self Model (PSM), which he describes as, *'an efficient way to allow a biological organism to consciously conceive of itself (and others) as a whole,'* enabling the organism, *'to interact with its internal world as well as with the external environment in an intelligent and holistic manner.'²*

Through the process of conceptualisation, we can objectify and therefore think, monitor and evaluate our thoughts, and anticipate the thoughts of others. The Buddha clearly understood and accepted the experience, or sense of agency, along with its convenient representation of the whole experience as a 'self'. What he did object to was the belief, identification with, and attachment to the belief in a 'self' that is substantial and inherent. Instead, the Buddha saw the transience and fallacy of that belief and let it go with all the accompanying consequence that led to the anatta, or 'no-self' doctrine. What the Buddha found in his intensive meditational investigation is that everything is impermanent. Our thoughts, affects, body and external environment are always in a dynamic flux. Even consciousness is impermanent, being as it has its basis in the physical world.

However, the Buddha experienced (and understood) through living, his sense of agency; that we all have a certain capacity to steer the 'rudder of the boat', to arrive at where we want to be. Through cognitive interventions within our cognitive apparatus we can alter and choose wholesome *versus* unwholesome thoughts and hence, behaviours. We have the ability through meta-cognition, to monitor and develop our cognitive apparatus in ways that enable us to purify our mind and attain awakening. The Buddha knew this and proceeded to teach from that perspective.

Unity of intentionality

Whilst the Buddha understood the body with its cognitive apparatus to be the matrix of our experiences, he did not specifically speculate on the biological origins of agency. Nevertheless, one can ask that if there is no substantive 'self' that is in control of all our personal activity, then what is the unifying cause of our being? Biological science has hypothesised that our awareness and capability to act freely, of agency, originates in the core of our biological being. Let us then suggest then, that an organism's spontaneous organising tendencies give rise to agency, and that the awareness of pure subjective experience springs spontaneously from this ground of organised biological activity. Or in other words, that agency arises from an organism's innate processes of using the environment to meet its current or projected biological needs.

The sense of a 'self' arises from the early awareness of environmental feedback associated with automatic, self-organised behaviour. The abstracted 'self', the representation of 'I' and 'I do' as the broader sense of 'I can do' is based on the awareness of such feedback. 'I-ness' originates from volitional spontaneity, and this abstracted, conscious 'I' later confers a measure of freedom, or choice to human action. To more specifically explain this process, biochemist Mae-Wan Ho of the Institute of Science in Society has proposed that:

> *'Quantum coherence is the basis of living*
> *organisation, and can also account for key*
> *features of conscious experience - the 'unity of*
> *intentionality', our inner identity of the singular*
> *'I', the simultaneous binding and segmentation*
> *of features in the perceptive act, the distributed,*
> *holographic nature of memory, and the distinctive*
> *quality of each experienced occasion.'*[3]

To live means to be capable of self-generated movement with intention. With further development of cognitive sophistication and ability, we can consciously perceive the intentions that accompany our actions, and our later responses are shaped by the memory of what we intended to do and the results obtained.

Recent developments in cognitive neuroscience emphasise the role of the acting body and of sensory-motor systems in shaping our cognitive schemas, thereby determining the way our mind represents reality. Our body is a highly interconnected and intercommunicating organism at all levels, from the intracellular to the sociological. It is an active participant, constantly responding to and transforming its inner and outer environment. An intuitive appreciation of our body's coherence is to think of the imagined 'I', or 'self', as our own essential nature. We know that our body is a multiplicity of organs and tissues, composed of billions of cells and vast numbers of molecules of many different kinds, all capable of working autonomously. And yet, amazingly, all of these elements coalesce into a singular being creating our individual experience. Or, as the Gestaltists point out, the whole is more than the sum of its parts. Metaphorically, it is like a very large jazz band where every player is doing his or her own thing whilst being perfectly in step and in tune with the whole.

In light of this, the inappropriateness of the questions, 'Where is the self?' or, 'Does the self exist?' is clear. These questions are meaningless when one understands what it is to be a coherent, organic whole, where part and whole, global and local are so thoroughly enmeshed as to be indistinguishable, with each part being in control as much as it is sensitive and responsive. What we have abstracted and called the 'self' is, instead, a coherent state that permeates the whole of our being with no definite localisations or boundaries – a 'pure experience' of inseparability. This integral state of existence and experience therefore implies the presence of an active whole agent that is ultimately free to act. To not have a degree of freedom to respond and act dooms any organism to death, since flexibility and appropriate response is *sine qua non* to life. Dualistically and egotistically, the idea of freedom becomes perverted when it is understood only as its possible expression - with 'myself' rising only in opposition to others. The Enlightened understanding of the representation called 'self' is that it is only a fictional character that we believe necessary in creating one's existence. Biochemist Mae Wan-Ho suggests:

> *'That a truly free individual is a coherent being that lives life fully and spontaneously, without fragmentation or hesitation, who is at peace with herself and at ease with the universe as she participates in creating, from moment to moment, its possible futures.'*[4]

Neuroscientist Jaak Panksepp presents a corresponding perspective by suggesting that the pure subjective experience of an individual existence, abstracted as 'I', is a biological agency based on affectively rich intention, similar to other organisms. This phenomenological level of 'I' is pre-cognitive, a 'pure experience'. Evidence from Panksepp's experimental work suggests that the core of the brain is much more relevant to biological intentionality than the higher neocortical areas. Panksepp calls agency, *'Primary process consciousness,'*[5] and describes it as residing in the basic action-readiness of the biological system.

Any organism within a specific niche is always solving a multitude of challenges, constantly adjusting its body and regulating its behaviours. The agency system identifies and incorporates as its own, all of the emotions and visual, auditory, and somatosensory systems of the midbrain.

Along with the consolidated motor actions of this agency, it is also likely that it provides a 'coherent matrix', in which a variety of sensory stimuli become either intrinsically attractive or aversive.

In other words, as was described also by the Buddha (and biologists), we establish attraction and aversion values. Therefore most of our basic awareness of a spatial-temporally located body in an environmental niche becomes imbued with positive and negative effects. These primary sensations of pain and pleasure are intimately integrated with the action-orientation of our motor systems. Our basic subjective experience is later labelled as 'I'. The affects and emotions that arise as learned survival modes then pervade our primary and secondary consciousness. Therefore, it is necessary for them to be integrated into our cognitive schema to operate effectively. Panksepp states that subjectivity resides first in the biological realm of intention and action.[5] Like the Buddha's, Panksepp's approach suggests that consciousness is an integral part of our physio-chemical system, and that many of our competencies are autonomic systems operating in the dynamic unconscious. From this perspective, the 'I' refers to the spatial-temporal extension of the primary biological agent that is the evolutionary response to the struggle for survival.

Another perspective which emphasises the biological system as the base for agency is Gestalt therapy. Gestalt therapy defines an organism's self-regulation as the creative adjustment that the organism (person) makes in relation to the environment; that is, the person's equilibrium with his or her environment. According to the Gestalt perspective, we regulate ourselves according to needs that arise from our natural organism functioning. Self-regulation is the process of making choices and responses. Organisms' needs are typically spontaneous impulses that comes from the 'whole'. When these impulses contradict each other or are not feasible at the same time, we make choices between them based on our priorities and environmental support. Natural self-regulation occurs when the choice is made holistically, with a natural integration of mind and body, thought and feeling, spontaneity and deliberateness.

Most of our interactions with the world are handled automatically and reflexively, with minimal awareness. Effective, updated self-regulation requires that the habitual be first brought to our awareness, and then monitored and altered as needed. Awareness is cognitive, sensory and affective. With awareness comes the possibility of a skilful, responsible choice. Responsibility entails owning; that is, a responsible person knows they have control over the expression of their own behaviour and feelings. According to the Gestalt perspective, awareness is grounded in, and energised by, the dominant present need or want of the organism. Any denial or distortion to avoid a situation and its demands is called a 'disturbance' of awareness. In essence, a disturbance represents ignorance of the possible influence one has in a specific situation. While a person may verbally acknowledge his situation, if he does not fully comprehend it, feel it, respond to it and monitor his response, he is not fully aware or in full contact. But the person who is mindful or has equanimity is aware of what they do and how they do it; they know that they have alternatives and that their acts are their own choices.

The dynamic, cognitively constructed 'I', or the 'autobiographical self', is constantly flowing and being reborn during every change in emotional, perceptual or cognitive content. Therefore, 'I' cannot be a substantial entity. To emphasise the biological basis of 'I', Philipp Rau wrote the following:

'[...] the self is at root a neurobiological-cognitive system which, long before socialization, allows the individual to be conscious of itself in the world. [...] the self, once emerged, can be shaped by socio-cultural factors. The processes contributing to the self are distributed across a number of neuro-anatomical structures. It is only their synchronous neural activity that generates a self. The core self of the neuro-cognitive theory only arises when the organism becomes conscious of itself interacting with the world. Thus, the self emerges precisely when the internal–external boundary is straddled. The phenomenal content of the neuro-cognitive self, however, corresponds to what Cartesian intuition would have us conceive of as an ontologically independent self. There is no such self independent of the brain and body, of course, but the self-representational processes described by the neuro-cognitive theory, in creating a conscious self-model, produce in us the illusion that there might be.'[6]

From the perspective of the biological regulation and coherence of an organism, the intuitive concept of a 'Cartesian Theatre' in the brain, wherein the self sits as a spectator on the world and acts as the CEO of all decision-making, is exposed as an illusion.

Figure 11.2 *Satirical representation of an observing 'self', acting from a command cabin, as separated from the rest of the organism. (http://faculty.humanities.uci.edu/michaelfuller/ NeuroscienceConsciousness/Images/CartesianTheater.png)*

Clearly the biologically based core functions of organisation, selectivity and coherence are necessary for survival. However, as the Buddha noted, it also appears that the conscious mind emerges at the interface between the brain, the body and social environment. Consciousness is primarily a physical reaction or response to external stimuli. As the Buddha stated, consciousness is created by, *'whatever condition through which it arises.'* For example, because of the eye and visible forms, there is a visual consciousness. The combination of experience, body, and external conditions is the main determinant of our conscious experience and of our ongoing adaptive activities in the environment. We are also capable of adapting and readapting our schemas in new and meaningful ways. The Buddha's view is that actions and environmental conditions are embedded in each other, such that the person and the environment are co-dependent.

A crucial issue for the Buddha's programme of the Eightfold Path and cognitive purification is the cultivation of new 'agent' executive capabilities that add new regulatory perspectives and skills, and thereby provide a wider range of options that increases our scope of action. In this manner, we have more possibilities for successfully realising desired outcomes, than those with fewer established resources of agent.

It is therefore clear that the new science in support of the Buddha's psychology proposes that we transform our interactions with the physical environment in such a way as to metamorphose it into our 'world', or into a place of clarity, meaning, and value. This transformation of an environment into our world happens through the constructive activity of our cognitive apparatus. Thompson and Stapleton describe this sense-making as the interactional and relational side of autonomy[7] and it represents the activity through which our cognitive apparatus learns about, thinks about, and makes sense of the world. It is the activity through which we have a 'world', and then engage in purposeful action, displaying the necessary characteristics of genuine agency.

Intentions or volitions, while being higher-level and neurologically embodied with emergent properties, are also affected by context-sensitive constraints that set control boundaries. These constraints can impact our behaviour, since interactive processes are defined by skills which both condition and are conditioned. Contexts provide challenges that are the catalysts for actions. A challenge is any circumstance that engages a person's abilities or resources to resolve a problem or threat, as well as to achieve the many goals defined by a hierarchy of needs. A biological approach to understanding how a person develops, focuses on the interface between the agent and surrounding environmental context as well as inner signals. Capability to act as an agentic requires a person to possess the needed knowledge, skills and belief that not only one *is* capable, but also if one acts, one can expect positive outcomes. Agent-enabling capacity largely involves the meta-cognitive skills of self-regulation and self-management that enables one to compare their current states with expected goal states and to monitor, evaluate, and regulate their progress. Although actions are purposeful (that is, performed to achieve an end), behaviours are governed by many interacting influences. In this sense, people are, '*contributors to, rather than the sole determiners of, what happens to them,*' and therefore, '*Agency refers to acts done intentionally.*'[8] For actions to possess a strong sense of personal empowerment, there is the quality of owning one's actions, and choices made are integrated with the organism's hierarchy of needs. As Deci has reasoned, '*Without choice, there would be no agency, and no self-regulation.*'[9]

Inherent spontaneous self-organising coordination tendencies give rise to an awareness of agency – the most fundamental kind of consciousness, the awareness of a self, springs from the ground of our spontaneous organised activity. In simple terms, we can say that the tendency of our physiological system to maintain internal stability, owing to the coordinated response of its parts to any situation or stimulus (homeostasis), is the origin of conscious agency. From the spontaneous, organised behaviour of the organism emerges a dualistically conceived self – 'I am', and 'I do'. From this point, a huge range of potentialities ('I can do') and restrictions ('I can't do'). The constancy of most incoming information guides, modifies and directs the system's mobility. This embodied repertoire enables activities to become habitual and to occur before we consciously make them happen. The bases of our decisions are mostly determined by non-conscious processes, which we normally act out in a habitual way. Only with consciously concentrated awareness and monitoring of our cognitive processes (mindfulness) can we influence and direct those processes and experience a heightened sense of agency.

Our preferred choices are made based on the memory of previous experiences, and what we have experienced within the larger framework of earlier choices in terms of like, dislike or neutrality. In our memory, the history of a firing pattern of any neuron determines its response. And yet, because of the plasticity of the brain, neuron sensitivity and hence its pattern of firing can be altered with each response. Whilst we are 'free' to choose, the skilful execution of choices is determined by our past, and our choices are emergent properties that arise from specific states of our brain and body.

So, as the Buddha taught, we are free to learn new information, rethink and update old information, make choices, and act and shape our own future – even though all of that takes place within the context of many different structures and hindrances.

Bibliography

1. Martinez, M. E. (2006). What is Metacognition? Phi Delta Kappan, 87(9), 696-699.

2. Metzinger, T. (2009). The Ego Tunnel: The Science of the Mind and the Myth ofthe Self. New York: basic books. p. 4–5.

3. Ho, M. W. (1997). Quantum Coherence and Conscious Experience. Kybernetes, 26(3), 265-276.

4. Ho M. W. (1996). The Biology of Free Will. Journal of Consciousness Studies, 3, 231-244.

5. Panksepp, J. (1998). The Periconscious Substrates of Consciousness: Affective States and the Evolutionary Origins of the SELF. Journal of Consciousness Studies, 5(5-6), 566-582.

6. Rau, P. (2011). The Self: Social Construct or Neurobiological System? M.A. Dissertation, University of Sheffield, Department of Philosophy.

7. Thompson, E., & Stapleton, M. (2009). Making Sense of Sense-Making: Reflections on Enactive and Extended Mind Theories. Topoi, 28(1), 23-30.

8. Bandura, A. (1997). Self Efficacy: The exercise of control. New York: Freeman.

9. Deci, E. L. (1996). Making Room for Self-Regulation: Some Thoughts on the Link Between Emotion and Behavior. Psychological Inquiry, 7, 220-223.

12

Dividing Existence – Duality

'... the world is steeped in the notion of duality. It grasps either this end, or the other end. Hard it is for the world to understand the stance of the Arahant couched in the cryptic phrase, "neither here nor there nor in between the two." The worldling is accustomed to grasp either this end or the other end.'

Bhikkhu K. Ñānananda[1]

'We experience ourselves and the world as subject and object only through conceptualization and language. This dualism, however, is only mental and not real. Mind produces this subject-object dualism. The subjectivity of our mind affects our perceptions of the world.'

Tom Arnold[2]

'Awakening is the discovery that the apparently objective is in fact "subjective", and the apparent entity has disappeared with the total appearance.'

Wei Wu Wei[3]

The dualistic perception: the separation of subject and object

One of the Buddha's most significant insights created through his Awakening to 'Pure Awareness' was that the 'self' is developed by a complementary dualist perspective, and this distinction between a subject and object is an arbitrary convention. Nonetheless, there is no denying that the belief of the innate substantiality of separation of subject and object is extremely persistent. As professor A.J. Diekman suggests, '*In fact, our experience is fundamentally dualistic – not the dualism of mind and matter – but that of the 'I' and that which is observed.*'[4] Yet, through the fallacy of there being a separation between subject and object, the majority of people persist in viewing the world this way.

There may be several reasons why this is so. One reason relates to the fact that once we begin to consciously discriminate our initial sense experience, we make a subject-object differentiation; there is always a bifurcation, a dichotomy. In our perceptual experience, we cannot avoid dividing the world between perceiving subject and perceived object. The human mind is predisposed to understanding the world by breaking it into smaller, more manageable pieces. Perception can be understood as the process of sensing, categorising and labelling the world in order to make sense of it.

For psychologist William James, this discrimination is the result of attention, which is a process of selection:

> '*Out of what is in itself an indistinguishable, swarming continuum, devoid of distinction or emphasis [...] Attention [...] picks out certain sensations as worthy of notice, choosing those that are signs to us of things which happen practically*

or aesthetically to interest us, to which we therefore give substantive names and to which we give the status of independence and dignity.[5]

However, human attention has a limited capacity. The focus of attention is often described by psychologists as a moving searchlight which enhances or brings into awareness certain categories at the expense of others. For example, while scanning a crowd for a friend's face, attention helps the observer to focus on the idea of their friend, including what they look like and so forth, while ignoring irrelevant features of the crowd. And as everyone knows, if one is not paying attention, we can easily fail to perceive people and objects right in front of our faces. This phenomenon is known as Inattentional Blindness.[6] It demonstrates that it's not until a sensation is cognitively recognised, named and interpreted that it moves into the realm of perception. It also highlights the fact that what we see is very much influenced by what we expect to see, which in turn depends on how we categorise the world.

Applying the preceding analysis of attention and awareness to concepts of the 'self', one begins to see how the innate capacities and limitations of the human brain play a role in establishing the 'self' as an entity separate from its environment. In only being able to attend to a few features or objects at a time, their separateness is emphasised. A similar logic is applied when the mind turns its perceiving and categorising apparatus back upon itself. As we have seen in the Buddha's analysis of the khandhas and his six–stage theory of the perceptual process, once we begin to consciously discriminate our initial sense experience, we cannot avoid the further step of dividing experience into perceiving subject and perceived object. If there is something seen, then there has to be one who sees. However, we do not merely perceive an external object; we simultaneously perceive ourselves in the act of perceiving the object. The object represents the content of one's knowing, whilst our perception of the subject (my perception of 'me') provides a clue about the underlying structure or schemata of one's knowing. There are consequently two aspects of this core, integral event – two poles (subject/object), with consciousness linking them together. After all, where there is an object of perception, there is a subject. In some sense, the concept of 'self' is implied by all of our sensory experiences.

The human tendency to categorise and classify, combined with the limits of human perception and attention, naturally leads us to postulate a distinction between subject and object. This is the psychological reality of dualism. If one rejects Cartesian mind/body dualism (as almost all modern scientists and philosophers do), one accepted view of the nature of the construct we refer to as the 'self' is that all cognitive processes, are emergent properties of lower-level physical processes within our brains and extended nervous systems. When physical systems of a certain type reach a certain level of sophistication, we gain the ability to think symbolically about the world, and this includes thinking about ourselves. The development of a 'self-symbol' becomes a belief or representation of itself as a unifying principle that links and is constant through all of an individual's experiences.

Another important aspect of our self-representation is its apparent status as a causal agent. Although our thoughts seem to cause actions, we cannot perceive the complex dynamics which cause thoughts to occur – they seem to spontaneously spring forth from our deepest inner natures. We postulate the idea of a 'self' and its various properties in part to explain how we think and act as we do (for example, 'I didn't run from danger because

I'm a brave person'). Rothstein explained the concept of 'I' as, *'The self-representation as agent,'* because it, *'conceives of itself as existing actively to pursue and insure its wellbeing and survival.'*[7] Meaning, our sense of self is further bolstered by our sense of agency.

While our belief in a 'self' becomes fixed, the nature of our self-representation is not static. Recall the formula from the previous chapter: *'Dependent on the eye and forms, brethren, arises eye-consciousness; the concurrence of the three is contact.'* In this linking function, consciousness dwells in the contact between the eye and object until the focus moves on to something else. Or, another way of putting this is that because attention has a limited capacity, we can only be conscious of a small number of distinct objects or categories at any particular moment. The extent of the dwelling of consciousness comes to depend on the strength of attachment and the craving or aversion as applied by the self's volition. That is to say, objects, people, or situations that have previously been rewarding or useful (the opposite being aversive and harmful), to our physiological needs, will tend to draw our attention towards them. These concepts become integrated into our self-concept by association. For example, one's preference for a favourite piece of music may feel like an important part of one's 'self'.

Throughout this process, the 'self' remains a purely hypothetical construct. There is no substantive reality to this 'self', but it remains useful shorthand. It's much easier to say, 'I love this piece of music', positioning a 'self' at the centre of the experience, than to say, 'This piece of music stimulated pleasure centres in the brain of the organism who is presently speaking.'

We each represent many different concepts and categories in our brains. Of all these concepts, arguably the most developed and extensive is the concept of 'I' or 'me', which is connected in some fashion to *all* of our perceptions. The concept becomes associated with countless other sensory impressions (to varying degrees), such as the taste of one's favourite foods, the sound of favourite song or the images of loved ones. However, despite its apparent centrality, the meaning of 'self' remains difficult to define; it only gains meaning when considered in relation to other ideas.

The cognitive mirror: resonating with others

In addition to thinking about the 'self', people also have the ability to entertain thoughts and ideas regarding other people who are assumed to have internal selves analogous to our own. When we are aware of other people's actions, emotional expression and experienced sensations, we are able to recognise a given behaviour through the senses, which we can subsequently interpret and logically analyse. We perceive others' behaviour as immediately meaningful because it is directly linked to the neural assemblies that preside over our own lived experience of the same behaviours (actions, emotions, and sensations).

Within these 'mirroring' processes, we are somewhat neutral about the identity of the subject-object and, quite easily, through a shared functional state, the 'other' becomes 'another self,' a 'like-me', who yet still maintains his or her 'other' character. The degree to which we can imagine these other selves is quite clearly dependent on experience. For example, it is much easier to imagine what a close loved one is thinking or to predict how they will behave, compared with a complete stranger.

The 'self-other' distinction has long fascinated neuroscientists (in addition to philosophers), and in recent times technology has improved to the point that we can directly observe certain brain processes corresponding to the self-other bifurcation process. There appear to be at least two large-scale neural networks that are involved in thinking about the relationship of 'self' and 'other'. The first network includes areas of the frontal and parietal cortex, which provides the basis for bridging the gap between the physical 'self' and others. Through simulation mechanisms it has been shown that similar neurones are activated whether an individual performs an action or is observing another person performing the same action. Neurons that behave in this manner have been dubbed 'mirror neurons', because the brain seems to be sympathetically mirroring the observed actions in a kind of mental simulation.[8]

The second network involves cortical midline structures which engage in processing information about the 'self' and 'others' in more abstract, evaluative terms. Recent evidence of the significance of our brain neural structures in the bifurcation process is supported by the discovery of the mirror-neuron system. This indicates that the neural systems of midline structures and mirror neurons show that 'self' and 'other' are two sides of the same coin, whether their physical interactions or their most internal mental processes are examined.

The mirror system provides a basis for identifying and, to a degree, sharing in the experience of others. As the experiences of the 'other' are shown to be shared with the 'self', the previously clear separation between 'self' and 'other' appears less distinct.' ... *when we witness the intentional behavior of others, embodied simulation generates a specific phenomenal state of 'intentional attunement'*[9] This, in turn, generates a peculiar quality of identification with other individuals, produced by establishing a dynamic relation of reciprocity between the 'I' and the 'thou'. By means of embodied simulation we do not just *see* an action, an emotion, or a sensation. Side-by-side with the sensory description of the observed social stimuli, internal representations of the body states associated with these actions, emotions and sensations are evoked in the observer, *as if* he or she were doing a similar action or experiencing a similar emotion or sensation. That enables our social identification with others. To see others' behaviour as an action or as an experienced emotion or sensation, specifically requires such behaviours to be mapped according to an isomorphic format. Such mapping is embodied simulation; private mental states can in fact be approximated.

Although mirror responses are to some extent neutral about the identity of the subject, they are more robust when the observer has more experience performing the action in question. For example, in one study skilled basketball players showed stronger mirror neuron activity in their premotor cortex (an area involved in planning actions) compared with novices when they watched a video of another person shooting baskets.[10] This sits well with the intuitive idea that the ease with which we can step into another person's shoes depends on their similarity to ourselves. Through this process, the subject or voyeur has the ability to simultaneously reflect upon the other as well as their own past actions as an agent with a certain amount of discernment.

This ability to reflect on oneself through the eyes of another is very important. In the Buddha's Eightfold Path of meditation, the process of reflecting on our thoughts and actions is recognised as the starting point for behavioural changes. And without reflection, change would be impossible.

The relationship of subject to object

From a cognitive science perspective, the dynamic nature of thought has been explained as:

> 'Thinking – the creation of information in the mind – is a transient non-stationary dynamic process. It corresponds to a flow of converging 'perching' (integrative phase-locking tendencies and individuation of brain areas) and diverging 'lights' (segregated decoupling tendencies and individuation of brain areas). Both tendencies are crucial: the former to create thoughts, feelings – information in general; the latter to release individual brain areas to participate in other acts of cognition and emotion. To be stuck in a phase-locked state is to be temporarily "trapped in thought," to be depressed in effect, in one stationary state or another, the limited repertoire of either/or… [complementary] pairs are fundamentally dynamical. There is no attraction without repulsion, no stability without instability, no persistence without change, etc.'[11]

Here, Scott Kelso and David Engstrom highlight how closely the scientific explanation of complementary brain dynamics parallels those descriptions that are based on the idea of dependent origination (that is, nothing exists independently of other things) that was at the core of the Buddha's teachings. Our cognitive apparatus depends on a variety of complementary processes. Attention, for example, is accomplished through a combination of excitation and inhibition of neural connections. Another (famous) example is the perception of bi-stable images: 'My Wife and My Mother-In-Law', an ambiguous visual image which can be perceived as either a beautiful young woman or an old hag, but which is very difficult to see as both at once.[12]

Figure 12.1 *"My Wife and My Mother-In-Law", a famous bi-stable image showing how visual perception can be tricked.*

It is important not to lose sight of the underlying unity of complementary psychological processes. In particular, let us focus on the notion that the subjective and objective components of experience are somehow opposite or irreconcilable processes. The argument to be made here is that the subjective and objective are really two complementary sides or poles of a single process. As Hamilton explains:

> 'The entire world of experience is one which is comprised of the polarity between subjectivity and objectivity. [...] The subjectivity and objectivity are mutually dependently originated [...] the subjective and objective aspects of our experience are in fact the linked "poles" of a single process.'[13]

'I' observing 'me'

As has already been noted, the act of observation immediately suggests a distinction between the observer and what is to be observed. Paradoxically, when one tries to observe the subjective 'self' or 'I', it immediately becomes an object. Here we have an observer effect, similar to as has been described in quantum mechanisms, in which the act of observing a substance causes the substance to change behaviours, thereby frustrating attempts at objective description. This may be one reason why 'self'-knowledge is so difficult. In any case, the act of 'self'-observation leads to an artificial splitting of the 'self' into two components – the subjective 'I' ('self' as subject) and the objective 'me' ('self' as object). Of course the subjective and the objective 'self' imply each other, that is, that there could not be a 'me' without an 'I'. Yet, through the acts of perception and verbal labelling, we establish the subject 'I' and object 'me' as distinctive concepts.

Early in life, a child's developing 'self' is conceived directly from this bifurcated, dualistic view of the self, the 'I' and 'me' distinctions that are being embedded in the structure of the child's language. One way to characterise the observed 'me' would be to say that it is the idea we construct about ourselves as a result of our many interactions with the world. For example, if a young woman observes that a particular young man often smiles at her, this informs the woman about the young man's emotional state ('He likes me'), but also informs her about herself ('I am likeable').

While our idea of 'me' may be more or less accurate within certain contexts, it is a fluid proposition at best. Through our interactions with the world, we develop an internal model of the world, as well as an internal model of ourselves, as we come to understand our 'self' and our place in the world. This system of interrelated observations constitutes a feedback loop of sorts. By interacting with others, or even in simply perceiving them, we can affect changes in them. Also, in the act of changing others, we also change ourselves. One can see that the subjective 'self', far from being independent from the objective world, interacts with it continually. Kelso and Engstrom depicted this concept as:

> 'The complementary aspects of a complementary pair (subject/object) are fundamentally mutual. They are distinguishable but coexistent. They are co-emergent, co-defining and complicated. Being mutually coupled, complementary aspects are also dynamic: they flow in and out of each other in subtle and seemingly mysterious ways. What one perceives affects what one does and what one does affects what one perceives. What we want influences what we think about and what we think about influences what we want.'[11]

For the Buddha, the interconnectedness that the previous examples demonstrate is all–embracing. To see the connectedness of all things is to see that no one thing has an independent existence. To understand *anything* (including the 'self'), one must understand that all phenomena are the result of a combination of conditions. The Buddha teaches that *pure experience* is the integral unit of awareness or consciousness. This preverbal awareness of our existence comes before any concept or opinion is developed about the 'self', and prior to any attempt to communicate the insight using words. In fact, the moment we attempt to put a label on our subjective or core experience, using the words 'self', 'I', 'me', or 'mine', we find that each of these limited notions fails to capture the reality of our core experience. The 'self' is not something that can be so easily defined, nor can it easily be identified with a particular brain structure or cognitive process. There are simply too many mutually dependent moving parts for an analytic understanding to be possible. To understand the nature of 'no-self', one must give up on labels and grasp the whole. At the moment of

Enlightenment the subject and object evaporate into nothing.

The stratification of 'I' and 'mine'

In our conventional Westernised ways, the dualistic level of thinking is absolutely indispensable. We normally function on a dualistic level, which means that we are continuously making complementary distinctions between concepts like tall and short, good and bad, hard and soft, subject and object. As Vitaliano cogently states:

> *'Dualism is the act of severance, cutting the world into seer and seen, knower and known [...]with the occurrence of the primary dualism, man's awareness shifts from the non-dual universal consciousness (pure experience) to his physical body.'*[14]

Distinguishing between useful categories is critical to progress in science, and by carving the world apart into different categories, deliberation and choices became possible as well as the pursuit of desires. Mental categories referring to (more or less) static concepts also help organise deliberate behaviour. However, these things come at a cost. Our cognitive apparatus is so preoccupied with the belief of a 'self' that stands separate from (or above) the rest of nature that we become fixated with the illusion of a substantiality and static identity and existence. We miss the point that all of life is a dynamic process. That is, we live in a world of concepts and 'I', rather than understanding the essence of 'emptiness' as a truth.

This has numerous negative consequences. Through our need to impose order on our environment, we seek and then often come to believe in causes for what are actually non-local. Or worse still, we may commit violence against others or against nature out of a desire to control and exploit for 'self' gain, forgetting that the 'self' is a static illusion and instead the universe and world in which we are embedded in operates on an ecological, interdependent mode, so our 'self' is always harmful, short-sighted and extremely limited in scope.

Our sense of separation from the world is also intimately tied to expressions of desire. According to the Buddha's psychology, once the 'self' is identified, the prolific process of concept-building, with its complex ramifications, takes hold. The concept of 'I', along with its complementary notion, 'not I', leads people to measuring, making comparisons and valued judgments. As Bhikkhu Nanananda explained in his collection of 33 sermons, Nibbana - the mind stilled[1], the Buddha's psychology explains how the intrusion of the 'self' into the previously undifferentiated field of sense perception, leads to expressions such as, 'delighted in', 'craving', 'asserting' and 'clinging to'. These cravings, conceits, and opinions further reinforce the distinction between subject and object. Already when one says, 'This is mine,' one has discriminated between 'this' and 'I', making them into separate realities. Only when there is an 'I', can something exist relative to that 'I', and that something, if it is *there*, is where 'I' am not present, or is at a distance from 'me'. If it is *yonder*, or *over there*, perhaps it is nearer to 'you' who is in front of 'me'. And if it is *here*, it is beside 'me'. Evidently, the original split between subject and object spawns a multitude of different points of view – likes and dislikes. These feelings lead to cravings and aversions, and in this way we quickly divide up our existence.

The more accustomed we become to the idea of ourselves as separate from everything, the more locked in this idea becomes. Because we feel estranged from the rest of the existence that constitutes all that is not 'me', we feel insecure. We desire permanence and security. This leads to futile attempts to establish permanent ideals, as opposed to embracing the continuous, dynamic unfolding of life. Static concepts describe forms which are exactly defined because they are unchanging. This facilitates the records of memory through the repetition of mental processes. The record of the past tends to determine the present. In this way, the division of the world into categories is self-sustaining. Filtered through the self-matrix, by far the most virulent and crystallised of these static concepts are inflexible, dogmatic views.

The notion of an independent 'self' awakens at the stage of sensation awareness, and duality develops until it is wholly embedded and justified at the conceptual level. However, normally we don't recognise the concept of 'self' as an intrusion because we regard the subject-object relationship as the very essence of cognition. So, what begins as a complex, conditionally arising physiological process, develops into abstract conceptions of subject and object. The concepts of 'I' and 'me' are then superimposed on the complex contingent process and serves as a convenient short-hand device. Yet, there is nothing substantial corresponding to these concepts. They are, instead, cognitive constructions, albeit constructions with far-reaching implications.

The vortex and the homeostatic dynamic

Amid all this discussion of the illusory nature of the 'self-other' distinction, it is important to recognise that the Buddha did not dispute the reality that humans are biological organisms possessing particular features and embedded in particular environments. There is no denying the biological boundaries that separate an organism's body from its external environment. Homeostatic processes are essential to all life, and some of these processes require implicitly distinguishing the body of the organism from other types of objects. Even plants have a primitive form of 'self'-recognition, such that the roots belonging to related plants show fewer competitive interactions compared with the roots of two non-related plants.[15]

Nevertheless, if homeostatic processes are real, why is the self-other distinction considered to be an illusion? Homeostasis is a physical process. The plant that behaves as if it recognises the roots of its kin makes no claims to be separate and independent from the rest. The Buddha's objection to dualist perspectives has little to do with the existence of physical boundaries, and more to do with the construction and propagation of a persistent, abstract 'self'.

In the Buddha's teachings, he describes how the belief of a 'self' is metaphorically comparable to a vortex, or whirlpool. A whirlpool does exist, in the sense that it can be observed and certain measurements can be taken. It even has physical boundaries, as one can discern its edges. However, it clearly has no existence independent from the medium (air or water) in which it manifests. Furthermore, the material of which it is made continually changes, as the water molecules flow in and out of the vortex. The same is true of biological organisms, as the cells which make up the physical substrate of our bodies are continually dying and being replaced.

Figure 12.2 *The vortex, a metaphor for the ever-changing self.*

The 'self-as-vortex' metaphor evokes the tension that comes about as a consequence of the subject-object duality. A vortex reflects a conflict between something *internal* and something *external*; a *tangle within* and a *tangle without*. Enlightenment brings about cessation of a vortex through insight into the false nature of the separation of duality. Release from this duality is at the same time release from grasping, attachment and identification; hence, also selfishness, greed and hate. When a vortex ceases, all those conflicts subside and a state of peace prevails. What remains is the boundless great ocean with no delimitations. It is a solitude born of full integration. The insight and mental state of pure emptiness undercuts clinging attachments and suffering, and instead, compassion and happiness are able to be nourished and brought to bear. Consequently, the conflict between subject and object and the tangle in between is resolved.

This is a psychological process and a difficult topic for the untrained to understand. It creates a lot of confusion to say that emptiness is a state of mind. We are so accustomed to our dualistic thinking that it is not easy to transcend this characteristic of our existence. However, the ultimate goal of the Buddha's Eightfold Path is Awakening – to understand the workings of the subjective, relative basis of polarity and transcend to a non-dualistic experience, or Emptiness. To achieve this we need to go beyond the normal boundary markers between 'self' and 'other' and open ourselves to the reality of our profound interconnectedness with all that is.

Bibliography

1. Nanananda B.(2003). Nibbana - The Mind Stilled. Dharma Grantha Mudrana Bharaya. pp. IX.

2. Arnold, T. (1999). The Identity of Subject and Object. Retrieved from http://www.hyponoesis. org/Essays/Essay/e029

3. Wei, W. W. (1982). Open Secret: Linguistic and Literary (Vol. 1). Hong Kong University Press.

4. Deikman, A. J. (1996). 'I'= awareness. Journal of Consciousness Studies, 3, 350-356.

5. James, W. (1884). II.—What is an emotion? Mind, 34, 188-205.

6. Mack, A. (2003). Inattentional Blindness Looking Without Seeing. Current Directions in Psychological Science, 12(5), 180-184.

7. Rothstein, A. (1980). The Ego: an Evolving Construct. The International Journal of Psycho-Analysis, 62(Pt 4), 435-445.

8. Rizzolatti, G., & Craighero, L. (2004). The Mirror-Neuron System. Annu. Rev. Neurosci., 27, 169-192.

9. Gallese, V. (2009). Mirror Neurons, Embodied Simulation, and the Neural Basis of Social Identification. Psychoanalytic Dialogues, 19(5), 519-536.

10. Aglioti, S. M., Cesari, P., Romani, M., & Urgesi, C. (2008). Action Anticipation and Motor Resonance in Elite Basketball Players. Nature Neuroscience, 11(9), 1109-1116.

11. Kelso, J. A., & Engstrøm, D. A. (2006). The Complementary Nature. The MIT Press.

12. Botwinick, J. (1961). Husband and Father-in-Law: A Reversible Figure. The American Journal of Psychology, 74, 312-113.

13. Hamilton, S. (2000). Early Buddhism: A New Approach: The I of the Beholder (Vol. 16). Psychology Press.

14. Vitaliano, G. (2000). A New Integrative Model for States of Consciousness. NLP World, 7, 41-82.

15. Callaway, R. M., & Mahall, B. E. (2007). Plant Ecology: Family Roots. Nature, 448(7150), 145-147.

13

Language Construction of Duality

'We live our lives in this shared virtual world [...] The doorway into this virtual world was opened to us alone by the evolution of language.'

Terrence William Deacon[1]

'The language production mechanism "takes a web of thoughts and outputs them in form of words spoken one at a time, without a conscious effort or formal instruction, and is deployed without awareness of its underlying logic."'

Steven Pinker[2]

'Instead of proving or disproving a theory, researchers in linguistic relativity now examine the interface between thought (or cognition), language and culture, and describe the degree and kind of interrelatedness or influence.'

Phillip Wolff & Kevin J. Holmes[3]

The universality of language in human culture

Human perception unquestionably categorises the world into discrete objects and concepts, and the most basic of these divisions is the duality between subject and object, between observer and what is to be observed; 'me' and 'you'. Cultural conventions embedded in the structure of our spoken and written language play an important role in constructing and reinforcing these concepts. Human beings are social creatures, and as such they need to communicate with each other. Our spoken and written languages evolved to answer this necessity. Language constructs a symbolic representation of reality, allowing individuals to express needs, ideas, concepts, perceptions and beliefs. For the human species, language is considered as a quintessential activity. It is universal and innate, in fact, in the absence of a received mother language, there is evidence that children spontaneously invent their own.[4] Communication through a form of language is therefore central to the human condition.

The universality of language in human cultures suggests that the ability to learn language is inborn, arising as a consequence of a shared biological heritage, which has endowed us with a basic set of cognitive structures apt to facilitate and delineate what we can normally see, feel and think. As humans, we share a common cognitive endowment; a human world that is different from, for example, that of cats or elephants. Furthermore, humans from different regions and culture, with a common language, share similar categorisations of objects and actions. And yet, according to the culture, there is a considerable variation with respect to tool use, body language, styles of dress, food preparation and so on.

What emerges then, is the creational aspect of language, not merely an instrument to express our cognitive world, but more a tool that shapes it, dividing reality through different categorisation processes depending on the language acquired. That is to say, different linguistic traditions construct quite different mental worlds. Therefore, to understand the mental construction of the self-identity, we need to understand the influences of human language and human culture.

The principle of linguistic relativity

Language is an intricate but habitual part of our existence and we mostly take it for granted. It is easy to think of language as a passive tool of thought, a means of sharing our pre-existing thoughts with others. However, this is not the view of most contemporary scholars. Language and the categories it creates are not simply added on to human consciousness after an event; they are constitutive of it. As neurophysiologist Terrence Deacon puts it:

> *'We cannot help but see the world in symbolic [linguistic] categorical terms, dividing it up according to opposed features and organizing our lives according to themes and narratives.'[1]*
> *In other words, language is not just a method for communicating thoughts; it also determines what types of thoughts are possible.[1]*

One implication is that language, despite its many uses, may constrain or limit thought in relevant ways. In *The Social Construction of Reality*[5], sociologists Peter Berger and Thomas Luckman proposed that a person's concept of reality is the result of what is socially negotiated. That the conventions through which people communicate establishes certain socially agreed-upon set of representations which constitutes the shared reality of a society. In psychology, the idea that the structures of language determine or influence the way individuals (and societies) think, is known as the 'principle of linguistic relativity'. Some linguists have gone so far as to say that since language is the means by which we express our perceptions of reality, then reality can be mostly described as a linguistic construction.[6]

Most people are familiar with the idea that certain languages lack words for concepts that are part of the standard vocabulary in other languages. For example, it would be extremely difficult to explain the concept of the internet using the language of an indigenous Amazonian tribe (without resorting to borrowed English words), because such a language would simply have no words for such a foreign concept. Environmental and cultural evolution lead to linguistic categories absent or built on the backs of previously defined experience and categories, allowing us to describe ever more complex patterns and relationships. Or as the sutta commentary explains:

> *'The seeds of the impressions of language give rise to conceptual proliferation since endless time, without which the new arising of the impressions of language would be impossible.' (MI.61.2)*

Another feature of language that influences how thoughts are expressed is the rules of grammar, or syntax. In linguistics, a theoretical distinction is often drawn between syntax (structure) and semantics (meaning) of a language. In practice, however, the grammatical structure of a language carries with it certain baggage, which can constrain the types of meanings that are expressible, or at least make certain meanings easier to convey than others. For example, consider a simple utterance such as, 'I see you.' As a sentence of written English, this sentence distinguishes a subject (I), which is understood to be distinct from the recipient of the action (you). However, an alien physicist might just as well describe the scene in question as a complex dance of atomic particles or wave forms without loss of information. There would be no need to distinguish subject and object in such a description, and given the equivalence of matter and energy in physics, one might even dispose of the distinction between nouns and verbs. Our alien physicist's description would likely be unintelligible to most humans, but this is precisely the point. The conventions of everyday language bias us towards a particular level of description (the macroscopic world), and also bias us to separate the scene in a particular way (nouns, verbs, subjects, objects). As the linguist Benjamin Whorf put it in his 1956 book, *Language, Thought, and Reality*, '*Formulation of ideas is not an independent process, strictly rational in the old sense, but is part of a particular grammar.*' [7]

Most linguists agree with the idea that language influences the way we think about and see the world, and maybe it completely determines such process. In fact, the influence is profound. Furthermore, the relationship between language and worldview is reciprocal. In other words, language both influences and is itself influenced by how we understand the world. Certain languages lack words for concepts that are part of the standard vocabulary in other languages. In addition, what we perceive when we look out onto our world, and reflect back about our 'self', does not reflect some inherent truth; it reflects only the effects of our sense organs, cognitive functions and our culture. In fact, even how we think about such foundational concepts as space and time is influenced by the relativity of language. While all cultures draw on spatial metaphors to represent the concept of time (such as clocks, calendars, time lines), cross-cultural studies reveal differences in how languages map time onto space.

In her study, Lera Boroditsky summarises that:

> '*How people conceptualize time appears to depend on how the languages they speak tend to talk about time – the current linguistic context, what language is being spoken, and also the particular metaphors being used to talk about time in the moment. Further, people who conceptualize space differently also conceptualize time differently, suggesting that people co-opt representations of the physical world/space in order to mentally represent more abstract or intangible entities. Taken all together, these findings show that conceptions of even such fundamental domains as time differ dramatically across cultures and groups; the results reveal some of the mechanisms through which languages and cultures help construct basic notions of time.*'[8]

The influence of language over thought patterns is deeply pervasive, affecting even basic concepts such as space and time. Much of this perception depends on one's acquired knowledge, partly because both verbal and non-verbal communication depends on performance memories which, once acquired, operate largely outside of conscious awareness. To illustrate this, try to explain to someone why you phrased an utterance in a particular way. Normally, unless one is speaking very deliberately, the reason for a particular choice of words is completely hidden to the speaker. Certain words or phrases are simply more accessible than others; they just come to mind naturally. This may be because surrounding influences, the speaker's idiosyncratic personal history, or a variety of other reasons. A minor point perhaps, but it is not to be underestimated the extent to which our thinking relies on symbols. The result is that we live in a consensually constructed reality whose structuring mechanisms are effectively outside our normal awareness.

How language supports the separation of 'self'

Once we have created names, or labels, we can develop categories and references. Language is clearly a subjective method for organising the incoming experiential data we access through our senses; those data are then processed by our systematic cognitive organisation into increasingly complex and refined levels in order to help us make sense of our constructed 'world.' If kept in our awareness, the initial, immediate data move to a second stage, where they are identified more completely. It is then, in the khandha of apperception and conception, that we identify things by naming them.

The subject-object dichotomy is an inherent characteristic of language, for in order to make sense of our experience, we need to objectify our experiential data. It is easy to give examples of how we categorise opposites in our world, and the linguistic arrangement of attributes in pairs of opposites shows the prevalence of such a thinking process. Below are just a few very common examples of how duality shapes our everyday linguistic habits, and so influence our cognitive schemas.

Observation and its Opposites

Cold	Warm
Bad	Good
Pain	Pleasure
Hostile	Friendly
Changing	permanent
Death	Birth

Likewise, it is easy to signify an imperfection of our world and to project an image of its absolute opposite. From the observed opposites in our world it is tempting to conclude that there must also be real equivalents to the phenomena that lack observable opposites.

Deduced opposites

Immortality	No birth
Conditioned	Unconditioned

The process of differentiation through labelling is a process of objectification that organises not only the abstract but the concrete perceptions that we take in and, in so doing, makes sense of the otherwise unknown. Words and concepts remain no more than cognitive constructions that help create the reality perceived in ordinary states of consciousness. There is always a degree of distortion of experience whenever the world is abstracted and expressed in words, and linguistic descriptions have no absolute truth-value. Nonetheless, pre-enlightened people consider their own representations of the world to be true and truly isomorphic with reality – it is through language that they describe this reality.

Bhikkhu K. Ñānananda gives this analysis:

> 'Worldlings have a tendency to tenaciously grasp the concepts in worldly usage, to cling to them dogmatically and lean on them. They believe that the words they use have a reality of their own, that they are categorically true in their own right. Their attitude towards concepts is tinctured by craving, conceit and views.'[9]

There is growing evidence as to the importance of language to functions such as empathy, theory of mind, sense of self, for thinking and communication, but we need to understand the fallacy of our use of language as a descriptor of an objective, static 'world' experience. Words, and all concepts, are like the cognitive constructions of the external environment. They are abstractions, not the objective reality they try to capture. As Rudolf Carnap explains:

> '[…] The formulation in terms of "comparison", in speaking of "facts" or "realities", easily tempts one into the absolutistic view according to which we are said to search for an absolute reality whose nature is assumed as fixed independently of the language chosen for its description. The answer to a question concerning reality however depends not only upon that "reality" or upon the facts, but also upon the structure (and the set of concepts) of the language used for the description.'[10]

For the Buddha, language is primarily a tool for communication and for pointing to the truth, a means to help us attain Enlightenment.

How we construct our language helps reinforce our belief in an encapsulated 'self' as a locus, or mindset, as well as our categorised static relationship with the external world. While this demarcation of a 'self' is a context for verbal knowing, it is only an sketchy abstraction. We recognise that the 'self' as context, a story, a fiction is in fact valuable, because from this standpoint, one can more easily disengage and dis-identify emotionally and cognitively from one's flow of experiences. As with identity of a 'self' and a belief that the words we use have a reality that is categorically true, concepts become influenced by craving, conceit and beliefs. It is easy to be judgmental about our psychological and environmental experiences.

The Buddha's psychology asserts that the conventional way of constructing and representing the world is deeply embedded in both one's culture and language. People are influenced to see, think, and feel through everyday expressions of language; and we are also subtly conditioned by the traditions and history of our primary social group. In the beginning, linguistic conventions are necessary in order to establish the ground rules for communication, which represented an impelling evolutionary need. People have the need to communicate with each other and the structure of the language has to be functional to this necessity. To this end, everyday speech delineates a mutually sanctioned world of separate objects and categories because our underlying cognitive structures have been 'infused' by the impressions of language, a shared medium that allows us to inhabit a 'shared virtual world.'

The first words that an infant learns are normally simple nouns with repeatable syllables, such as 'puppy', 'papa', 'mama'. However, as the number of concepts and sounds in a child's repertoire increases, language becomes progressively abstract. As we grow from infancy to maturity and develop our capacity for language and critical evaluation, we naturally categorise experiences into classes that share certain characteristics, for example: 'animal', 'vegetable', 'mineral'. The game of 21 questions nicely illustrates this process. As we gain experience, and this continues through all phases of our active, mentally engaged life, we both place experiences into already defined categories, such as: animal – dog or cat, and create new categories where we don't find the existing ones convenient. Each of these classes, and there is an exacting logical science for classification, is a level of abstraction. As the class of objects grows, new subclasses, more abstract formulations, occur. Carried far enough and we have, as in the field of natural history, the story of life on this planet and an array of scientific subjects, an encyclopaedia of species, and specializations that fill a catalogue.

However, scholar Korzybski identified a problem with abstractions. The further along the chain you go, then the greater the distance you get from the original, first order, experience. Reality loses its solidity and cohesion, which is the foundation of a sane, rational mind. One major problem with this process is that we tend to think that the word represents the thing itself. Ultimately you get into philosophical debates about whether categories, or forms, have an independent existence and also the mind-body split, a phenomena Korzybski concluded was one of the major pathologies of modern life. Related to this pathology are all-ness, identification and elementalism. The Buddha calls this process of mental construction papañca, that is, elaboration, embellishment, or conceptual proliferation.

For the Buddha, the elaborations block out the presentational immediacy of phenomena; they let us know an object only 'at a distance', not as it really is. But the elaborations do not only screen cognition, they also serve as a basis for projections. The deluded mind, cloaked in ignorance, projects its own internal constructs outwardly, ascribing them to the object as if they really belonged to it. As a result, what we know as the final object of cognition, what we use as the basis for our values, plans, and actions, is a patchwork product, not the original article. But the product is not wholly illusory. It takes what is given in immediate experience as its groundwork and raw material, but along with this it includes something else: the embellishments fabricated by the mind. In the end, the original direct experience has been overrun by ideation, and the presented object appears only dimly through dense layers of ideas and views, like the moon through a layer of clouds.

Language then, enables us to conceive and express about objects and relationships with no concrete physical referents. Examples include hypothetical relationships, mathematical concepts and highly complex social constructions such as 'liberty' or 'justice'. Once constructed via language, these mental entities, rules, obligations and expectancies govern human thought and action to a remarkable degree. In short, language shapes not only communication, but also understanding. As stated by many cognitive psychology studies, and in particular by the famous linguist Binjamin Lee Whorf, our, *worldview is inescapably shaped by our language*.'[7] Language clearly draws our attention to certain aspects of the world and also influences our judgement about it.

When a name given to an object for purposes of easy communication has the sanction of others, it becomes a convention. There would be no shared world in common to all human beings if there were no shared dimension of this subliminal awareness. It is only through conceptual categorisation that we are able to objectify ourselves in contrast to others and in relation to remembered pasts and anticipated futures. '*It is a final irony*,' Deacon concludes, '*that it is the virtual, not actual, reference that [linguistic] symbols provide, which gives rise to this experience of self. This most undeniably real experience is a virtual reality.*'[8] Most of this, though, occurs quite without our awareness of it. Our 'shared virtual world,' which arises in correlation with the common cognitive structures and linguistic categories is so deeply engrained and so utterly habituated that it occurs almost automatically and nearly unconsciously in every moment. Human worlds are a collective and consensual (yet unconscious), construct, and the concepts are invested with the necessary flexibility and set on their tracks to proliferate. The uninstructed, average person succumbs to it; the disciple training on the Eightfold Path resists it; and the Emancipated Ones transcend it. Concepts for them are, '*Merely worldly conventions in common use, which he made use of, without clinging to them.*' (DN. I. 202) The Buddha reminds us that language is only based on conventional usage and that these worldly usages are not to be taken with an absolute perspective.

Over the course of a lifetime, this shared world of linguistic concepts becomes deeply engrained in our thought and speech patterns. These concepts are unavoidable when we learn to speak and live as members of a specific culture. Of these concepts, perhaps the most elaborate and deeply engrained psychological category is our concept of the self, which evolves and is defined in relation to a complex web of other concepts. Since language provides the vast majority of these concepts to us, one can easily agree that in large part our sense of 'self' reflects our particular cultural inheritance, the shared reality that we tacitly agree upon with others.

Our concept of the 'self' arises from a perceived division between subject and object, which contains yet further divisions within itself. On the one hand, there is the 'self' as agent, the subjective 'I' who performs various actions in the moment. On the other hand, there is another view of the 'self', the objectified 'me', as an enduring entity with a particular set of personality traits which we evaluate and judge according to cultural norms. This split becomes evident when people say things such as. 'I am a very intelligent person.' Such an expression is only coherent if we accept a split between our 'self' in the moment, and a deeper, more permanent and reflective 'self'. At this point, it is significant to remember that the human brain is a rather creative storyteller, which uses language to organise the world of conscious experience, efficiently making sense of an otherwise overwhelming volume of perceptual information processed by the nervous system. In building stories to describe the world of concepts around us, we at the same time are defining ourselves, an idea referred to as the *narrative self*.[11] To put it more simply, as we gain mastery of our native language, we begin to use words to tell stories, and in these stories we create what we call 'ourselves'. This ongoing and reflective personal narrative constructs the fiction of a time-bound, continuous 'self'. The great drawback to the structure imposed by language is that our words emphasise the individuality of *things* at the expense of perceiving the unity of experience.

Transcending the dualism of language

For the Buddha, the central snare of language is that we become confined in the misconception of the identifications of the 'self', which are encouraged from the grammatical use of agent and object. Once we establish the intentional '*I*' as part of our lexicon, I-related thoughts enter our inner dialogue of mental chatter. We select the '*I*' thoughts that build and maintain a story about ourselves that we are willing to accept; we are all creative writers in the service of the 'self'. As a result, our reality is filtered through the selective, and often self-serving vision of our subjective 'I' lens. Engrossed and compelled as we are in our stories of 'I', 'me', and 'mine' (which are founded on dualism), we cannot comprehend the actuality of existence. This in turn leads to our state of suffering.

In the Buddha's psychology, the term Nāma-rūpa, or 'name-form', is used to describe the interplay of psychological and physical processes, which defines a human being. Nāma (name) refers to the psychological dimension, and includes processes such as feeling, attention and perception. Rūpa (form) refers to physical substance and provides some consistency and recognisability to the individual, giving shape to abstraction. However, in keeping with the doctrine of anatta, neither nāma nor rūpa have any meaning or significance without the other: they are complementary, or mutually necessary. Rūpa can secure a basis in consciousness only in collaboration with nāma, and vice versa. In other words, without an observer there is no an object. We perceive the world in dualistic terms because language helps make any unity experience elusive to our cognitive apparatus. Enlightenment becomes possible when one understands that the shared social world, which includes a self, is a construction and becomes open to directly experiencing the unity which underlies Nāma-rūpa and other apparent dualities.

Importantly, this unity cannot be fully grasped by exercising one's intellectual faculties alone because that inevitably brings symbols and concepts back into the picture, which is self-defeating. Instead, Buddhist meditative practice teaches disciples to clear their mind of concepts in incremental stages, gradually dissolving the illusory boundaries that confuse us. Through a systematic meditative practice, we can free our perceptions from all the restraints and burdens of the pre-enlightened mind and achieve Awakening – a non-verbal appreciation of the world as it continuously comes into being.

So, Awakening involves seeing and reflecting on things just as they are, impartially, without exclusion, bias, attachment, obstructions or distortion. The grasper-grasped relationship ceases. When this transcendence is achieved, in the *seen* shall only be the *seen*, in the *heard* only the *heard*, in the *sensed* only *the sensed*, in the *cognised* only the *cognised*.

Bibliography

1. Deacon, T. W. (1998). The Symbolic Species: The Co-evolution of Language and the Brain. WW Norton & Company.

2. Pinker, S. (1994). The Language Instinct. New York: William Morrow and Company.

3. Wolff, P., & Holmes, K. J. (2011). Linguistic Relativity. Wiley Interdisciplinary Reviews: Cognitive Science, 2(3), 253-265.

4. Senghas, A., Kita, S., & Özyürek, A. (2004). Children Creating Core Properties of Language: Evidence from an Emerging Sign Language in Nicaragua. Science, 305(5691), 1779-1782.

5. Berger, P. L. & T. Luckmann. (1966). The Social Construction of Reality: A Treatise in the Sociology of Knowledge. Anchor Books.

6. Grace, G. W. (1987). The Linguistic Construction of Reality. New York, NY: Croom Helm.

7. Carroll, J. B. (ed.) (1956). Language, Thought, and Reality: Selected Writings of Benjamin Lee Whorf. Cambridge, Mass.: Technology Press of Massachusetts Institute of Technology.

8. Deacon, T. W. (1998). The symbolic species: The co-evolution of language and the brain. WW Norton & Company.

9. Nibbana: The Mind Stilled, Sermon 4 p. 78 Nanananda (2003). Nibbana - The Mind Stilled (Vol.1) (PDF). Dharma Grantha Mudrana Bharaya. pp. IX. ISBN 955-8832-02-2.

10. R. Carnap. truth and confirmation, 1936, philosophy of science 3: 419-471.

11. Gazzaniga, M. S. (1995). Principles of human brain organization derived from split-brain studies. Neuron, 14(2), 217-228.

14

Identification

'Without identification we can live with care, yet we are no longer bound by the fears and illusions of the small sense of self.'

Jack Kornfield[1]

'Ignorance is equivalent to the identification of a self […]'

Ringu Tulku[2]

'I identify with, therefore I am.'

Timothy Morton[3]

'Sense of becoming or feeling oneself one with another.'

Anonymous

In the Buddha's investigation and discovery of how the 'self' and identity are mentally constructed, he identified the importance of the phenomena of identification or tammayatà. In psychology, identity is distinguished from identification – identity is a label, whereas identification refers to the process. Identity is best understood as being both relational and contextual; while the act of identification is best viewed as inherently procedural. In fact, the formation of one's identity occurs through one's identifications with significant others (primarily with parents and other individuals and also with groups of people during one's lifetime of experiences).

In and of itself, identification is a natural, biological phenomenon that also influences our ability to empathise and offer care. Identification can be defined as, *'the process by which a person assimilates an aspect, characteristic or attribute of an other and is transformed, wholly or partially, by the model the other provides.'*[4] So the core meaning of identification is, put simply – to be like, or to become like another, as can be seen when an individual idolises a famous star by dressing, walking and gesturing in a similar way to that person. The identified characterisations are no longer cognitively separate and become part of an expanded identity – from a smaller 'I', to a larger 'us' or 'me'.

This proliferated and expanded 'self' is always a bifurcation of the world into 'self' and 'other', or 'myself' and 'us', the world is increasing experienced as a dichotomised 'other'. Naturally, the identifying subject has a increased feeling of specialisation and separation between 'self' and the larger 'world', which creates more self-encapsulation or constraint. Objectification of what is cognised creates judgments of liking; to crave, to acquire and possess that which is liked; or aversion to and the desire to expel what is disliked. Furthermore, the liked object is often imagined to be possessed as `me/mine', and the disliked object as 'not me/mine'. These resulting value judgements (for example, 'I like and identify with these people, but not with those people') often lead to embracing 'group think', and as a result, narrow judgemental attitudes, envy and conflict.

Through the process of identification, an identity is created when one becomes (through craving, conceit and views) attached, emotionally entangled, affected and united with concepts judged in the perceptual process as liked (or the opposite, disliked). In modern terms, this phenomenon has been described as identifying with the 'in crowd', or clique, in contrast to disliking the 'squares', or other disparaging labels. The process of identifying with the external world has therefore, implications for the experience of 'myself'.

Mechanisms of identification

There have been many interesting scientific discoveries in recent years regarding the psychological, social and neurological processes that contribute to identification. A particularly fruitful area of research has focused on the processes by which we understand and identify with other people. From an evolutionary perspective, these adaptations are thought to constitute a major difference between humans and our closest great ape relatives, and may have been critical to the development of human civilization, language and higher-level consciousness. For example, comparative psychologist Michael Tomasello argues that humans have evolved a very special set of cognitive adaptations, which allows us to understand that other individuals have similar rational lives to our own. This ability may provide the foundation for language and shared intentionality, which are necessary for human-level culture.[5, 6] Indeed, the ability to identify with others is highly adaptive, as it supports learning by observation as well as other social functions such as empathy.

Humans have an intrinsic ability (and need) to identify with other people. One of the earliest expressions of this need is imitation, or copying a behaviour. Imitation is not unique to humans, but no other animal seems to do it as much as we do. Children in particular take obvious delight in imitating adults, and newborn infants have been observed imitating facial gestures less than one hour after birth, suggesting an innate faculty for imitation.[7] Although the matter is far from settled, many researchers argue that this capacity to identify with other bodies could act as an entry point for identifying with other minds. In this case, imitation may lay an early foundation for the more sophisticated identification processes that come later, such as perspective-taking, empathy, and 'theory of mind' (that is, holding beliefs about other people's beliefs).

Imitation is not limited to infants and children of course. Social psychologists have long appreciated the contributions of shared facial expressions and body posture to adult social interactions. The automaticity of perception-behaviour results in default tendencies to act in the same way as those around us. This is known in social psychology as the chameleon effect.[8, 9] People tend to adopt the physical behaviours (such as posture, facial gestures, arm and hand movements) of the strangers with whom they interact. This unconscious imitation facilitates association and bonding between the individuals. Unconscious mimicry promotes identification with others. Identification is different to imitation as it may involve a number of behaviours being adopted, whereas imitation usually involves copying a single behaviour.

In 1977, Albert Bandura developed Social Learning Theory.[10] He was one of the first psychologists to study how behaviour is learnt from the environment through the process of observational learning. However, observational learning is not the same as pure imitation or merely copying another's behaviour. Observational learning describes the concept of behaviour acceptance (or avoidance), which occurs as a result of witnessing another person, but is performed later and cannot be explained as having been taught in any other way. Whether there is learning of behaviour, acceptance or avoidance depends on the nature of a consequence on the observed behaviour received in the original scenario. Cognitive processes must be at work, else observational learning cannot occur. The term 'identification' as used by Social Learning Theory, involves internalising another person's behaviour. This occurs with another person (the model) and involves adopting observed behaviours, values, beliefs and attitudes of the person with whom you are identifying. In fact, Bandura found that children will have a number of 'models' that possess qualities seen as rewarding and with whom they become attached to and identify with. These may be people in their immediate world, such as parents or older siblings, or could be fantasy characters or people in the media. The motivation to identify with a particular model is that they have a quality which the individual would like to possess.

The mirror neuron system

The recently discovered mirror neuron system provides an intriguing biological basis for imitation and other forms of identification. As previously noted, mirror neurons are so named because they respond similarly to either executed, observed or imagined actions. Furthermore, mirror responses are more robust when people observe familiar rather than unfamiliar actions. From this, it is tempting to postulate that social identification, or the process by which we identify with others, is reflected by some underlying neural synchrony among members of the 'in-group'. Although this is speculative, there is at least explanatory evidence that the ease of simulating another's behaviour depends in part on how 'similar to you' the other person is.[11] Indeed, the shared inter-subjective, 'we-centred' space mapped by mirroring mechanisms, is likely crucial in bonding neonates and infants to the social world. Yet it also acquires a different role – it provides the 'self' with the capacity to simultaneously entertain 'self-other' similarities and differences. Once the crucial bonds with the world of others are established, this becomes the adult conceptual faculty of socially contrasting and comparing likenesses and differences. Social identification, the inner feeling of 'similar-to-you' triggered by our encounter with others, is the result of the preserved shared 'we-centred' space.

This common relational character of actions, emotions and sensations, the earliest constituents of our social life, is created at the cognitive level by shared mirroring neural networks. Research indicates that mirror neurons in our brain respond to actions that we observe in others by firing in the same way when we recreate that action ourselves. Besides simple imitation, they can create many sophisticated human behaviours and thought processes. Mirror neurons create a direct link between the sender of a message and its receiver. Thanks to the mirror mechanism, actions performed by one individual become messages that are understood by an observer without any cognitive mediation. The observation of a person dancing is immediately understood because it evokes the same motor representation in the parieto-frontal mirror system of the observer. The shared 'we-centred' space, enabled by the activation of mirror neurons, is paralleled by the development of the capacity to distinguish 'self' from 'other', as long as sensory-motor 'self'-control develops. In such a way, infants progressively carve out an agentive, subjective perspective onto the world.

We have seen how people's action systems are tuned in to the expressions and behaviours of other people. This tuning facilitates both overt imitation and covert mental simulations, both of which can eventually lead to a kind of identification with others that is fundamentally rooted in bodily action. Inanimate objects can also prime particular actions. For example, many studies have shown how ambient stimuli (such as the perception of a hammer) automatically prime us to physically interact with the world (perform a power grip).[12] Self-other physical and mind-based interactions are shaped and conditioned by environmental limitations. Another example would be that in order to properly drink from a cup, one must grasp it and then move it to the mouth and drink – these simple examples show how environmental interactions, in countless ways, modify and standardise human interactions to create 'similar-to-you' experiences. The spontaneous activation of action plans is obvious in neuropsychological syndromes in which patients are incapable of suppressing actions that are elicited by environmental, action-related objects. These are known as 'utilisation behaviours'.[13] The human brain is strongly disposed to unconsciously, selectively resonate, both figuratively and literally, to particular objects and people in our environment. This provides a basis for identifying with the external world, and for deciding to what degree people and objects are 'like me' or 'important to me', or vice versa.

How identification contributes to the development of the 'self'

The perception-action links that enable early-in-life imitation appear to play an important role in bonding between infants and their caregivers, and in developing motor control. While the earliest instances of imitation may be more akin to a reflex than to strategic or intentional modelling behaviour, research is indicating that before the use of language, young infants already impress the likeness between acts of 'me' and 'other'. However, as Meltzoff suggests:

> *'The use of the English word 'me', is not meant to suggest that the young infant has an adult sense of self. I think that the adult notions of 'I', 'me', and 'self' develop. The 'like me' notion could be rephrased by purging the theoretically laden word, 'me', and saying that the infant recognizes: "that looks like this feels".'*[14]

This basic registering of similarity, influences the infant's first interpretations of the social world and they imbue the behaviour of others with felt meaning. Once the human brain has registered the 'similar to me' stimuli, infants and young children go on to learn a great deal about how their bodies work by a reflexive bi-directionality of caregivers and fellow children. Meltzoff suggests that there is a very close relation between perception and production that allows young infants to move in two directions – from 'self' to 'other' and from 'other' to 'self'. This is manifested by the imitation of novel acts that infants have not previously performed.[15] The capacity to imitate others' actions provides the ability to simultaneously identify with others whilst maintaining an awareness of differences.

Psychological theory explains that early identifications are critical to the development of a child's self-concept. Typically, children adopt the characteristics (appearance, attitudes, and behaviour) of the people who play a significant role in their lives as they grow up. The individual may aspire to incorporate the people, ideas and things which are experienced as beneficial into their own identity. An example would be the internalisation of the values of an admired institution (a process often termed 'idealistic-identification'). At the same time, one may also begin to define oneself in opposition to aspects of the world that one wishes to reject ('defensive contra-identification').[16]

Children most often identify positively with those they perceive to be emotionally warm, dominant or powerful. Also, children tend to be fascinated by questions such as, 'What is your favourite colour?' Or, 'What is your favourite animal?' Such questions encourage children to select various objects and traits which they might like to incorporate into their emerging identities.

As the child grows older and increases in self-awareness there is a cognitive shift from preoccupation with concrete physical attributes like hair colour, height or their favourite activities, to more abstract likes and dislikes. By the age of around nine years old, children shift to more abstract, internal or psychological descriptions of themselves, including their competences and skills compared with others. By adolescence, the individual increasingly defines themselves by a web of identifications coloured by associated feelings, thoughts and beliefs. In cognitive psychology, the term 'self-schema' is used to refer to a collection of stable and entrenched memories that forms the basis of a person's beliefs, which they consider important to their self-definition. A person's self-schema (a belief or idea about oneself that is self-perpetuating) with regards to sociability might be, 'I am shy', reflecting how the individual has decided to categorise his or herself in relation to others on the basis of formative experiences. The full scope of this capacity is seen in the adult world of social comparisons, which is populated by a combination of friends, family and allies who are 'like me', but also enemies and others 'not like me'.

Once a self-schema has been developed, it is stored in long-term memory and acts as both facilitator and a bias (or filter), influencing what the individual attends to, remembers, and is willing to accept as true about them. For example, if a respected yet insensitive teacher tells a student they won't succeed academically, the student may choose to pursue non-academic activities, even though in truth they have sufficient capability to succeed academically. The self-schema becomes self-perpetuating when the individual chooses activities based on expectations instead of desires. Nevertheless, a person's self-concept can, and does, change over time when schemas are updated or reassessed. While there is debate in psychology over the timeline of self-concept construction, there is wide agreement that one's self-concept has an important influence on how people behave, as well as influencing cognitive and emotional outcomes such as self-esteem, academic achievement, anxiety, levels of happiness, social integration and life-satisfaction.

Atammayatā (non-identification)

A person's identity created through identifications can be a strong motivating force in a person's life, but it is also inherently encapsulating and unstable because of continual fluctuations created by their social and cultural underpinnings. Inevitably, our views of the world change as we progress through life. What is important in the early years of our life may become less important later, and occasionally our views in the senior years become diametrically opposed to earlier-held views. Alliances shift, friends become foes or vice versa. For these reasons, our identity cannot provide the permanent sense of security and safety that many people desire. If we persist in clinging to our affiliations in hopes of finding lasting security, the futility of the exercise is more likely to result in additional suffering and anxiety. For while it is in the permanent that

we attempt to establish our identity, identifications and
the social and cultural world upon which they are based
are always changing, and so continually undermining any
attempts to achieve a lasting stability, security, status and
favour. As Physicist David Bohm says:

> *'We have all sorts of representations of ourselves
> which are really rather superficial. And we try to
> identify with them. But then once we do that, we
> have this quality of thought which infuses it into
> perception. We apparently perceive the thing we
> are representing - it seems to be there. It's like the
> rainbow; we see a rainbow, but what we have is
> drops of rain and light - a process. Similarly, what
> we 'see' is a self; but what we actually have is a
> whole lot of thoughts going on in consciousness.
> Against the backdrop of consciousness we are
> projecting a self, rather than a rainbow...if you try to
> touch the self, it will be the same difficulty as trying
> to touch the rainbow. We have a representation
> of the self, which is really arising in a process. We
> don't know the process very well; but the attempt to
> treat the self as an object is just not going to mean
> anything.'[17]*

In modern society in particular, constant marketing, media
and social pressure to accept new identifications creates
much stress and suffering, if taken seriously, in both our
intra-psychic and emotional lives as well as with our
interactions with other people.

In the end, our attempts to construct and maintain
an enduring identity, entangled as it is with grasping at
attachments, cravings and ignorance, creates suffering
and anxiety in the face of the truth of impermanence and
the interrelatedness of all phenomena. For these reasons,
the Buddha advised against, *'building one's house'* (that
is, identity) on the impermanent and shifting sands of

identifications. We will understand ourselves and our world more realistically and profoundly if we think of the self in terms of dynamic patterns of relationships or, as the Buddha advised, in terms of dependent origination rather than of static substantial essences or entities. Our pursuits can be most successful if we are not encapsulated by our past and can easily update and adapt to our shifting social landscapes. If we don't adapt and instead reinforce whatever we identify with, in the end it controls us. In the words of Ferrucci, our identifications, *'can submerge us, control us, limit our perceptions, and block the availability of all other feelings, sensations, desires and opinions.'*[18]

However, when we release ourselves from the shackles of our identifications, then we no longer allow ourselves to be controlled by these attachments. This is why the Buddha enjoined that one should cultivate an attitude of atammayatā, or non-identification, by engaging in a course of training (Eightfold Path) for the emancipation of the mind from such imaginings and proliferation. The purpose of non-identification is to liberate consciousness from the confines of the constructed 'self' so we have a clearer perspective and can then make better choices. Those who do so are liberated from the anxiety caused by an insecurity of a belief in a static 'self', and simultaneously expose the falsity of the dichotomy between 'self' and 'other'. They are not swept away by the uninhibited emotions of like and dislike depending on the biases established through identifications with different people, groups and ideas. In Buddhism, the Arahant is called atammayatā, one who avoids identifying themselves with anything. They are liberated from the unconscious belief in a 'self' and have exposed the falsity of the 'I'. With non-identification one has insight, understanding and therefore the ability to transcend the entangling phenomenon of identification or tammayatà and become non-attached. When attachments or entanglements are avoided, a person more easily remains unaffected, calm, peaceful and sublime.

Bibliography

1. Kornfield, J., & Siegel, D. J. (2011). Bringing Home the Dharma: Awakening Right Where You Are. Shambhala Publications.

2. Tulku, R. (2005). Daring Steps Toward Fearlessness: The Three Vehicles of Buddhism. Snow Lion Publications, Incorporated.

3. Morton, T. (2015). I identify with, therefore I am. Blogpost from http://ecologywithoutnature. blogspot.it/ June 18, 2015

4. Laplanche, J., & Pontalis, J.-B. (1973). The Language of Psychoanalysis. London: The Hogarth Press and the Institute of Psycho-Analysis.

5. Tomasello, M. (2000). First Steps Toward a Usage-Based Theory of Language Acquisition. Cognitive linguistics, 11(1/2), 61-82.

6. Herrmann, E., Call, J., Hernández-Lloreda, M. V., Hare, B., & Tomasello, M. (2007). Humans Have Evolved Specialized Skills of Social Cognition: The Cultural Intelligence Hypothesis. Science, 317(5843), 1360-1366.

7. Meltzoff, A. N., & Moore, M. K. (1983). Newborn Infants Imitate Adult Facial Gestures. Child Development, 54(3), 702-709.

8. Dijksterhuis, A., & Bargh, J. A. (2001). The Perception-Behavior Expressway: Automatic Effects of Social Perception on Social Behavior. Advances in Experimental Social Psychology, 33, 1-40.

9. Chartrand, T. L., Maddux, W. W., & Lakin, J. L. (2005). Beyond the Perception-Behavior Link: The Ubiquitous Utility and Motivational Moderators of Nonconscious Mimicry. In Hassin, R. R.. Uleman, J. S., & Bargh, J. A. (Eds.). The New Unconscious, 334-361. New York: Oxford University Press.

10. Bandura, A. (1977). Social Learning Theory. Prentice Hall.

11. Knoblich, G., & Flach, R. (2001). Predicting the Effects of Actions: Interactions of Perception and Action. Psychological Science, 12(6), 467-472.

12. Tucker, M., & Ellis, R. (2001). The Potentiation of Grasp Types During Visual Object Categorization. Visual Cognition, 8(6), 769-800.

13. Archibald, S. J., Mateer, C. A., & Kerns, K. A. (2001). Utilization Behavior: Clinical Manifestations and Neurological Mechanisms. Neuropsychology Review, 11(3), 117-130.

14. Meltzoff, A. N. (1988). Infant Imitation after a 1-Week Delay: Long-term Memory for Novel Acts and Multiple Stimuli. Developmental Psychology, 24(4), 470.

15. Meltzoff, A. N. (2007). 'Like Me': A Foundation for Social Cognition. Developmental Science, 10(1), 126-134.

16. Weinreich, P., & Saunderson, W. (Eds.). (2005). Analysing identity: Cross-cultural, societal and clinical contexts. Routledge.

17. Bohm, D. (1992). Thought as a System (transcript of seminar held in Ojai, California, from 30 November to 2 December 1990). London: Routledge.

18. Ferrucci, P. (2000). What We May Be: Techniques for Psychological and Spiritual Growth. Tarcher.

15

The Buddha's Compassion

'Go forth, bhikkhus, for the good of the many, for the happiness of the many, out of compassion for the world, for the good, benefit, and happiness of men.'

Vimånavatthu I, 20

'Of all the teachings, the ultimate is emptiness, of which compassion is the very essence. It is like a very powerful medicine, a panacea that can cure every disease in the world. And just like that very powerful medicine, realization of the truth of emptiness, the nature of reality, is the remedy for all the different negative emotions.'

Atiśa Dipankara Shrijnana (980–1054 CE)

Karunā (compassion)

The Buddha often spoke of karunā (compassion) – understanding that there is suffering and doing what will best help to alleviate that suffering – as the most beneficial and moral of all behaviours. Knowing that there is dukkha is the strongest incentive for living a life of compassionate behaviour toward ourselves as well as toward others. Compassion for our 'self' and compassion for others are not mutually exclusive.

Karunā is an important an aspect upon the Path to Wisdom. As we advance on the Path to Enlightenment by progressively developing purified mental dispositions and behaviours, we gain insight into the subjectivity of our identity and how we confound our understanding of the world through the misconception of an inherent dualistic reality. In conjunction, as we become less enchanted and fascinated with our 'I' and we begin to detach from our cravings and identifications, we develop both wisdom and compassion. Like two wings that work together in flight, each of these qualities supports the other. Wisdom distinguishes the beneficial from the non-beneficial; compassion moves us to action.

In his discussions of these two attributes, the Buddha was essentially speaking of having empathy for another's suffering and the desire to alleviate it. Modern psychology asserts that empathy both precedes and is a prerequisite for compassion. Fundamentally, to have empathy is to understand another's feelings. It is to put ourselves emotionally in the place of another. The ability to empathise, however, depends on our capability to feel our own feelings and identify them, because to recognise them in others we first need to be able to recognise them in ourselves. To play with the clichés that capture this notion, empathy is, 'walking in another's shoes or hearing with someone else's ears'. We can understand the common connotation of empathy in this way. Nevertheless, it is useful to break the idea down and consider its more specific components.

Empathy for you and me

Scholars who study empathy have noted several ways in which the word can capture the variety of emotional and cognitive responses it suggests, such as recognising someone else's internal state, including the other's thoughts and feelings; intuiting or projecting oneself into another's situation; feeling empathic concern upon witnessing another person's suffering; and wanting to help the person. One capacity, while still hotly discussed as to its nature and origin, is called 'meta-representational abilities'. As we have learned, our cognitive systems have the ability to construct and process representations of objects and situations. The branch of cognitive science that studies *how* we represent and try to understand our and others minds is called the 'Theory of Mind'. Human beings have a natural basic comprehension of our cognitive functions such as perception and memory. We can also attribute to one another beliefs and desires. In fact, humans may be the only living creature to succeed in meta-representing other people's thoughts as well as our own.

Meltzoff and Moore suggest that from a very early age, possibly from birth, there are innate links between a child's perception of the actions of others and their perception of their own internal body states.[1] Young babies also have an unlearnt ability to hear fine differences between consonant sounds and to perceive them categorically. Newborns are able to perceptually represent and imitate another person's movements. For example, the neonate will imitatively stick out his or her tongue after observing an adult make this gesture. Infants respond differently to people than they do to objects and seem to expect people to behave differently than objects do. In fact, at only five to eight weeks old, babies will imitate mouth openings and tongue protrusions produced by an adult, but not mimic similar-looking behaviours when they are produced by an object. Infants try to retrieve a just-disappeared object by reaching toward its place of disappearance but try to retrieve a just-disappeared person by vocalising. Very young infants indicate special preferences for certain human faces and voices, and engage in complex nonverbal communicative interactions with others. Butterworth has shown that by nine months old, infants begin to follow the gaze of others and to point objects out to them.[2] In the behaviour known as 'social referencing', infants who are faced with an ambiguous situation turn to check the adult's facial expression and regulate their actions in accordance with it.[3]

These very early abilities suggest that there is a strong innate component to our Theory of Mind. As children mature, they develop a succession of theories about the mind that they use to explain their experience and the behaviour of themselves and others. These simple theories provide predictions, interpretations and explanations through postulating mental entities and regulations. The theories change as children discover counterevidence, gain new data, and test their assumptions. Therefore, fairly soon they discover that the 'I' authority can be incorrect and, perhaps, eventually, the insight that what we know about our minds is as much a construction or assumption as what we can know of the minds of others can arise – *'Your thoughts are not who you are.'*

A belief represents the world, like a picture in the head. If this representation matches up with the accepted norm of the world, then the belief is considered true. A false belief is thought to misrepresent the world. When we believe we know about another person's beliefs and desires, we automatically infer mental states (desires, perceptions, beliefs, knowledge, thoughts, intentions and feelings) from their behaviour. This inference ability is very adaptive because we predict other people's behaviour based on what we know about them. An ability to predict, explain and interpret other people uses an internally represented knowledge structure often called a 'folk psychology'.

Our understanding of mental states develops from childhood into adulthood. So to reason hypothetically, a person must be able to represent a belief as separate from the world it is representing. This is the so-called 'decoupling skill' – the mental ability that allows us to mark a belief as a hypothetical statement of the world rather than a real one. As Harris has argued, '*We mirror our understanding of the mind which reflects an increasing ability to imagine the experiences of others.*'[4] In other words, we begin to *assume* knowledge of others feelings and thoughts. We become empathetic. So meta-representation (the representation of one's own representations) allows self-critical perspectives to develop; this is unique to human cognition. Beliefs about how well we are forming beliefs become possible because of meta-representation, as does the ability to evaluate one's own desires.

Growing evidence suggests that the mirror neuron system plays a vital role in our ability to empathise and socialise with others. Evolution has given us general abilities, called 'contextual priming', for survival and reproduction, and culture and early learning fine-tune these adaptive unconscious processes to the specific local conditions we grow up in. This is what allows us to make accurate adjustments to present time events and people by automatically activating our cognitive representations of them, and concurrently, all of the information (goals, knowledge, effect) that we associate with that. This process of a close, automatic connection between perception and behaviour has been discovered. The mirror neurons in the pre-motor cortex, which becomes active both when we perceive a type of action by another person as well as when we engage in that action ourselves.[5] Neurons with this capacity to match similar observed and executed actions, code not only the observed actions of 'my action' and 'your action', such as grasping a cup, but also codes the intention behind the action – 'That's a grasp to drink', or, 'That's a grasp to accept the pouring of a liquid into the cup.'

This finding suggests that mirror neurons allow us to determine other people's intentions as well as their actions. For example, with the facial expression of a smile, whether we observe it or make it ourselves, the same regions of our brain become activated. The more active our mirror neuron system, the better we are at interpreting facial expressions. Along with the sensory description of the observed stimuli, internal representations of the body states associated with them are evoked in the observer, 'as if' he/she would be doing a similar action or experiencing a similar emotion or sensation. So, the embodied simulation is based on our experience/contact with the world, while the second mechanism is an abstraction or cognitive description of that experience. The proposed, cognitively 'mind-reading' ability is built on the embodied experience.

This ability of sharing the intentional relations of others, by means of the shared neural state, produces intentional harmony, which then produces the quality of familiarity that we identify with others. This is 'being empathic'. By means of a shared neural state that obeys the same morphological-functional rules, the 'objectified other' becomes a 'similar to self'. This cognitive ability, so natural and immensely engaged in almost every moment of our life, is a very important evolutionary development that promotes human survival and community.

When we perceive others expressing an emotion, be it joy or sadness, the same brain areas are activated as when we also experience the same emotion. Similarly, direct matching has also been described for the perception of pain and touch. So taken together these results suggest that our capacity to empathise with others is mediated by embodied simulation processes; that is, by the activation of the same neural circuits underpinning our own emotional and sensory experiences.[6] These data support the idea that mirror neurons are important for the effortless, automatic understanding of the mental states of other people,[7] and may also be the basis of automatic imitation.[8] While a deficient ability of these processes could have a responsibility for autistic spectrum disorders[9], it cannot now be assumed as the necessary cause of autistic dysfunction. However, when the simulation process is not present or malfunctioning, there is empathic impairment in autism indicated by a reduced tendency toward automatic imitation and a small, detached consideration of the social experiences of others.

Emotional responses elicited by and consonant with the welfare of others and oneself may include sympathy, compassion, tenderness and the like, and all of these aspects of the basic condition of empathy are consistent with the varied experiences that the Buddha described as indicating the presence of compassion. The Buddha taught that the wisest way to practice altruism is to help people help themselves while giving them emotional support as well as skill development when possible. It is not unusual, however, for pre-enlightened, altruistic behaviour to become enmeshed with selfishness and greed, thereby creating problems for others instead of helping them. As long as our 'I' and 'self'-interest are involved, we tend to look for some kind of payback or self-gratification for our actions. Therefore, we need to scrutinise carefully our intentions behind our altruistic behaviours.

The Buddha emphasised that a necessary beginning for the cultivation of empathy includes empathy for oneself as well as empathy for the well-being of others. The Kandaraka Sutta, for example, describes the correct path as that of a person who *does not torment himself or others.*' Until we are able to accept ourselves and feel empathy toward ourselves, we cannot correctly understand what others feel and so cannot show them empathy with wisdom. It is critical to understand here that altruism toward the 'self' is not egoism (the enemy of altruism). Egoism seeks to use others for one's material welfare and gain. Its concern is possessive and manipulative. As selfishness is minimised and empathy develops, altruism becomes real. Recognising and cultivating empathy towards the 'self' and towards 'others' is a critical step in removing egotism (with its focus on separation and alienation), and increasing selflessness, happiness and affinity with the other sentient beings inhabiting this world.

Bibliography

1. Meltzoff, A. N., & Moore, M. K. (1977). Imitation of Facial and Manual Gestures by Human Neonates. Science, 198(4312), 75-78.

2. Butterworth, G. (1991). The Ontogeny and Phylogeny of Joint Visual Attention. In Whiten, A. (Ed), Natural Theories of Mind: Evolution, Development and Simulation of Everyday Mindreading, 223-232. Basil Blackwell.

3. Campos, J., & Sternberg, C. (1981). Perception, Appraisal, and Emotion: The Onset of Social Referencing. In Lamb, M., & Sherrod, L. (Eds.). Infants Social Cognition: Empirical and Social Considerations. Hillsdale, NJ: Erlbaum.

4. Saarni, C., & Harris, P. L. (1991). Children's Understanding of Emotion. Cambridge University Press.

5. Frith, C. D., & Wolpert, D. M. (Eds.). (2004). The Neuroscience of Social Interaction: Decoding, Imitating, and Influencing the Actions of Others, (pp. 133-135). Oxford University Press.

6. Gallese, V., Keysers, C., & Rizzolatti, G. (2004). A Unifying View of the Basis of Social Cognition. Trends in Cognitive Sciences, 8(9), 396-403.

7. Iacoboni, M. (2009). Imitation, Empathy, and Mirror Neurons. Annual Review of Psychology, 60, 653-670.

8. Cross, K. A., Torrisi, S., Losin, E. A. R., & Iacoboni, M. (2013). Controlling Automatic Imitative Tendencies: Interactions Between Mirror Neuron and Cognitive Control Systems. NeuroImage, 83, 493-504.

9. Gallese, V. (2006). Intentional Attunement: A Neurophysiological Perspective on Social Cognition and its Disruption in Autism. Brain Research, 1079(1), 15-24.

16

Memory

There is little direct commentary on the function of memory in the Buddha's teaching. It is taken for granted that our existence is accumulative; that is, nothing is really forgotten, and our present state is continually filtered through the experiences of the past. The Buddha explains that memory is of dual importance. Firstly, the Buddha attributed much importance to habituation and schemata in the cognitive processing that creates our reality. Without memory we cannot establish a habit. Secondly, memory is essential to learning new habits (and pursuing the Buddha's teachings). For example, there are two aspects to Right Mindfulness (or right memory, right monitoring or right attention) – being aware of the instructions on the Eightfold Path teachings.

The Buddha laid out an extensive programme of change detailing how best to reach the goal of nibbana. Since memorising and reciting the texts were (and still are), a method of instruction and teachings, an effective memory was essential. A wise mediator must remember the instructions and act on them with diligence or 'Right Effort'. These two aspects of mindfulness – remembering and monitoring the knowledge and application of the instruction – are essential in the direct application of the Buddha's teachings.

Mediators who practice mindfulness whilst monitoring their thoughts can become aware of an unwholesome mental state. The skilful application of a learnt intervention can halt the defilement, but if the unwholesomeness continues to take hold, a stronger method must be employed to evict and replace it. Unwholesome states rob us of our peace, wisdom and happiness. Teachings need not only to be recalled but also monitored and given a person's full awareness in relation to the application of the teachings. This process creates an imprint, or a new memory, which later becomes a habit in our mind. The more we do this the more a teaching becomes easier to remember and the more likely that new wholesome mental states will be established.

The Buddha's psychology is now supported by evidence generated using modern scientific methods. Cognitive science confirms the Buddha's theory that memory is a powerful influence on our perception of the world and ourselves. Our memories are not objective or unbiased, but they are easily influenced by personal feelings, interpretations, or prejudice. As Damasio states:

> *'Our memories are prejudiced, in the full sense of the term, by our past history and beliefs. Perfectly faithful memory is a myth, applicable only to trivial objects. The notion that the brain ever holds anything like an isolated "memory of the object" seems untenable. The brain holds a memory of what went on during an interaction, and the interaction importantly includes our own past [...]'[1]*

Our personal histories, as memory, constantly influence us, persistently filters and guides our feelings and thoughts, and we often follow them seemingly blindly. For example, when we worry, the root conditions of the worrying lie in the past. Even our views are generated and perpetuated by these latent tendencies deeply stored in our unconscious. In the end, the original direct experience has been overlaid by ideation and the original data is understood through overlying dense layers of ideas and views, in a way similar to how we view the moon through a thick layer of clouds. The Buddha calls this process of mental elaboration papañca, or 'conceptual proliferation'. The foundations for this process of fabrication, are unconscious memories hidden from view; the latent tendencies.

So even though we assume that we are always directly aware of the present, without bias or interpretation, this is an inaccurate belief. In ordinary consciousness, our mind has an initial impression of the given moment, but it does not stay that way. Instead, the immediate impression becomes a springboard for building mental constructs which obscure it from the original data because, as we have seen, the cognitive process is interpretative. Then, immediately after grasping the initial impression, the sense data is made intelligible. Concepts are woven into constructs – that is, sets of mutually corroborative concepts – and then the constructs are woven together into complex interpretative schemas.

Memory is essential for our ability to survive. It is so important that without memory we would not be able to perform basic functions, have abstract thought, create our own identities or communicate with others. Memories are the foundation of our habits and way of life. Much of who we presently are is formed from what we have learnt and thought before. Compared with many other organisms, we have the advantageous ability for our survival to recall past memories in order to imagine the future and to plan future courses of action.

The memory system

Memory is our ability to encode, store, retain and subsequently recall information and past experiences. It is a complex system of diverse processes carried out in various areas of our brains. For the brain to process information, it must first be stored. To begin with, information is encoded according to the type of sensory stimuli. The different memory systems operate in parallel to support behaviour. The various specific memory systems can be distinguished in terms of the different kinds of information they process and the principles by which they operate. Sherry and Schacter suggested that multiple memory systems have evolved because they serve distinct and functionally incompatible purposes. There are multiple types of memory, including sensory information storage (SIS), working or short-term memory (STM), and long-term memory (LTM).[2]

Once information is stored, it must be maintained. Each memory type differs with respect to function, the form of information held, the length of time information is to be retained and information-handling capacity. There is not yet a universally accepted knowledge organisation model, because each has strengths and weaknesses. Some animal studies suggest that working memory, which stores information for roughly twenty seconds, is maintained by an electrical signal looping through a particular series of neurons for a short period of time. Information in long-term memory is hypothesised to be maintained in the structure of certain types of proteins. Researchers also believe in the existence of an interpretive mechanism and an overall memory monitor or control mechanism that guides the interaction among various elements of the memory system.

Once stored, memories will eventually be retrieved from storage. However, remembering past events is not like watching a recorded video. Rather, it is a process of reconstructing what may have happened based on the details the brain chose to store and was able to recall. Recall is triggered by a retrieval cue, an environmental stimulus that prompts the brain to retrieve the memory. Evidence shows that the better the retrieval cue, the higher the chance of recalling the memory. It is important to note that the retrieval cue can also make a person reconstruct a memory improperly. Memory distortions can be produced in various ways, including varying the wording of a question. For example, merely asking or suggesting to someone whether a red car had left the scene of a hit-and-run can make the person recall having seen a red car during later questioning, even if there was never a red car.

Sensory information storage

The stimuli detected by our senses either can be not attended and remain undetected, or perceived and enter our sensory memory. This selection process is usually outside of conscious controls: the brain must filter information that is unconsciously judged by us as necessary or not. When information is perceived, it is automatically stored in sensory memory. However, sensory memory degrades very quickly and cannot be prolonged even via rehearsal. Images are held in SIS for several tenths of a second after they are received by the sensory organs and before fading. This allows the brain to process a sensory event for longer than the extremely short duration of the contact, which explains why a movie shot at sixteen separate frames per second appears as a continuous movement. Even though it lasts for a short time, sensory information storage is an essential first step for storing information in short-term memory.

Short-term memory

Most neuroscientists would agree that information passes from SIS into STM via the process of attention (the cognitive process of selective concentration on one aspect of the environment of interest and ignores other things), where again it is held for only a short period of time – a few seconds or minutes, pending further processing. Whereas SIS holds the complete image, STM stores only an abstraction of the image. This processing includes judgements about meaning, relevance and significance, as well as the cognitive processing necessary to integrate information into long-term memory. If we immediately forget some information just received or given, this is because it was not transferred from short-term to long-term memory. Short-term memory acts for temporary recall of the information which is being processed at any point in time.

An important element of STM is the limitation of its capacity (typically around seven items or even less) of keeping information in mind in an active, readily-available state for a short period of time (typically from ten to fifteen seconds, or sometimes up to a minute). What is actually held in short-term memory, though, is not complete concepts, but rather links or pointers (such as words) that the brain associates with other stored knowledge. So, when we choose where to focus our attention, we can concentrate on remembering, or interpreting, or taking notes on information received just a moment ago. Alternatively, we can pay attention to immediately received information. Since the information has never left the conscious mind, retrieval of information from STM is direct and immediate. Therefore, information can be maintained in STM by a process of over and over repetition, called rehearsal. But while rehearsing, we cannot simultaneously add new information so there are strict limitations on the amount of information able to be retained in STM at any one time.

Long-term memory

Some information retained in STM can become LTM through the process of consolidation. The information of past experiences may be filed away in the mind for a long period of time and must be retrieved before it can be used. Over time, very little decay occurs in LTM; a large amount of information can be stored almost indefinitely. Whilst LTM mostly encodes information for storage based on meaning and association, it does encode to some extent by sound.

Although not completely understood, a physiological process called Long-term Potentiation is what is believed to establish LTM. It involves a process of physical changes in the structure of neurons or nerve cells in the brain. When something is learned, circuits of brain neurons, known as neural networks, are created, altered or strengthened. These neural circuits are composed of a number of neurons that communicate with one another through special junctions called synapses. The communicative strength of certain circuits of neurons is reinforced through recurrent use, involving the creation of new proteins within the body of neurons, and the electrochemical transfer of neurotransmitters across synapse gaps to receptors. The efficiency of these synapse connections then increases, facilitating the passage of nerve impulses along particular neural circuits, which may involve many connections to the visual cortex, the auditory cortex, the associative regions of the cortex. Forgetfulness occurs in LTM when the formerly strong synaptic connections among the neurons become weak, or when the activation of a new network is superimposed over an older one causing interference in the older memory.

Yet in a study conducted by researchers at the University of California, Los Angeles, it was found that traces of a lost memory might remain in a cell's nucleus, perhaps enabling future recall or at least the easy formation of a new, related memory. These results are surprising because it suggests that a neuron 'knows' how many synaptic connections it is supposed to form, meaning that it encodes a crucial part of memory. The researchers also ran an experiment in which they found that a LTM could be totally erased (as gauged by its synapses being destroyed) and then re-formed with only a small reminder stimulus – again suggesting that some information was being stored in a neuron's body.[3]

While these three memory processes (SIS, STM, LTM) comprise the storehouse of information that we call memory, the total memory system includes other features as well. To explain the operation of the total memory system, while little agreement exists on many critical points, most psychologists posit the existence of an interpretive mechanism, a sort of monitor or central control mechanism that guides and oversees the operation of the whole system.

Organisation of information in memory

On average, the human brain has about 100 billion neurons and many more neuroglia (or glial cells), which serve to support and protect the neurons. Each neuron may be connected to up to 10,000 other neurons, passing signals to each other via 1,000 trillion synaptic connections. Computational neuroscientists' estimate of the human brain's memory capacity vary from ten terabytes to 2.5 petabytes (or one million gigabytes).

A few months after birth no new brain cells are formed, although existing ones may increase in size until the age of about eighteen years old. They are designed to last a lifetime, so our memory can record a lifetime of experience and thought.

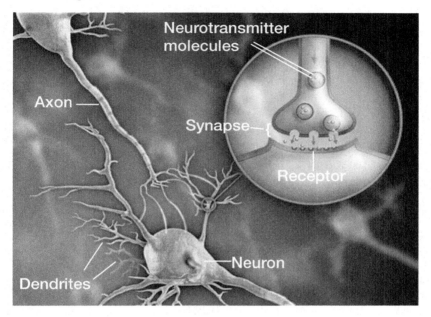

Figure 16.1 *Synaptic transmission. The neurons are capable of storing information. Each neuron has long, feathery filaments attached to the cell body called the dendrite and a special, extra-long, branched cellular filament called the axon.*

A message within the brain is converted, as it moves from one neuron to another, from an electrical signal to a chemical signal (and back again), in an ongoing chain of events that is the basis of all brain activity. Briefly, electrical impulses flow through the dendrites and axons and are carried by neurotransmitters of various types across what is called the synaptic gap between neurons (Figure 16.1). Memories are stored as patterns of connections between neurons. When two neurons are activated, the connections between them are strengthened. The whole process takes less than one five-hundredth of a second. For example, reading this page is actually physically changing your brain. George Johnson states, *'In a matter of seconds, new circuits are formed that can change forever the way you think about the world.'*[4] This massive system must have an organisational structure, an indexing system; otherwise information that enters the system could never be retrieved.

Most current research focuses on which sections of the brain process various types of information (for example, Broca's area of the brain is primarily involved in speech, and language processing as opposed to Wernicke's area, which is involved in language comprehension), but none of the current theories explains the full complexity of memory processes, including memory for sights and sounds, for feelings, and for belief systems, which integrate information on a large number of concepts. To illustrate simply its interconnectedness and complexity, imagine memory as a massive, multidimensional spider's web. It is possible to start at any one point in memory and follow a complex path to reach any other point on the web tracing through the network of interconnections to the place where the memory is stored. The ability to retrieve memories is influenced by the number of locations in which the information is stored, as well as the number and strength of pathways from this information to other concepts that might be activated by incoming information. The more frequently a path is followed, the stronger that path becomes and the more readily available the information.

Once people have started thinking about a problem one way, the same mental circuits or pathways get activated and strengthened each time they think about it. This facilitates the retrieval of information. These same pathways, however, also become the mental ruts that make it difficult to mentally reorganise the information and see it from a different perspective. If one has not thought about a subject for a long time, it may be difficult to recall details. After consciously thinking our way back into the appropriate context and finding the general location in our memory, the pathways are found more readily. Hence, we begin to better remember what was apparently forgotten.

Factors that influence what is remembered

Factors that influence how information is stored in memory and the likelihood of its being retrieved in the future comprise being the first-stored information on a given topic, the amount of attention focused on the information, the credibility of the information and the importance attributed to the information at the moment of storage. By influencing the content of memory, all of these factors influence the output analysis. Bias describes how availability in memory influences judgments of probability. The more instances a person can recall of a phenomenon, the more reliable the authenticity of that phenomenon seems to be. This is true even though the ability to recall past examples is influenced by, amongst other things, the vividness of the information, how recently something occurred and its impact upon one's personal welfare.

Memory rarely changes retroactively

Memories act as structures to facilitate the repetition of the mental processes by which the particular memory was formed. The formative process works via a positive feedback loop, whereby as memory structures form they then facilitate their own further development. If the memory systems did not facilitate their own development there would be disorder. This is why records of the past tend to dominate the present. This process is a development of continual adjustment. Receiving new information should, logically, cause these processes to automatically update the credibility or significance of previous information, and ideally the earlier information should become more salient and readily available in memory.

Memory, however, does not work that way. Instead, *every* perception is influenced by *all* that has gone before. Mental processes become habitual and automatic, and memories are seldom reassessed or reorganised retroactively in response to new information. The difficult task of learning new schemata usually requires the unlearning of existing ones. It is always easier to learn a new habit than to unlearn an old one. Understanding how memory works provides insight into the nature of creativity, a person's openness to new information, and breaking mindsets. All involve spinning new links in the spider's web of memory – links among facts, concepts and schemata that previously were only weakly connected, or not at all.

Schemas

From the perspective of cognitive psychology (that is, understanding the internal processes of the mind, which has become highly influential in all areas of psychology), our responses to natural and social stimuli appear to be mediated through an established cognitive framework or concept that helps organise and interpret information. This is referred to as schema. Schemas are necessary because through them we create shortcuts in interpreting the vast amount of information that is available to us in our environment. As a result, these cognitive frameworks cause us to focus mainly on things that corroborate our already existing biases and ideas.

They contribute to maintaining stereotypes and any new information that does not conform to our established ideas about the world is often difficult to retain. Schemata give a sense of order and predictability to the world because they organise our current knowledge and provide a framework for understanding future inputs.

Schemas are stored in long-term memory and exercise a powerful influence on the formation of our perceptions from sensory data. A schema describes a pattern of relationships among the information stored in memory, which are often compared with other links in the 'spider's web' of memory that are connected so strongly that they can be retrieved and used more or less as a single unit. Any memory point may be connected to many highly complex, different, overlapping schemata.

This concept of a schema emphasises the important point that memory does have structure. Recent research carried on by the Gallant Lab has shown that mental categories are organised in the brain by following the principle of semantic similarity – objects and concepts that have something in common are physically stored closely within the brain circuits.[5]

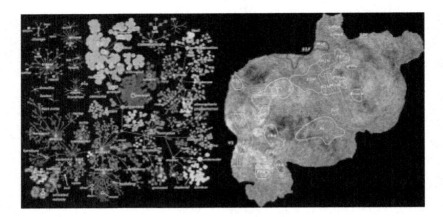

Figure 16.2 *Representation of objects and actions across the cerebral cortex.*[5]

The way that knowledge is connected in memory is very important in determining what information is retrieved in response to any stimulus, and how that information is used in reasoning. Schemas are the organising framework that allows us to direct our attention to information that is consistent with an established schema to process information more quickly and to have a greater recall capability for schema-consistent *versus* schema-irrelevant information.[6]

This ability to immediately perceive patterns enables us to more efficiently process many bits of information together as a coherent pattern.

If information does not fit into what we know, or think we know, we have greater difficulty processing it. Schema help us to filter the information we get from our environment in order to make sense of it. *'A schema is a structure for screening, coding, and evaluating the stimuli that impinge on an organism.'*[7] So schemas are a key factor because they determine, *'what we notice, attend to, and remember of our experiences.'*[8] Even though concepts and schemata begin developing in response to life events that occur during childhood, LTMs are neither fixed nor inflexible, but are constantly being adjusted as our schemata evolve with experience.

There are several commonly used metaphors that describe how schemas shape the way in which we view ourselves and the world, for example, schemas as lenses; a metal crusher; a cut-out; magnet and a prism (Figure 16.3).

In other words, schemas are the cognitive foundation of purposeful thought and action. They are considered active structures that shape perceptions, memories, emotional and behavioural responses. Often they are categorised in one of three ways: 'self-schemas', 'other-schemas', and 'world-schemas'. These structures help a person to describe themselves, others and the world around them. Self-schemas process, integrate and summarise the array of information received from the self-relevant stimuli often encountered. Through self-schemas, we construct stable knowledge structures about our 'self'.

In fact, the structure of different schemas that presently mould and inform our cognition have played an indispensable role in shaping human culture and behaviours and even the 'worlds' humans have experienced and built. Throughout the history of the human experience, each generation's cognitive-based worlds have been layered on the schemata of the previous countless generations' experiences and activities, and will continue to do so into the future. Here we see the application of volition, kamma and the fruits of kamma based on a broader societal and cultural level.

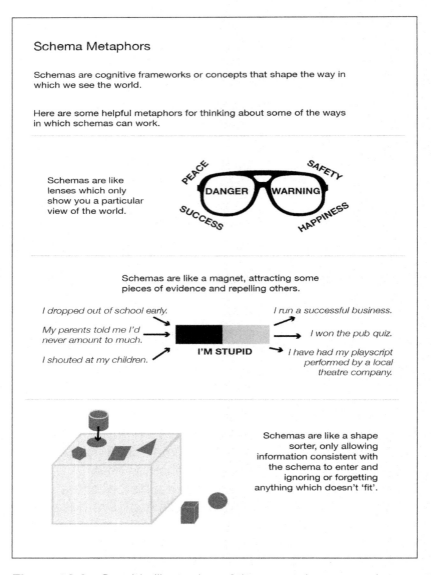

Schema Metaphors

Schemas are cognitive frameworks or concepts that shape the way in which we see the world.

Here are some helpful metaphors for thinking about some of the ways in which schemas can work.

Schemas are like lenses which only show you a particular view of the world.

PEACE SAFETY
DANGER WARNING
SUCCESS HAPPINESS

Schemas are like a magnet, attracting some pieces of evidence and repelling others.

I dropped out of school early.

My parents told me I'd never amount to much.

I shouted at my children.

I'M STUPID

I run a successful business.

I won the pub quiz.

I have had my playscript performed by a local theatre company.

Schemas are like a shape sorter, only allowing information consistent with the schema to enter and ignoring or forgetting anything which doesn't 'fit'.

Figure 16.3 *Graphic illustration of the way schemas work through the use of metaphors.*

Not only do people have available in their memory conceptions of who they were in the past and are in the present, but also visions of who they might be in the future. Less fully elaborated self-conceptions may fluctuate in their accessibility in response to the current social context. The 'self'-concept refers to a person's total collection of cognitions about the 'self' including self-schemas, possible selves, and other less fully elaborated self-images. From this, we can see that the Buddha's teachings and cognitive psychology with its empirical background of analysis, proposes a similar framework of understanding how the mental processes of humans work, and that it is comparable to the Buddha's perceptual process comprising the six stages.

From a cognitive perspective then, 'self' is a fluid construct continually being re-constituted through interactions. The 'self'-concept is the set of all an individual's beliefs about his or her personal qualities and visions of what the 'self' is differs between cultures. In cultures emphasising individuality, the individual characteristics are valued; in cultures emphasising interdependence, the social roles are more important. In all cases, the 'self'-concept as a schema provides the structural foundation of the information processing sequence which serves as a guide in adaptation, directing the focus of attention and serving as the internal framework that shapes interpretation and response to incoming stimuli.

A person's construction of an imagined self-image is created mostly unconsciously and unintentionally. For example, we are usually not consciously aware that we often try to conform to the image that we imagine other people want from us. Finally, the construct of the working self-concept emphasises the importance of the environmental, social, and cultural impact on a person's emotional and behavioural responses.

What is different from the Buddha's insight of 'no-self' is that, according to psychology, the conviction of an inherent and substantial 'self' is not a quandary. In fact, it is not engaged at all. Paradoxically, while significant pieces in psychological literature explain that the 'self' is a cognitive construct like any other, the same literature also highlights the need to protect and promote a healthy 'self'. The fact that we are taking a process, a fabrication, and creating it into a substantial object in our minds is simply not addressed. Nevertheless, the belief that this organising process is a real, permanent 'me' can diminish with insight, and the recognition that what is identified as 'self' is indeed only an abstraction built on the sense of agency.

The Buddha's Eightfold Path is a training, or purification of the mind involving a range of unconscious processes, creating new schemata and then reinforcing these new mental codifications with habituation. The techniques the Buddha taught help us to recognise and then transform our codified perceptual and cognitive biases, and unwholesome and unskilful habits of mind. With the recent discovery of synaptic plasticity and how connections between neural systems are constantly being changed by experience, we now appreciate how bhavana or mental culture promotes learning. By changing our perspective of an object (physical or mental), we change our mental state. This might mean changing a negative view to a positive one. So as we become more aware or mindful of our patterns of reactivity and then change a reaction, such learning has physiological consequences and, with habituation, lasting changes in the neural networks does occur.

In the Buddha's psychology the mind is conditioned by the objects of attention. We attend to those conditions which stimulate our emotional responses, in that we desire or don't desire the stimulus, then we identify with it or reject it. While objects which are physical are more commonplace, abstract things like ideas or concepts can be powerful in conditioning our mental states. With intensive training, humans have the ability to become free agents, able to choose their own destiny and to become aware of and act according to a moral and ethical framework. The Buddha offers us a clear insight into the possible development of uplifting potentialities that are inherent in our nature.

Bibliography

1.   Damasio, A. (2010). Self Comes to Mind. Pantheon.

2.   Sherry, D. F., & Schacter, D. L. (1987). The Evolution of Multiple Memory Systems. Psychological Review, 94(4), 439.

3.   Cosier, S. (2015). Where Memories Live. Scientific American Mind, 26(14). Published online: 9 April 2015 |doi:10.1038/scientificamericanmind0515-14b

4.   Johnson, G. (1991). In The Palaces of Memory. Vintage.

5.   Huth, A. G., Nishimoto, S., Vu, A. T., & Gallant, J. L. (2012). A Continuous Semantic Space Describes the Representation of Thousands of Object and Action Categories Across the Human Brain. Neuron, 76(6), 1210-1224.

6.   Markus, H. (1977). Self-schemata and Processing Information about the Self. Journal of Personality and Social Psychology, 35(2), 63-78.

7.   Beck, A. T. (1967). Depression: Clinical, Experimental, and Theoretical Aspects (Vol. 32). University of Pennsylvania Press.

8.   Padesky, C. A. (1990). Schema as Self-prejudice. International Cognitive Therapy Newsletter, 6(1), 6-7.

17

The Unconscious

'It is difficult indeed then to understand how conscious awareness can effectively guide action without massive support by unconscious guidance systems.'

J.A. Bargh[1]

'The psychological unconscious refers to mental structures and processes that influence a person's ongoing experience, thought, and action outside of conscious awareness.'

J.F. Kihlstrom[2]

'We must give up the insane illusion that a conscious self, however virtuous and however intelligent, can do its work singlehanded and without assistance.'

Aldous Huxley[3]

The unconscious workings of our brain

For most of human history, the proposition of the supremacy of conscious thought and intentional behaviour has been foremost in psychological theory, even though a persisting hypothesis existed about the importance of unconscious causes of human behaviour.

Contemporary psychological science remains attached to a conscious-centric model of the higher mental activities, supporting the idea of the unconscious as a system that is primarily a subliminal stimulation from the environment. This concept perpetuates the idea that our conscious self-promoting processes are most important and significant, representing the causal force of human judgment and behaviour. As John A. Bargh wrote, '*Today, most theories of goal pursuit emphasise conscious choice and guidance of behaviour on a moment-to-moment basis.*'[4]

But many of our actions, in fact, are not fully determined by our conscious mind, but, rather, we more often than not act habitually and without conscious awareness. Moreover, it is not only our brain but our whole body which is very busy maintaining itself and our relationship with the world autonomously. Such processes are unconscious and continue even when we are engaged in conscious calculations. Many processes are going on in the unconscious not only because we need to filter out stimuli and impulses, but also because many of our cognitive operations function so quickly that they are beyond our cognitive awareness.

The term 'the unconscious' refers to the existence of sophisticated, flexible and adaptive, outside-of-awareness behaviour guidance systems. Something formed by a combination of biological and environmental influences. It is a process – a way of constructing perception, memories and other kinds of cognition that changes systematically as we develop and experience life. While our consciousness does play a significant role in our ability to transform, manipulate and convey information, it is nevertheless (even when we are alert and attentive), our body (which includes the brain), that processes a vast amount of information automatically and without our awareness. We are often unaware of implicit precepts, memories and thoughts that affect our ongoing experience, thought and action.

The Buddha attached great importance to the psychological unconscious in his analyses of mental processes, and called it the anusaya, or 'latent tendencies'. They are defined as being latent because they have the potential (and are likely) to manifest when stimulated by a sufficient cause. In fact, the so-called 'unconscious' mind is not without an awareness ability. For example, it is always conscious of bodily sensations, and it reacts to them. If they are unpleasant, it reacts with aversion. If they are pleasant, it reacts with desire. This is the habit pattern, the behaviour pattern, of the so-called unconscious. Similarly, Bargh writes:

> *'What this means for present purposes is that not only did sophisticated unconscious modules evolve that give us today the building blocks of adaptive motives, preferences, and behavioural impulses, all operating unconsciously; there also evolved (indeed, had to evolve) a mechanism to integrate or interface these separate, parallel inputs into serial behavioural and judgmental responses. (Indeed, it has been proposed that the primary function of consciousness is to integrate the outputs of different action oriented systems that are vying for skeletal muscle control).'*[4]

Mindfulness and unconscious psychological processes

In his formulation of the six senses, the Buddha recognised how our initial perception of things occurs through the higher (yet still unconscious) cognitive processes of recognition, or giving names and forms to the impinging sense-data. These mental processes are given structure and meaning by cognitive schemas derived from past sensory and conceptual experiences. In this way, we construct our present, based on our past knowledge, which is then either transformed or substantiated by the present experience. Much of the time our lives are driven on autopilot, based on the direction of our habitual tendencies, selective memories and biased perceptions.

For the Buddha, the mental purification needed to attain Awakening was aimed at transforming the mental processes by mindfully examining the persistent psychological and physiological structures, such as sense organs, faculties, dispositions and traits. A significant conclusion of the Buddha was that mental representations (precepts, memories, knowledge acquired through learning, and thoughts) can exist outside the conscious awareness, and, importantly, that they dominate our ongoing cognitive experiences and actions. The resulting formed habits are involved in how these vital processes exist, and conscious awareness, so that it can effectively guide our actions, needs an extensive buttressing by the unconscious systems.

In response to the contact of sense stimuli, impulses are generated which activate unconscious operating motives, preferences and their associated approach (like) and avoidance (dislike) tendencies, emotional reactions and related motivations. The generation of responses of the possible reaction/action is largely unconscious, even though we usually (inaccurately) believe that the decision of an action is consciously generated. There are two ways that non-conscious processes can trigger a response to surface. Firstly, when we respond emotionally, based on latent tendencies, which bias the mind state; or secondly, when during the process of perception, there are thoughts from which often-obsessive conceptual proliferation can result.

The process of developing latent tendencies within our memory structures typically occurs as within the following example. When we do something enjoyable, like eating delicious food, it affects both our bodies and minds in pleasurable ways. These experiences create and/or reinforce specific neural pathways in the brain and body, which encourage their being used again. We come to experience physiological and psychological desires and cravings for the sensations that they provide, and thus we tend to repeat them over and over again. A common satisfying summer activity for many is eating ice cream. Our first taste of enjoyment as a child has us seek out again a similar ice cream, over and over. Then we may be adventurous and try new flavours, repeating those we like and avoiding the ones we find distasteful. So whenever we recognise an ice cream shop sign or see someone else eating some, we are automatically stimulated to go to the ice cream shop and satisfy our desire of tasting our favourite ice cream. If there isn't the possibility of satisfying our wish immediately, we can use our thoughts at least to indulge in the lesser, yet still satisfying fantasy of having and eating our favourite ice cream flavour. This desire can be easily activated. In this way, actions (going to the ice cream shop and eating ice cream) gradually reinforce the conditions that participate in their repetition, resulting in the psycho-physiological complexes (latent tendencies), which are stored and then activated unconsciously in the mind under the right conditions.

The most problematic latent tendencies (or dispositions), important in the Buddha's psychology of relieving suffering, are called the Three Poisons of Greed, Hatred and Ignorance, all of which lead to unwholesome effects in the present and future. In Buddhist teachings, these latent tendencies are often categorically expanded to a set of seven, which includes sensual desire, aversion, conceit, wrong views, doubt, craving for existence and ignorance. They are considered to be ingrained, unwholesome patterns of mind that are harmful to a person's wellbeing. These unwholesome latent tendencies lie dormant in the mind and, yet, are easily activated to be the source of one's addictions and deep clinging, holding the mind in a state of attachment and, as a result, in suffering.

For each latent tendency there are three levels of activation:

1. The deepest is the latent level, a subtle gross level of defilement, where they remain as latent disposition in the life continuum. We are not aware of it, unless it is stimulated by an encountered stimulus.

2. The intermediate level of adherence or habituation, an obsession level, a level of defilement, where they arise and become Mental Intoxicants to obsess and addict the mind, yet it has not been overtly expressed physically or verbally.

3. The transgression level, a level of defilements that lie dormant, but are easily activated and create difficulties because they instigate and causes a person to express unwholesome physical or verbal actions with greed, hatred and spuriousness.

In general, through the programme of cognitive transformation (the Eightfold Path) defilement by, or activation of, the unwholesome lapse tendency is inhibited by observing the moral precepts (sila).The habitual level of obsessive defilement is overcome through mental cultivation (samadhi). The deepest levels of latent tendency are conquered by insight wisdom (Panna)(Vism 1.13/5). These three levels of defilement are mentioned often throughout the Commentaries. The latent tendencies are transcended by the practitioner gradually, level by level. To transcend with the right view, one does not consciously foster by fixation and clinging to any kind of mindset associated with an unwholesome latent tendency. The Buddha taught that if we purify and nullify our unconscious dispositions, through observation and equanimity to our feelings, then we realise truth as it is, and can become wholesomely free. This realisation is also called Wisdom, which is cultivated through Insight Meditation. The defilements are totally eradicated by the fully Awakened and partially eradicated by the other four types of Noble Disciples (1. Stream-enterer – sotāpatti; 2. Once-returner – sakadāgāmitā; 3. Non-returner – anāgāmitā; 4. Arahant - arahatta).

According to William Waldron, craving and views are types of mindset, or mental standpoint, which are the foundation for the mind.[5] They are linked to our motivation because they stay in the mind and lie there dormant. They are considered potent as a force of motivation. Whichever personality traits dominate and lie latent within a mindset is subsequently how a person is regarded – that is, by those defining characteristics. For example, if we have a dominant latent tendency towards a form of conceit, then we will have the tendency to respond to the world with arrogance, self-importance and over-estimation of one's abilities. This is an important idea to be considered when in pursuit of purification of the mind and personality in order to reach our goal of Awakening. The Buddha taught that each predominate, unwholesome personality trait or tendency could be countered by an intervention that specifically targeted that characteristic, such as greed with generosity.

The Buddha's emphasis on the importance of continual mindfulness, or awareness of cognitive processes in order to transform and purify those processes, shows both his understanding of the crucial influence of unconscious processes and their effect on the total cognitive and action processes. It also highlights the Buddha's insight into the role of awareness as the monitor and gatekeeper of consciousness. If a habitual, non-conscious behaviour pattern is not disrupted, there will be continued reactions of craving or aversion, from which, as Buddha taught, suffering arises. Therefore, unwholesome latent behaviour patterns must be changed. With intervention, over time, and with effort, the whole habit pattern of the mind can change at the deepest level. Indeed, the Buddha's insight into a foundation of cognitive processes corresponds with contemporary theories and biological research, in which unconscious forces are understood to motivate the behaviour of all living organisms.

Neuroscientist Pessiglione and colleagues have shown how regions of the brain and cognitive processes are invoked in unconscious, as well as in conscious goal pursuits, and that conscious goal pursuit makes use of pre-existing unconscious motivational structures.[6] The pursuance of a goal can operate independently of any conscious awareness, which implies a distinction between the executive control structures in the brain responsible for the continual running of that goal's programme and from those that facilitate conscious awareness of the goal pursuit. For example, the often-said expression, 'I will sleep on it,' belies the wisdom of letting the unconscious process the decision information to gain a better perspective before rushing to act. Also, the unconscious use of body movement through space supports the notion of the separateness of conscious awareness and intention from the unconscious operation of complex behavioural processes. As the Buddha had learned, modern science has now shown that unconscious processes are significant in the moment-to-moment operation of our cognitive processes and actions.

In the Buddha's psychology, the unconscious processes that generate our actions are considered to be volitionally motivated, and as such are actions that create expected consequences. The Annatara Bhikkhu Sutta 1 (S 22.35) records the Buddha as giving this teaching to the monk: *'Bhikshu, one is reckoned by whatever lies latent in one. One is not reckoned by what does not lie latent in one.'* Even so, though mindsets are habitual; below conscious awareness, they are still considered as being deliberately formed.

The formation of these latent cognitive processes is via volitions, decisions and integrations, which in turn create memories and habits. Actions gradually reinforce the conditions that are conducive to their own repetition, resulting in the psycho-physiological complexes called anusaya (in Pāli), dispositions or underlying tendencies. Latent tendency can be qualified as being, *'[tendencies] that have not been abandoned in the mental continuum to which they belong and because they are capable of arising when a suitable cause presents itself.'* (M 1995, 1241, n. 473) Therefore, at the centre of the Buddha's motivational psychology, actions are called 'formations' (saṅkhā-ra) and are considered closely connected to the deeper latent tendencies (or dispositions).

For example, the process of one latent tendency the Buddha mentioned in particular is that of sensual craving (kāma, rāgânusaya). This is a biological potential because we are our six senses – the eye, ear, nose, tongue, corporal and mind, which are continuously seeking gratification from their corresponding sense-objects – forms, sounds, smells, tastes, touches and mind-objects. Sense-desire is essentially a craving at its most instinctive;

a 'pulling toward' factor. Our senses hold on to pleasant sense objects and once sated, release them and seek a new one, just as a monkey swings from branch to branch through a forest. (Assutava Sutta 1. S 12.61) The Buddha and the texts state (M I 303) that through contact with sense objects, a feeling, or sensation (vedanā) occurs, arousing one of the dispositions so that we respond to pleasure with craving, to discomfort with aversion, and to neutral feeling with indifference. These affective responses evoke actions whose effects reinforce the very conditions that supported their arising in the first place. As these patterns are repeated, they gradually become more entrenched; habits that are increasingly difficult to break, latently persisting in memory relatively independent from the changing contents of conscious awareness, ever ready to reactivate when a suitable cause stimulates them.

Some traditional clarifications about latent tendencies

1.   The latent tendency of sensual craving lies latent in the two feelings (pleasant and neutral) of the sense-sphere. This most common manifests itself as the lust for sense-pleasures, the collecting of sense-experiences perceived as pleasant.

2.   The latent tendency of aversion lies in painful (bodily and mental) feeling. Aversion is a pushing away factor.

3.   The latent tendency of conceit lies in the two feelings of the sense-sphere, and in those of the form sphere and the formless sphere.

4.   The latent tendency of views lies in all states related to identity (sakkāya).

5.   The latent tendency of doubt lies in all states related to identity (sakkāya).

6.   The latent tendency of craving for existence lies in the form sphere and the formless sphere and has the most powerful influence. It is the abiding self-love which functions as self-construction, 'I am'. 'Self' is the deepest stratum of psychological life and is the last to be transformed on the path toward liberation.

7.   The latent tendency of ignorance lies in not knowing the four truths, or a kind of blurred or distorted vision of them (sakkāya).[7]

The habit hardens into character

An untrained mind is habitually and mostly impulsively ruled by the senses because of the programmed, embedded interaction of the body with the physical environment. It is the untrained and un-awakened mind that keeps craving pleasant objects, rejecting what it considers as unpleasant, and ignoring what is neutral. This situation is enhanced and strengthened by our use of language, which creates virtual, static objects for us to desire or reject. While ignoring their actual dynamic, impermanence and insubstantial nature, we eagerly grasp at every pleasant sense stimulus.

Contrary to our belief, however, these experiences are not pristine pleasures – we tend to repeat the past even when it seems the present. To desire what we identify as lasting, pleasant, essential or good means to recognise what we are familiar with. They become adhered to fixed mental standpoints, mindsets or biases. Therefore, we mostly repeat ourselves in all of our lives. The Buddha called this tendency abhinivesa, adherence or habituation, in reference to the habitual level of behaviours that is intimately linked with the adherence of our yearning for the arising of pleasant sense feelings. So, what one chooses and repeats again and again becomes a natural disposition and then a habit. Even at a physical level, my repeated movements become a basic sense habit because of their recurrent patterning.

Since habits originate through our chosen and continued repetition of actions, this clearly indicates the significant cognitive dimension in both the formation and the maintenance of habits. Intertwining of routine, motivation and action originates in the mind that becomes excited by expectations. Or, as a passage echoing the Buddha expresses it:

> *'The thought manifests as the word,*
> *The word manifests as the deed,*
> *The deed develops into habit,*
> *And the habit hardens into character.*
> *So watch the thought and its way with care,*
> *And let it spring from love*
> *Born out of concern for all beings.'[8]*

However, the Buddha also distinguishes between two kinds of pleasures: the craving after pleasant sense experience versus other pleasant feelings such as the bliss of meditative absorption, which does not activate the sense based latent tendency. Even though the basis of the pleasant sensation is different, one must treat them the same in terms of non-clinging and adherence for in both cases they are impermanent and subject to dis-ease when ending. Nevertheless, the Buddha's ability to discriminate between the impacts of these two different pleasant-based experiences led him to the Middle Way, and ultimately Awakening.

The Buddha also taught that obsessive and reactive behaviours can be overcome through mental cultivation. Although we have our six senses and the six corresponding sense-stimuli, and our feelings and perceptions of them, these are not permanent; they all change in time. An emotionally reactive person impulsively reacts to both internal and external stimuli. To perceive an injury or to fear one means to try to eliminate the source of pain, attempt escape or seek protection. Such reactive behaviour is not only unskilful but also predictable. People act as if they have no choice, while, of course, ultimately, they always have a choice. The obliviousness created by habit includes not looking for or considering facts, perspectives or ideas that are different from what is known and accepted – going outside one's 'comfort zone'.

Latent tendencies, as unconscious sources of motivation, work with one another. The latent tendency of arrogance also functions with craving for existence and with strong and biased perspectives. They are all interconnected in the matrix of self-identity that can range from a harmless sense of self-satisfaction to an exaggerated self-glorification. Actually, all pretentions are ultimately self-defeating, because although a conceited person is self-centred, he or she does not have a secure sense of 'self'. In fact, such an individual is always dependent (and hence insecure), on how others define and approve or not of them. For the Buddha, the deepest, most obstinate, yet crucially important disposition is the 'I am', or the belief that we are substantial, enduring entities. Buddha declared if, '*that view of self-existence has become habitual and is not eradicated*,'[9] then our suffering would be endless.

From an evolutionary perspective, knowledge (both physical and cognitive) gained from experience represents short-cut processes that appear as *a priori* knowledge. It saves us from continually working out what is good or bad, helpful or useless. We don't always have to reinvent the wheel every time we have problems to be mastered. Therefore, thankfully, the conscious mind is mostly unconsciously activated and is not the source of most of our behaviour. Instead, consciousness acts as a gatekeeper that allows us to reflect on, evaluate and to make sense of our interactions. That is, the impulse is firstly unconsciously generated, and then consciousness or awareness permits what is appropriate and so experiences it.[10-14]

The Buddha's method of mind transformation and purification doesn't suggest elimination of dispositions or latent tendencies or habits, as that is impossible. Instead, he describes a programme of refining and uprooting unwholesome and ignorant tendencies and developing wholesome and skilful ones. If the latent tendencies are not purified, they keep us in a loop of ignorance and illusion that feeds on itself, transforming us into self-inflated beings, which crave and loath objects that truly signify nothing. We desire and hoard temporary and impermanent objects seeking a safe, pleasurable, static, predictable and permanent world that does not exist – it is only an illusion of an ideal. Once we understand this dilemma, we can start working on earnestly healing and purifying ourselves and eventually achieve our Awakening.

Bibliography

1. Bargh, J. A., & Morsella, E. (2010). Unconscious Behavioral Guidance Systems. In: Agnew, C., Carlston, D., Graziano, W., & Kelly, J. (Eds.). Then a Miracle Occurs: Focusing on Behavior in Social Psychological Theory and Research (pp. 89-118). Oxford University Press.

2. Kihlstrom, J. F. (1987). The Cognitive Unconscious. Science, 237(4821), 1445-1452.

3. Huxley, A. (1956). The Education of an Amphibian. In: Adonis and the Alphabet and Other Essays, (pp. 9-38). London: Chatto & Windus.

4. Bargh, J. A., Gollwitzer, P. M., Lee-Chai, A., Barndollar, K., & Trötschel, R. (2001). The Automated Will: Nonconscious Activation and Pursuit of Behavioral Goals. Journal of Personality and Social Psychology, 81(6), 1014.

5. Waldron, W. S. (2003). The Buddhist Unconscious: The Alaya-vijnana in the Context of Indian Buddhist Thought. Routledge.

6. Pessiglione, M., Schmidt, L., Draganski, B., Kalisch, R., Lau, H., Dolan, R. J., & Frith, C. D. (2007). How the Brain Translates Money into Force: A Neuroimaging Study of Subliminal Motivation. Science, 316(5826), 904-906.

7. Nyanatiloka, M. (1938; 2nd ed. 1957; 1971). Guide Through the Abhidhamma-piṭaka. Yam 268; pp104. Kandy: Buddhist Publication Soc.

8. Dhammananda, K. (1989). Sri. How to Live Without Fear and Worry. Kuala Lumpur: Buddhist Missionary Society.

9. Waldron, W. S. (2003). A Buddhist Unconscious: The ālaya-vijñāna in the context of Indian Buddhist Thought. RoutledgeCurzon.

10. Eagleman, D. M. (2004). The Where and When of Intention. Science, 303(5661), 1144-1146.

11. Gazzaniga, M. S. (1985). The Social Brain. Psychology Today, 19(11), 28.

12. James, W. (1890). The Consciousness of Self. In: The Principles of Psychology.

13. Libet, B. (1986). Nonclassical Synaptic Functions of Transmitters. Federation proceedings, 45(12), 2678-2686.

14. Wegner, D.M. (2002).The Illusion of Conscious Will. Cambridge, MIT Press.

18

Habits

The brain has a natural tendency to tune out, ignore and habituate to stimuli deemed insignificant. In popular terms, habit is often thought of as a deadening, destructive, automatic behaviour. However, in and of itself, habituation is not negative; it can be understood as positive and necessary, for if we had to pay conscious attention to every stimulus we would never be able to function effectively. We only have so much attention to give. Habit affords us an economy and efficiency of action by allowing us to perform well-learnt behaviours while being sensitive to, or giving attention to more demanding or interesting stimuli. As a survival strategy therefore, our brain and nervous system easily pays attention to what is presented to us as novel, and as long we continue to believe that a stimulus is important, we remain vigilant and do not habituate to that stimulus.

Habituation and sensitisation can be viewed as homeostatic processes which optimise an organism's ability of detecting and then assessing the importance of a stimulus in a new situation or changes in an established one. So, contradictory to common belief, critical features of a system of habituation are not rigidity, fixation and compulsivity, but rather that the learning and formation of habits, with the resulting habituation and automaticity, can operate as skills and be functionally compatible with autonomy, giving us the freedom to think of other things and even do other things, while on 'cruise control'.

People who can more effectively maintain the more wholesome and skilful behaviours can be more effectively maintained by transferring more behaviour regulation over to non-conscious processes. A meta-analysis of the effects of self-control on a wide range of behaviours showed that self-control is more strongly linked to non-conscious behaviours than to consciously regulated behaviours.[1] Indicating therefore, the usefulness of self-control training as a means of enhancing non-conscious regulation of physical activity through the formation and maintenance of strong habits. This supports Hagger and colleagues' proposition that self-control can act on behaviour through non-conscious means.[2-3]

If well-learnt automaticity is interrupted, the results can be devastating. There is a short poem – *The Centipede's Dilemma*, which aptly describes this effect that is often called the 'Centipede Effect', or 'Centipede Syndrome'.

The Centipede Effect occurs when a normally automatic or unconscious activity is disrupted by intense, critical awareness directed at it or through reflection upon it. For example, a basketball player thinking too closely about their dribbling the ball can find their performance of the task impaired (hyper-reflection). As Aristotle observed (as cited above), with the perfection of learnt automaticity in, for example, sports, art and dance, comes an ability, which provides both the foundation for and the instrument of the freedom and creativity of human action.

The Buddha identified habituation (or adherence) as a significant unconscious process that needed close attention for the purification of the mind, since habit can either promote wholesomeness and wisdom or the opposite As Buddhist monk and writer Thich Nhat Hanh identified:

> *'Suppose someone says something that angers you. Your old pathway wants to say something to punish him. But that makes us victims of our habit energy. Instead, […] with just one or two seconds of looking and seeing the suffering in him, compassion is born. […] With the practice, we can always open new neural pathways like that. When they become a habit, we call it the habit of happiness.'[4]*

For the Buddha, personality is a transitory structure, it is guided only by certain broad schemata, a pattern imposed on complex reality or experience to assist in explaining it, mediate perception, or guide response, based on accumulated learned tendencies or habit-formations. It is through habit-forming that we learn either unskilled and unwholesome tendencies, or positive and wholesome ones. We shape our own psychology through the accumulated actions of our learning and effort. The Buddha encouraged ethical behaviour to promote wholesome habits; he taught the development

of wholesome habits and the deconstruction of
unwholesome ones in the Eightfold Path.

But what are habits?

*'As behaviours are repeated in a consistent context,
there is an incremental increase in the link between
the context and the action. This increases the
automaticity of the behaviour in that context.'*

W. Wood.[5]

*'Features of an automatic behaviour are all or some
of: efficiency, lack of awareness, unintentionality,
and uncontrollability.'*

J.A. Bargh.[6]

Behaviours we repeat most often are ingrained into
our neural pathways, so a habit becomes automatic
behaviour that occurs without much or any conscious
thought. The natural tendency is to habituate to the
surrounding world, to substitute abstract cognitive
patterns or perceptual preconceptions for the sensory
experience. It is an important mechanism that allows
organisms to adjust smoothly to their environment by
the filtering out of irrelevant sensory information, thereby
allowing us to focus on and devote our attention to more
crucial stimuli, a prerequisite for many cognitive tasks.

Habituation is considered one of the simplest forms of
learned behaviour, since it occurs after repeated exposure
to a particular stimulus. Sensitisation is the opposite of
habituation, and it leads to an increased behavioural
response, especially if the sensory stimulus is aversive.
Both habituation and sensitisation are two sides of one
coin, a process of the primary internal homeostatic
processes, which optimises an organism's likelihood
of detecting and assessing the significance of a new

stimulus. So called 'high responders' (those who initially react more strongly) have a lower threshold for detecting and assessing the significance of a stimulus than low responders (those who initially react more weakly).

Habituation develops when a changed, new or abrupt stimulus is encountered, which we react to and direct our attention toward (an orienting response), such as when we turn our head toward a strange sound. If the same stimulus is presented repeatedly, then the orienting response habituates. Habituation of the orienting response is a simple form of learning that depends on a memory process and acts as an attention-filtering mechanism allowing us to selectively attend to what is presently significant and, in doing so, adapt to the immediate environment.

Individual differences in memory abilities can affect rates of habituation. Those individuals with good working memory ability often adapt to their environment more quickly. Our habit-making behaviours are created in a part of the brain called the basal ganglia, a region believed to be central in the development of emotions, memories and pattern recognition. Habits can be formed not only by simply repeating behaviours, but also by being 'rewarded' with a positive result. Dawkins noted that even as an infant, we are able to absorb, automatically, *'an already invented and largely debugged system of habits in the partly unstructured brain.'*[7]

Decisions are made in a part of the brain called the prefrontal cortex, but this decision-making area of the brain goes into a 'sleep' mode as soon as a behaviour becomes habituated. Writer Charles Duhigg says:

> *'In fact, the brain starts working less and less[...]*
> *The brain can almost completely shut down. [...]*
> *And this is a real advantage, because it means*

*you have all of this mental activity you can devote
to something else... You can do these complex
behaviours without being mentally aware of it at all.'[8]*

He goes on to say, '*And that's because of the capacity
of our basal ganglia: to take a behaviour and turn it into an
automatic routine.*'[8]

This makes it easy, for example, to focus on the day's
plans while you are driving your car.

Research carried out in 2013 by Tobii Technology, using
eye tracking technology to explore the phenomenon of
driving without awareness, (DWA), demonstrated that
DWA is more likely to occur when the driving is done in
combination with other tasks. All participants who had
experienced phases of subconscious driving on the regular
intercity road said that they had been thinking about,
or concentrating on things unrelated to their driving –
organising their work, decisions they had to make and so
on. The fact that drivers do not remember everything that
they saw or that occurred during the journey reflects the
role of cognitive resources savings. Although the drivers
may be paying attention at the time, they do not allocate
resources to store this information for later recall because
unconsciously, it is not considered necessary. However,
they may remember some stimulus that is striking but
irrelevant. This reinforces the idea that subconscious
driving is restricted only to control repetitive actions
known to the driver himself. The study concluded that
DWA reduces attention to the act of driving, but is not
necessarily a general security and road safety concern.

Shiffrin and Schneider distinguished between automatic
or habituated mental processes and controlled ones.[9]
Automatic processes can be engaged by specific
environmental stimuli, regardless of our conscious
intentions. Some processes are innately automatic,

whereas others become automated after extensive practice. In either case, as we have seen in the example of the DWA, the efficiency of the operation of an automatic process consumes no attention-demanding resources, nor does it interfere with other ongoing cognitive processes or leave any trace of itself in memory. Repeated practice allows tasks that initially require a great deal of attention (driving a car or riding a bicycle) to eventually be performed habitually.

In a familiar environment we will perform automated behaviours the same way every time. In an unfamiliar situation however, we do not rely on old habits even though our actions are well-learnt, which is why a vacation is often stimulating; we pay attention differently and break our usual routine behaviour.

The Buddha's interest in habituation was twofold: the benefit of breaking acquired unwholesome habits and the development of new wholesome and skilful ones. He found that when our minds operate habitually, many latent tendencies contrary to the path to the goal of nibbana are easily activated, and consequently they control our lives, such as our craving towards pleasurable sights, sounds, smells, flavours, touches, and thoughts, and aversive habits like hate, anger, irritation, opposition, resistance, rigidity and stubbornness. Speculative views – as in believing that an action has no future effects – and sceptical doubt demonstrated as a lack of faith and conviction in the Buddha's Enlightenment, conception of 'I am,' which assumes the hidden existence of a constant core identity of 'I-me', the craving for 'becoming' as in the hoping for a future existence, and ignorance as not understanding and not knowing the Four Noble Truths – all of these tendencies create false views, alienate ourselves from others and the world and give us a sense of our minds as being separate from our bodies, a fascination to sense stimulation – craving of pleasure and aversion from pain, our anger when frustrated, our fear of the unfamiliar, and our many identifications. Moreover, our sense of self as an autonomous being is ascribed, and our attribution of an inherent existence to it, is habitually acquired (Saṃyutta Nikāya IV, 102; Majjhima Nikāya I, 130).

The Buddha emphasised the necessity for a crucial transformation. That is, if a person doesn't uproot and replace these unwholesome latent tendencies based on ignorance by wholesome and wise ones, they won't be able to cease their dis-ease and awaken. Through the correct application of wise skills, effort and persistence one can develop good rather than bad habits. You can change a habit by learning a new one that eventually supersedes the previous behaviour pattern. Altering the unwholesome latent tendencies requires paying fresh attention to them or being mindful of how a habit operates, what sustains it, and what its consequences are. We learn to become aware and be our own mindfulness or awareness agents. As unlearning habits is very difficult, new schemata or habits are learned most successfully in one of three ways:

1.   Disuse – Habits fade over time if not used.

2.   Superseding – The brain selects the most reinforced habit, or learning a new, stronger, competing action that overrides older weaker ones.

3.   Stopping behaviour – The brain has a mechanism for suppressing an activity once initiated. In this case, the habit is still there, but a new habit attempts to stop execution of the previous habit, such as when you go to do something automatically, but then stop yourself because you remember the bad consequence.

With concerted, disciplined effort over time (depending on the difficulty of the activity being learnt and the level of commitment on the part of the individual), your experience becomes easier. New, frequently repeated behaviours become automatic, so new wholesome behaviours can become habits. Research suggests that on average, most new habits succeed within 66 days, with the need for a new behaviour to be rewarded/increased in learning being greatest at the beginning. After the 66-day mark, the repeated practice of those activities hit a plateau of learning, and the behaviours became as automatic as they possibly will be. They are automatically embedded into the brain's neural pathways.

Once new wholesome habits are maintained, there is a positive, life-changing support to your wellbeing, leading eventually to the achievement of nibbana. It is through the Buddha's change programme, or the noble Eightfold Path, that the unwholesome and harmful habits or latent tendencies can be uprooted and replaced with wholesome and beneficial ones. When good habits become part of our life, they can keep alive in us a wholesome and skilful way, even when difficulties strongly challenge us.

Bibliography

1. de Ridder, D. T., Lensvelt-Mulders, G., Finkenauer, C., Stok, F. M., & Baumeister, R. F. (2012). Taking Stock of Self-control A Meta-analysis of how Trait Self-control Relates to a Wide Range of Behaviors. Personality and Social Psychology Review, 16(1), 76-99.

2. Hagger, M. S., & Chatzisarantis, N. L. (2014). An Integrated Behavior Change Model for Physical Activity. Exercise and Sport Sciences Reviews, 42(2), 62-69.

3. Hagger, M. S., & Luszczynska, A. (2014). Planning Interventions for Behaviour Change: A Protocol for Establishing Best Practice Through Consensus. European Health Psychologist, 16(5), 206-213.

4. Retrieved from https://www.facebook.com/pages/Thich-Nhat-Hanh-gems/319228401438031

5. Wood, W., & Neal, D. T. (2007). A New Look at Habits and the Habit-Goal Interface. Psychological Review, 114(4), 843.

6. Bargh, J. A. (1994). The Four Horsemen of Automaticity: Awareness, Intention, Efficiency, and Control in Social Cognition. In: Wyer, R. S., & Srull, T. K. (Eds.). Handbook of Social Cognition: Vol. 1 Basic Processes, pp. 1–40. Lawrence Erlbaum Associates Publishers.

7. Dawkins, R. (1976). The Selfish Gene. Oxford University Press.

8. Duhigg, C. (2013). The Power of Habit: Why we do what we do and how to change. Random House.

9. Shiffrin, R. M., & Schneider, W. (1984). Automatic and Controlled Processing Revisited. Psychological Review, 91(2), 269-276.

19

Cognitive Biases

'Sometime, somewhere, you take something to be the truth. If you cling to it so much, even when the truth comes in person and knocks on your door, you will not open it.'

~ The Buddha

'The self-serving bias is widespread in Western cultures such as the United States and Canada, but it is much less common in East Asian cultures such as Japan, China, and Taiwan. Unlike Americans, the Japanese tend to attribute their successes to luck and their failures to lack of ability or talent. The self-serving bias may be embedded within a cultural ethic in the United States and other individualistic cultures that place a premium on self-esteem.'

~ Nevid, 2013

The logical illusion of the self

Most people like to think of themselves as having an objective, logical and in-charge 'self', capable of taking in and evaluating correctly the information available about the world around them and therefore are confident that they make accurate and valid judgements and decisions. The truth is that when we are taking in information and making judgements about the world and events around us, we usually don't evaluate and construe these things objectively. We acquire and process information by filtering it through our own likes, dislikes and experiences – this is called 'cognitive bias'.

Cognitive biases can greatly hinder how we evaluate information and arrive at decisions making our judgements and decisions often riddled with errors. In fact, the pervasive cognitive biases play a role in some fundamental aspects of personality and normal personality functioning. While these significant, unconscious cognitive processes, also called 'thinking errors', lead to distortions of how we interpret and respond in our world, they actually serve an adaptive purpose. They allow us to make quick decisions in spite of the fact that our brain is constantly busy processing information and carrying out a myriad of mental processes. This shortcut, which allows for quick decision-making is called 'heuristics'. The human brain has, over a long evolutionary period, developed the ability to perform many mental processes that cogitate information efficiently and in ways that can be applied across various circumstances.

There is a difference between a logical fallacy and a cognitive bias: a logical fallacy grows from incorrect reasoning and concludes with a misconception, whereas a cognitive bias has its roots in thought-processing errors. Cognitive errors in processing information may develop as a result of errors of memory, social attribution or miscalculations – all are possible flaws in judgment and can lead us to make serious mistakes. For example, research suggests that the recall and evaluation of past interactions can be significantly influenced by a person's mood at the time when the past interactions were made – if one is depressed at the time of an interaction with a friend, then the recall of that situation will be easily biased by the perception developed through the depressed 'lens'. So, just a transient change in mood, which interacts with certain cognitive categories, can significantly bias assessments and create many different interpretations of even simple and observable social acts.

Three main categories for cognitive biases

The different types of cognitive biases are often grouped into one of three categories:

1. Egocentricity – This can be described as that condition when we think that the way we see things is exactly the way things are. Often egocentric people have an inability or unwillingness to consider others' points of view, and refuse to accept ideas or facts that would prevent them from getting what they want or think they want.

2. Beneffectance – This corresponds to perceiving oneself as responsible for desirable outcomes but not responsible for undesirable ones.

3. Conservatism – The resistance to cognitive change.

There is much evidence that these biases operate in the organisation of 'self'-construction. Biases are maintained because they preserve the cognitive schemas in which they exist. Schemas are crucial, because they enable easy and consistent access to the storage and retrieval of a large amount of information, rather than the disruption or confusion caused by a continual revision of the schema's coding structure.

If we think about language, for example, vocabulary and syntax are organised into schemas and scripts, which our brain links and stores together. Such a stable interactive schematic structure allows us to store, retrieve and use information rapidly and economically, making language a fast and efficient cognitive process.[1] However, conservatism limits our ability to update and revise information in the system. It is more efficient to maintain consistency within that scheme than revising it every time new significant information becomes available.

Together, egocentricity and conservatism biases can provide a protection, a static orientation, a certainty that preserves the core belief of not only the validity but correctness of the central entity – the person I call 'myself'. The conservatism bias ensures that information encountered over time is encoded into the same categories, retracing the same neuronal paths, and thereby achieving cognitive consistency, conviction and stability of mind. Biases are therefore pervasive, recognised again and again, and habituated. This explains why we are easily at risk of forming cognitive biases. They are recognisable, though; in being mindfully aware of when they arise we can carefully evaluate and alter our judgments and actions as needed.

Some examples of common cognitive biases

Psychologists have identified many cognitive biases in our everyday thinking. The list below is long, yet not complete from the Wikipedia Cognitive Bias[2] page. Nevertheless, here are some important examples for understanding common sources of our thinking errors:

- **Availability heuristic** – Estimating what is more likely by what is more available in memory, which is biased toward vivid, unusual or emotionally charged examples. This leads to using hasty generalizations and anecdotal evidence in arguments.

- **Bandwagon effect** – The tendency to do (or believe) things because many other people do (or believe) the same. Related to 'group-think' and 'herd instinct'.

- **Confirmation bias** – The referencing only those perspectives that fuel our pre-existing views, while at the same time ignoring or dismissing opinions – no matter how valid – that threaten our worldview.

- **False consensus effect** – The tendency for people to overestimate the degree to which others agree with them.

- **Hawthorne effect** – The tendency of people to perform or perceive differently when they know that they are being observed.

- **Herd instinct** – The common tendency to adopt the opinions and follow the behaviours of the majority to feel safer and to avoid conflict.

- **In-group bias** – The tendency for people to give preferential treatment to others they perceive to be members of their own groups.

- **Negativity Bias** – People tend to pay more attention to bad news – and it's not just because we're morbid. Social scientists theorise that it's on account of our selective attention and that given the choice, we perceive negative news as being more important or profound. We also tend to give more credibility to bad news. More evolutionarily, heeding bad news may be more adaptive than ignoring good news.

- **Omission bias** – The tendency to judge harmful actions as worse, or less moral, than equally harmful omissions (inactions).

- **Rosy retrospection** – The tendency to rate past events more positively than they had actually been rated when the event occurred.

- **Self-fulfilling prophecy** – The tendency to engage in behaviours that elicit results, which will (consciously or not) confirm our beliefs.

- **Self-serving bias** – The tendency to claim more responsibility for successes than failures. It may also manifest itself as a tendency for people to evaluate ambiguous information in a way beneficial to their interests.

- **Semmelweis reflex** – The tendency to reject new evidence that contradicts an established paradigm.

- **Stereotyping** – Expecting a member of a group to have certain characteristics without having actual information about that individual.

- **Trait ascription bias** – The tendency for people to view themselves as relatively variable in terms of personality, behaviour and mood while viewing others as much more predictable.

- **Wishful thinking** – The formation of beliefs and the making of decisions according to what is pleasing to imagine instead of by appeal to evidence or rationality.

We tend to perceive what we expect

One way we bias our perceptions is that we usually think of perception as a passive process and that the sense stimuli which stimulate our senses are basic and true. We believe that we are objective and so record what is actually there. Yet, as we have seen already, perception is a very active rather than a passive process; it constructs rather than records 'reality.' Perception is a process of inference in which we construct our own version of reality based on the building blocks provided through the five senses. What we perceive and how readily we perceive it, is strongly influenced by our beliefs, preferences, past experience, education and cultural values, as well as how well a stimulus is recorded by our receptor organs. Much research has been conducted which confirms that the extent to which information is obtained and organised by an observer depends significantly upon the observer's own assumptions and preconceptions.[3]

One illuminating study by Sheri R. Levy, *et. al.*, investigated how people who begin their process of social perception from the different starting assumptions of either fixed (entity) or dynamic (incremental) theories of human nature, pursue different patterns of perception, inference, judgment and behaviour when regarding other people. The researchers found that either theory influences a susceptibility to certain biases; that is, stereotyping, perceptions of group homogeneity, the ultimate attribution error, intergroup bias, and discriminatory behaviour. It was concluded that we fundamentally need both theories to give meaning or understanding to our social world.[4]

A significant aspect of this function is to be able to pay attention to information that is perceived as relevant and then providing a framework of beliefs and inferences that assist in interpreting this information and predicting new events. However, in this way, the established systems usually generate a self-perpetuating cycle. The framework leads to a particular social understanding and that social understanding in turn bolsters the validity of the framework.

In fact, as one might expect, Unger, *et. al.*, demonstrated that people seek out experiences to confirm their theories by enrolling in courses or careers that support their world belief.[5] The research emphasised how stereotypes are energy-saving devices, which serve to simplify information processing and speed up response generation, helping to release cognitive resources to perform other cognitive tasks [6-8] A fixed, static mode is primarily trait- and stereotype-oriented, and a dynamic mode is more concerned with active processes which can give context-based explanations for a group member's behaviour. By knowing a person's preferred theory of human nature, it is then easier to understand how people arrive at their idiosyncratic, yet comprehensible, opinions of individuals and groups.

The Expectancy Thesis and establishing mindsets

Experiments have shown that our patterns of expectation become so deeply embedded, they continue to influence our perceptions even when we are alerted to, and try to take account of, information that does not fit our preconceptions. This has been called the Expectancy Thesis. What is actually perceived in the flow of information we receive daily, and how we interpret it, depends in part on our own expectations. Information that is consistent with our expectations is perceived and processed more easily than information that contradicts our prevailing expectations. This information tends to be ignored or distorted in an unconscious process of perception. Perceiving what we expect seems to be more compelling than the tendency to perceive what we may want. There are many sources that influence what kind of information we pay particular attention to and how we organise and interpret this information in certain ways. The intention to be objective does not ensure accurate perception. These patterns form a mindset that predisposes us to think in certain ways.

Mindset can be defined as a person's or group's well-established cluster of assumptions that are a mental tendency, or habit, which predisposes a person's or group's interpretations of, and responses to, situations.

A mindset is like a lens through which we perceive the world. Nevertheless, a mindset or a schema is not necessarily 'bad' or 'wrong', or to be avoided. Instead, it is an inevitable biological necessity. Mindsets are unavoidable, since there is no possible way of coping with the volume of stimuli we are constantly exposed to, or with the volume and complexity of the data we have to interpret, without some sort of simplifying preconceptions about what to expect and what is important. We cannot avoid preconceptions to achieve objectivity; that would be ignorance or self-delusion. There is no such thing as just the 'facts' of a situation; there only perceptions and assumptions that make up our reality.

As the Buddha taught, only Awakening, or Pure Experience, which transcends conceptual duality, allows us to observe dispassionately the world and our 'self'. The only thoughtfully objective approach is by pragmatically and empirically making any basic assumptions and reasoning as explicit as possible, so that their relative validity can be challenged and mulled over by ourselves as well as others.

Mindsets are characterised by some crucial features, which make them strongly anchored into our cognition. First of all, mindsets tend to form quickly but are resistant to change – once events have been perceived in one way, there is a natural resistance to adopt other perspectives. Earlier but incorrect impressions tend to persist because the amount of information necessary to invalidate a hypothesis is considerably greater than the amount of information required to make an initial interpretation. The problem is not that there is an inherent difficulty in grasping new ideas (actually, we often form impressions on the basis of very little information). Rather, the resistance is to reject or change them once they are formed, unless significant evidence is obtained.

Initial exposure to opaque stimuli interferes with us making an accurate perception even after more and better information becomes available. However, this we can limit by resisting making a judgement for as long as possible, until no more new information is being received. Once a mindset or an expectation concerning the phenomenon being observed has been formed, then this conditions our future perceptions of that phenomenon. It explains why it often happens that the first time observation or 'beginner's mind' may generate a more accurate insight, or a 'fresh perspective' that has been overlooked by others who have worked on the same problem for longer periods of time.

A fresh perspective is sometimes useful as earlier experiences can handicap by familiarity. Perception is also influenced by the context in which it occurs. Different circumstances evoke different sets of expectations. A good example of the role played by context is the difference in meaning attributed to hearing footsteps behind us when walking along a dark, empty alleyway at night.

Bhikkhu Ñanananda explained how, in the Buddha's psychology, the final important stage of cognitive processing is conceptual proliferation (abstraction, speculation or papañca) – cognitive biases and distortions are examples of this. In fact, to simplify processing and make it more efficient, the cognitive apparatus develops language as well as ways of thought. Concepts are strongly adhered to and formulated into logical categories, assumptions and theories called diññhijâla, or a 'veritable networks of views' or schemas and mindsets. Such a key idea of a network structured to organise thoughts is not unknown in cognitive psychology. One of the most famous psychological models for cognition and memory, conceived by Collins and Quillian in 1969, represents mental processes as pathways of a well-organised network, where items or concepts are labelled, categorised and linked for a better navigation in the network.[9]

The proliferation of cognitive constructions creates not only a network of concepts but also various perspectives through the processes of recognition, memory and reflection and speculation. This network of concepts, with its apparent objectivity, beguiles and ultimately obsesses and stupefies. The Buddha used the metaphor of a magician's trick or illusion to describe this web of concepts. All views, being filtered through the self matrix, are speculative and biased; but by far, the most pernicious and calcified are dogmatic views.

The Buddha taught clear thinking, sense control, wholesome behaviour and meditation. When regarding thoughts from the Buddha's base of the 'actuality of knowing', all thoughts are representational of either an internally- or externally-based world of stimuli. Cognitive biases are seen as runaway conceptualisations and yet are not commonly understood for their subjectivity. We are controlled by these unchecked proliferations, which create many thinking errors and biases, and hence difficulties. In fact, the person who does not have a reflective and critical attitude goes through life enmeshed in prejudices derived from common opinion, from the habitual beliefs of the age or 'in-group', and from convictions that have uncritically evolved in the mind as being truth. To such a person the world becomes obvious, finite and definite; that which is unfamiliar is contemptuously avoided or rejected and common assumptions are not questioned.

But, in knowing that an interpretation is always a subjective creation and is influenced by many personal factors, the Buddha recommended that we should keep a critical attitude and consider carefully the opinions of others and ourselves. We need to judiciously review a topic and examine it with equanimity from all perspectives. Only then we can arrive at the best-reasoned and possible decision or evaluation. By applying mindfulness or awareness, we can maintain a humble attitude with a composed and evaluative mind and protect ourselves from being dominated by preferences, anger, conceit, praise and blame; and from becoming attached to and biased in our opinions.

Bibliography

1. Aitchison, J. (2012). Words in the Mind: An Introduction to the Mental Lexicon. John Wiley & Sons.

2. Full article at: https://en.wikipedia.org/wiki/Cognitive_bias

3. Heuer Jr, R. J. (1999). Psychology of Intelligence Analysis. Center for the Study of Intelligence, Central Intelligence Agency. Retrieved from www.odci.gov/csi

4. Levy, S. R., Plaks, J. E., Hong, Y. Y., Chiu, C. Y., & Dweck, C. S. (2001). Static versus Dynamic Theories and the Perception of Groups: Different Routes to Different Destinations. Personality and Social Psychology Review, 5(2), 156-168.

5. Unger, R. K., Draper, R. D., & Pendergrass, M. L. (1986). Personal Epistemology and Personal Experience. Journal of Social Issues, 42, 67–79.

6. Fiske, S. T., & Neuberg, S. L. (1990). A Continum of Impression Formation, from Category-based to Individuating Processes: Influences of Information and Motivation on Attention and Interpretation. Advances in Experimental Social Psychology, 23, 1-74.

7. Macrae, C. N., Bodenhausen, G. V., Milne, A. B., & Jetten, J. (1994). Out of Mind but Back in Sight: Stereotypes on the Rebound. Journal of Personality and Social Psychology, 67(5), 808.

8. Allport, G.W. (1954). The Nature of Prejudice. AddisonWesley.

9. Collins, A. M., & Quillian, M. R. (1969). Retrieval Time from Semantic Memory. Journal of Verbal Learning and Verbal Behavior, 8(2), 240-247.

20

Meta-cognition and Mindfulness

Meta-cognition refers to a person's ability to think about thinking. It is the knowing, the monitoring, regulation and control of thoughts. It supervises the realisation and the management of goals. Meta-cognition involves both executive management and strategic knowledge. Executive management processes involve planning, monitoring, evaluating and revising one's own thinking processes and products. Strategic knowledge involves knowing what (factual or declarative knowledge), when and why (conditional or contextual knowledge) and knowing how (procedural or methodological knowledge) to control cognitive processes. As stated by H. J. Hartman, *'Both executive management and strategic knowledge meta cognition are needed to self-regulate one's own thinking and learning.'*[1]

While cognitive strategies (such as repetition and using imagery for memorisation) are used to help us achieve a particular goal, meta-cognitive strategies guarantee or evaluate if we have reached that goal. Furthermore, they aid in regulating and overseeing learning. In his work, *How to Teach for Metacognition,*[2] R. Fogarty suggests that meta-cognition is a process that spans three distinct phases:

1. Develop a plan before approaching a learning task, such as reading for comprehension or solving a math problem (*What am I supposed to learn? What should I do first?*).

2. Monitor one's understanding; use 'fix-up' strategies when meaning breaks down (*How am I doing? What information is important to remember? What can I do if I do not understand?*)

3. Evaluate one's thinking after completing the task (*How well did I do? Did I get the results I expected? What could I have done differently? Can I apply this way of thinking to other problems or situations?*)

Such strategies are executive processes, which include planning and monitoring cognitive activities and their outcome, as well as figuring out how to do a particular task and then making sure that the task is done correctly. Through meta-cognition, we are able to devote a sufficient part of our mental life to evaluating our mental performance and predicting how well (or badly) we can do, have done or are doing. Such processes are typified when we look back and analyse an effort (such as performance in a task), remember an instruction or correctly predict our ability to attain some cognitive goal, such as learning a foreign language or making effective plans in a new situation. Helping us to focus on the ways in which we process information – like using self-questioning, or reflective journal writing – and discussing our thought processes and results with other learners, are among the many ways that learners can examine and develop their meta-cognitive processes.

Meta-cognition as a tool for the Eightfold Path

The use of meta-cognitive as well as cognitive strategies is vital for the successful accomplishment of the Eightfold Path, and consequently Enlightenment. A learner receives instruction both for the ideas from the Buddha's teachings (the Right Perspective) and for the necessary skills to capably maintain wholesome thoughts and behaviours through learning the regime of Right Desire, Effort, Energy and Intention. Once one has monitored and evaluated whether these skills have been correctly learnt, it is possible go forward with increased confidence in oneself, the process and the validity of the programme. Another benefit of advancing the training of mind development is to increase one's ability to collect the ordinarily scattered streams of mental states to create a more concentrated, unified one.

A unified mental state inspires open-mindedness and serenity, facilitating our inclination to insight, honesty and objectivity about our intentions. Once the cognitive ability of a unified mental state is achieved, the Buddha's programme is better assimilated. Any new skill applications need oversight and practice, while previously learned 'right' skills can be generalised to other situations and maintained. In the application of meta-cognition, one needs to practice heedfulness, maintain a balanced and watchful mind and to be monitor oneself in an objective, non-attached mindful manner.

A mindful mind

The meta-cognitive function of the Eightfold Path factor of Right Mindfulness includes not only observation and monitoring, but also the skills of discrimination, refinement and maintenance of having wholesome rather than unwholesome, and skilful versus unskilful thoughts, feelings, and behaviours, in addition to the integration of skills acquisition with the other 'right factors'. If we neglect mindfulness or monitoring, we can neither ask ourselves the essential questions that promote and maintain wholesome thoughts, nor put aside unwholesome ones. Right Effort and Right Mindfulness go together to keep in check the arising of unwholesome thoughts and to develop and promote good ones. If craving, envy and aggression flare up, we must first diligently monitor them as they arise in our mind and then energetically counteract them by using the strategy of promoting the other side with honesty, benevolence and kindness.

A mindful person is constantly monitoring his or her thoughts, words and actions. With Right Mindfulness, we guard against deviating from wholesome thinking and we can therefore continue to skilfully do any of the prescribed and necessary interventions to behave virtuously. The Buddha recommended that Right Mindfulness be applied to everything we do. In all of our movements, we are expected to remain observant – to be mindful. When we walk, stand, sit, speak, eat, keep silent and drink, all of the detailed motions that we perform are to be overseen mindfully and 'wide awake,' or with full consciousness. The Buddha said, '*Mindfulness, good monks, I declare, is essential in all things everywhere.*'[3] Pristine mindfulness comprises the balancing of attention and concentration to discipline a wandering mind; and awareness with introspection to understand kamma, or volition. As the Buddha explained:

> '*One is mindful to abandon wrong view and to enter and remain in right view. This is one's right mindfulness...*
> *One is mindful to abandon wrong resolve and to*

enter and remain in right resolve: This is one's right mindfulness...
One is mindful to abandon wrong speech and to enter and remain in right speech: This is one's right mindfulness...
One is mindful to abandon wrong action and to enter and remain in right action: This is one's right mindfulness...
One is mindful to abandon wrong livelihood and to enter and remain in right livelihood: This is one's right mindfulness...'

MN 117

The commentary of a verse in the Dhammapada explains further, 'The wise person is always mindful. Through this alertness he discards the ways of the slothful. The monk, as the seeker after the truth, is frightened of mindlessness because he knows that if one is unmindful, one is caught up in the unending suffering of saṃsāra. Therefore, he forges ahead diligently and mindfully burning away those bonds that fetter people to worldliness.'

(Dhammapada V.28)

We clearly see that Right Mindfulness has the function of monitoring in the present moment and, more importantly, self-regulation. H. J. Hartman has written about the benefits of mindfulness, such as:

'Promoting executive-level functioning in detecting when the mind has wandered (meta awareness) further reduces lapses in attention. Mindfulness practice promotes a form of meta-cognitive insight of learning to emotionally disengage from distracters (frustration; anxiety). This form of top-down cognitive control leads the Mindfulness practitioner to more readily focus on the present task leading to better performance.'[1]

In the Dhammapada, the word 'heedfulness' or 'heedful' is used often (which means having or showing a close attentiveness to avoid danger or trouble) and is substituted for 'mindfulness'.

Self-observing and self-reflection: metacognition and the introspective programme

Throughout the suttas or Buddhist texts, it is clear that Buddha taught a skills-acquisition, goal-oriented, introspective bhavana (or mental cultivation/training programme) using meta-cognition. We can say it is primarily an introspective programme because its primary plan is the monitoring and evaluation of any number of one's own mental states, including sensory, bodily, cognitive and emotional states. Highlighting the importance of mental cultivation, the Buddha is reported to have said, *'The training of the mind is good, a mind so tamed brings happiness,' 'The tame mind brings bliss,' 'All that we are is the result of what we have thought; it is founded on our thoughts, it is made up of our thoughts,'* and finally, *'We will develop mindfulness immersed in the body. We will pursue it, hand it the reins and take it as a basis, give it grounding, steady it, consolidate it, and undertake it well. That is how you should train yourselves.'*

The taming of the mind that the Buddha is talking about is realised through mindfulness, which has been likened to that of the trainer who subdues an unruly animal. Therefore, what is being discussed in the early Buddhist description of mindfulness is not a passive, sense-based, non-judgmental skill, but more accurately concerns meta-cognition, engaging cognitive-reflection and referring to the monitoring and control of thought, especially over specific processes used in learning, which enhances problem-solving ability.

Meta-cognitive regulation refers to processes that monitor and control thought, especially those that coordinate cognition. It is a term used to describe skills involved in monitoring learning and making changes in either how or what one studies. These include both bottom-up processes, called cognitive monitoring (such as error detection, source monitoring in memory retrieval) and top-down processes, called cognitive control (for example, conflict resolution, error correction, inhibitory control, planning, resource allocation).[4, 5] Meta-cognition is linked to executive function, which comprises the ability to monitor and control the information processing that is necessary to produce voluntary action.

So, meta-cognitive skills (or executive functions) help maintain the motivation and effort needed to see a task to completion, and the ability to monitor and skilfully intervene when unwanted internal and external stimuli occur. Meta-cognition by engaging in self-reflection or introspection enhances the monitoring of any lapses in knowledge and the correcting of them. Right Mindfulness, when understood as meta-cognition, plays a critical role in successful 'right' skills acquisition, 'right' skills consolidation and application training, as well as the generalisation and maintenance of the 'right' factors of the Eightfold Path.

Furthermore, mindfulness has other benefits, such as:

'Promoting executive-level functioning in detecting when the mind has wandered (meta awareness) further reduces lapses in attention. Mindfulness practice promotes a form of meta-cognitive insight of learning to emotionally disengage from distracters (frustration; anxiety). This form of top-down

*cognitive control leads the Mindfulness practitioner
to more readily focus on the present task leading to
better performance.'[6]*

Mindfulness as memory

In the Dhammapada, mindfulness is compared with
the treasurer of a king who remembers the royal
possessions in detail, daily, at night and in the morning.
The mindfulness of the aspirant to achieve Enlightenment
remembers the three pillars of the teachings of the Buddha
– Virtue, Concentration and Wisdom. The value of this
recollected activity of mindfulness is seen in the increasing
awareness of the essentials of 'right' living in the aspirant's
mind, and the growing strength of purpose for realising
these within him or herself.

The early Buddhist definition of mindfulness considers
the executive functions and meta-cognition of the learning
programme called the Eightfold Path. We have seen that
to proceed on the Eightfold Path, practitioners need to
assess whether or not retrieved information is relevant to
the life experience they are trying to skilfully master, given
that:

*'Successful differentiation of relevant from irrelevant
memories is key to problem solving, planning,
and other complex tasks. Planning requires
reflecting on which course of action is necessary
to achieve a goal, and as such planning is part of
metacognition.'[6]*

Action planning requires the establishment of a main
goal (Enlightenment) and a hierarchy of sub-goals that
must be satisfied for the main goal to be obtained (ethical
behaviour, concentration, learning the Four Noble Truths).
The main goal usually guides the sub-goals, so that we
can adopt a definition of mindfulness as a method by

which we skilfully and intentionally focus our attention to monitor and evaluate our behaviours, perceptions, feelings, thoughts, and mental processes in the present moment, with the right intention of purifying the mind as prescribed in the Eightfold Path.

Bibliography

1. Hartman, H. J. (2001). Metacognition in Learning and Instruction: Theory, Research and Practice. Kluwer Academic Publishers.

2. Fogarty, R. (1994). How to Teach for Metacognition. IRI/Skylight Publishing.

3. Thera, P. (2006). The Seven Factors of Enlightenment. Access to Insight (Legacy Edition).

4. Nelson, T. O., & Narens, L. (1990). Metamemory: A Theoretical Framework and New Findings. The Psychology of Learning and Motivation, 26, 125-141.

5. Reder, L.M. & Schunn, C.D. (1996). Metacognition does not Imply Awareness: Strategy Choice is Governed by Implicit Learning and Memory. In: Implicit Memory and Metacognition (Reder, L., ed.). Erlbaum.

6. Brown, A.L., J.D. Bransford, R.A. Ferrara and J.C. Campione. (1983). Learning, Remembering and Understanding. In: Flavell, J. H., & Markman, E. M. (Eds.). Handbook of Child Psychology, Cognitive Development, pp. 77-166. New York, Wiley.

21

Automatic Influences on our Actions and Perceptions

'No doubt, the rule, "As little outside world as possible," only as much as is absolutely necessary is apparent in evolution. It is valid for all descendants of the primeval cell and therefore for ourselves. Without doubt, the horizon of the properties of the tangible environment has been extended more and more in the course of time. But in principle only those qualities of the outside world are accessible to our perception apparatus which, in the meantime, we need as living organisms in our stage of development. Also our brain has evolved not as an organ to understand the world but an organ to survive.'

Hoimar von Ditfurth[1]

The truth of a 'self' is an enduring assumption of humankind, and if asked how one knows they have a 'self', often the reply is, '*I can make decisions, I can choose; I can voluntarily move, therefore, I know there is an "I" who is the chooser, the actor, the agent behind my choices.*' But how much is the conscious agent or cognitive executive really in charge of our physical, emotional and thought processes?

Survival through filtering

The latest research in neuroscience and biology indicates that besides some significant cognitive elaborations on the original phenomena, cognitive selectivity and choice is a function based on an organism's biological and evolutionary need to minimise and sort out all possible, *'blooming, buzzing confusion,'*[2] that would occur without the body's filtering system. Every second, we are inundated with information from the many stimuli in and around us. In order to keep the brain from becoming overwhelmed by the steady stream of data competing for attention, brain cells work together to organise and prioritise information.

To sort the important from the not-so-important needs, the brain functions in a hierarchical way comprising many levels. The brain selects and pre-processes the information introduced by sensory stimuli and constructs a meaning. The cognitive meaning is then translated into commands that control an appropriate action. Under normal conditions, our focus is concentrated on just those objects, situations or sensations that we habitually have learned are of importance to us. For example, our eyes are continuously bombarded by an exceptional number of visual information – colours, shapes and motion – but seeing is usually effortless because our brains perform automatic visual smoothing over time. If we were sensitive to every little change, our brains wouldn't be able to cope.

A study has found that for most of the time, our brain's visual perception fails to notice small, environmental changes over a fifteen-second period of time. *'What you are seeing at the present moment is not a fresh snapshot of the world but rather an average of what you've seen in the past ten to fifteen seconds,'* said study author Jason

Fischer, a neuroscientist at the Massachusetts Institute of Technology.[3] This means that what you see around you – your pet's face, the cup of tea, the book you read – may be a time-averaged composite the past and now. Fischer calls this filter a continuity field, which allows our visual system to average out what is mostly 'noise'. The benefit of this filtering (despite sacrificing some accuracy), is that it helps to stabilise incoming visual information, so we are not distracted by the constant stream of visual stimuli that is bombarding us over the daily course of our lives, and our brain doesn't have to waste energy noticing less dramatic or startling shifts in the environment. Therefore our perception of the world is very different from the true input that the eye receives. Fischer suspects that our brains learn that the world follows certain rules, and that in considering what is essential to our survival, deduces that small changes don't matter most of the time.

Another well-known example of the filtering phenomena has been called, '*The Cocktail Party Effect*'. This refers to the ability of being able to focus one's, say, auditory attention on a particular stimulus whilst filtering out a range of other stimuli, similar to how a partygoer can focus on a single conversation in a noisy room. The ability to pay attention to relevant information while ignoring distractions is a core brain function, without which we could not perform effectively.

A study conducted by researchers from Dartmouth's Geisel School of Medicine and the University of California Davis, investigated communications between synaptically-connected neurons under conditions where subjects shifted their attention toward or away from visual stimuli that activated the recorded neurons.[4] The results identified a novel cognitive mechanism, whereby attention shapes perception by selectively altering pre-synaptic weights to highlight sensory features among all the noisy sensory input. How the brain achieves this ability to choose and focus attention is believed to be connected with what is called 'efficient selection', which is likened to a filter. Important sensory information is routed to higher-order perceptual areas of the brain while disruptions from irrelevant information are suppressed.

In support of this idea, Justin Gardner and colleagues at the RIKEN Brain Science Institute, found that sensory signals were efficiently selected.[5] They held that stimuli which are particularly disruptive to our ability to focus and evoke high neural activity are preferentially passed on to perceptual areas of the brain, because stimuli with high contrast that evoke large sensory responses, such as flashing lights or loud noises, can easily disrupt our ability to focus.

Researchers have also found that it is possible to predict from brain signals which options study participants will take, up to seven seconds before they consciously make their decision.[4] The fact that decisions can be predicted so long before they are made goes against our usual intuitive sense that we always make our decisions with conscious deliberation, and that this deliberate process is a foundation of our 'self'.

With the belief in a 'self' comes the idea that what we experience and how we respond to it is directly created by our conscious substantial 'self', rather than automatic and unconscious forces. This egotistical presumption simply isn't true. However, the unconscious mind is still viewed by many psychologists as the shadow of a real, conscious 'self'. This 'conscious-centric' bias is owed, in part, to the operational definition within cognitive psychology, which often equates unconscious thought processes with subliminal, unintentional nature. In fact, contemporary social cognition research has demonstrated the existence of several independent unconscious behavioural guidance systems – perceptual, evaluative and motivational. We now know that a large percentage of our experience in life is created by unconscious and automatic processes which are biologically determined. We learn, cognitively, to predict outcomes on the basis of past experience, although most of such learning is not obvious to us as we live the experience. While our conscious minds are usually poor at dealing with probabilities, unconsciously we can estimate probabilities about the future, using incoming information along with prior beliefs that are based on past experience.

The functioning of the brain can be characterised by two different types of cognitive systems – the autonomous set of systems (known as TASS),[6] and the analytic thoughtful system. TASS refers to the autonomous systems because (a) the systems execute rapidly, (b) their execution is mandatory when the triggering stimuli are encountered, (c) they are not under conscious control, and (d) they are not dependent on input from the analytic system. As Stanovich explains:

> 'Included in TASS are processes of implicit and instrumental learning, over-learned associations, processes of behavioural regulation by the emotions, and the encapsulated modules for solving specific adaptive problems that have been posited by the evolutionary psychologists. Most TASS processes can operate in parallel with each other and with the analytic system. In contrast, the analytic system carries out critical processes of abstraction, decoupling, decontextualisation, and second-order self-regulation, which are important in determining rational thought and action—and indeed, for achieving an examined life. The analytical processing system supports hypothetical reasoning

*that involves the representation of possible states
of the world rather than actual states and it involves
many reasoning tasks, from deductive reasoning, to
decision making, to scientific thinking.'[6]*

Theorists have argued that early meta-representational thinking of hypothesised intentional states of other individuals is an evolutionary adaptation for allowing the checking of the consistency of statements with behaviours of other people to enable us to develop a valid measure of trust. These mental, meta-representational checking procedures might also have developed for self-evaluation purposes, to assess internal consistency.

Understanding the biological determinism of TASS helps confirm the Buddha's insight that many of our actions, emotions and thoughts that are intuitively and culturally believed to be the direct result of an acting substantial, static entity called a 'self' isn't the case. Nevertheless, this analytic system allows for us to reflect, analyse and choose our thoughts, emotions and behaviours that are necessary to work the programme and change through the Noble Eightfold Path.

Automatic principles influencing our perceptions and actions

As an example of how our automatic regulating systems influence our perceptions and actions, let us look to the highly complex processes underlying the mechanisms of the visual system.

The area of the brain responsible for visual perception is called the visual cortex. When we look at something, light reflecting from that object is focused by the cornea and lens of the eye onto a layer of light-sensitive cells at the back of our eyes called the retina. Information from the retina is conveyed via the optic nerve and dorsal lateral geniculate nucleus to the visual cortex in the occipital lobes, which generate an image of the visual world.[7] The visual cortex contains certain groups of neurons called columns, which correspond to receptive fields in the retina containing information about specific movement and shape orientations in the visual field. The brain combines the information that is perceived from different parts of each eye to create a complete image, and then sends information out to other areas in the brain.

Higher visual processing within the brain comprises two specific paths. The first leads to the parietal lobes, and provides us with spatial information referring to the analysis of motion and the location of an object. The second path leads to the temporal lobes, which are responsible for higher-level analytical processing and object recognition.

Sometimes, how a scene or an object is perceived and interpreted results in an illusion. Modern science distinguishes between two types of illusion: one the product of a physical cause and the other resulting from incorrect application of one's knowledge.[8] Physical causes include illusions arising from flaws in light perception, which occur when sensory signals reaching the eye are disturbed, and are known as ambiguities and distortions (like when we believe a rope to be a snake). In comparison, cognitive illusions occur when knowledge is wrongly applied and sensory signals are misinterpreted. In 2008, Mark Changizi stated that the human visual system tries to predict the future in order to compensate for the small delay (slightly less than one-tenth of a second) between when light reaches our retina and when this information arrives in the visual cortex.[9] According to this theory, geometric optical illusions that contain certain shapes are translated by our brain in the wrong way because of a wrong interpretation.

The end result of what we eventually see can be explained in terms of two different types of cognitive processing: bottom-up processing, in which we make good decisions without thinking about them first, versus top-down processing, when our brain is active first and completes what we see, making this form of processing knowledge-based.[10]

A good example of the top-down processing principle is the well-known phenomenon of the Gestalt laws in cognitive psychology. Gestalt theory can be defined as a theory of mind and brain postulating the operational principle of Law of Prägnanz, or that we order our experiences in a way that is regular, orderly, symmetric and simple. The Gestalt principles explain the way that visual perception physically and conceptually composes our experience. These principles are active in many aspects of our everyday life. Specifically, the Gestalt effect is the form-generating capability of our senses, particularly with respect to the visual recognition of figures and whole forms, which allows our ability to acquire and maintain meaningful perceptions instead of just a reduced collection of separate simple lines and curves. This helps us to complete the visual organisation in a predictable and efficient way.

Gestalt laws allow for the prediction of the interpretation of sensation, which is perception. The visual system does more than just interpret forms, contours and colours. It recognises patterns, which reflects a central principle of Gestalt psychology – that the mind considers objects in their entirety before, or with, perception of their individual parts; 'The whole is more than the sum of its parts'. While Gestalt psychology focuses on describing these principles, cognitive neuroscience, using brain-imaging techniques, has confirmed the important role of the underlying mechanisms of higher level brain processing during visual perception.

Gestalt principles

One application that illustrates how important the Gestalt laws are is the close relationship between design and Gestalt principles. To work well, a design has to consider not just the single element but the totality of how it is perceived. Gestalt principles help in focusing attention and organising contents in an effective way. The designer constructs products based on social patterns, with the resulting product based on the need to create a feeling. Gestalt principles influence how we move in groups, how we match clothing and their colours, how we think and perceive a whole from elements. Gestalt theorists have described how different elements in a field reorganise themselves in a solidarity system by following certain rules.

Here is a list of the six rules the Gestalt theorists have found, followed by illustrations demonstrating the explained principles.

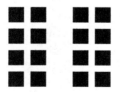

Proximity – Distance plays a key-role in determining the elements perception. Things that are close together are perceived to be more related than things that are scattered apart. The concept underlying the concept of proximity is the group. Proximity occurs when elements are placed close together and they tend to be perceived as a group. Elements which are close to each other are perceived as a shape.

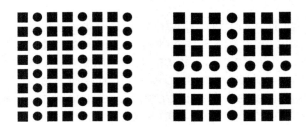

Similarity – There is a natural tendency to put together similar elements more than dissimilar ones. They can be, for example, be similar by shape, colour or dimension. Similarity occurs when objects look similar to one another. We often perceive them as a group or pattern. Perceiving similarities not only helps us to assume what elements are related to one another, it also implies a structure based on an emerging pattern. Those kinds of objects which share some characteristics create cohesion in the design because our brains automatically search for patterns.

Closure – Closure occurs when an object is incomplete or a space is not completely enclosed. If enough of the shape is indicated, people perceive the whole by filling in the missing information. Looking at a complex arrangement of individual elements, we tend to first look for a single shape obtained from recognisable outlines.

Closed shapes can be obtained by real lines, colour or contrast, or even lack of them. Closure Law occurs when an object is incomplete or a space is not completely enclosed and the brain activates some mechanisms to complete the figure by filling in the missing information.

Common Fate – Elements moving in the same direction are perceived as a group more than those which are a steady group because they show more coherence. A collection of distinct objects in a layout that seem to move all together toward a common goal, definition, conclusion or direction are generally perceived to be related to each other.

Figure Ground Relationship – The human brain tends to interpret ambiguous or complex images as simple and complete. In an image, the composing elements are perceived as either figures or ground. Background and foreground can be exchanged and in both case they assume a precise meaning. Balancing figure and ground can make the perceived image clearer. Using unusual figure-ground relationships can add interest and subtlety to an image. This visual illusion is produced by the tendency of ambiguous perceptual between two or more alternative interpretations. In order to clear the image it needs to balance the figure-ground area.

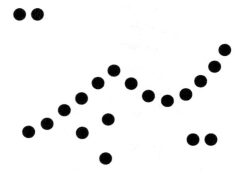

Good Continuation – All elements are perceived as part of a coherent object so if they are arranged in a line they are considered more related than detached elements. Continuation occurs when the eye is compelled to move through one object and continue to another object.

These six laws of perceptual organisation mechanisms of higher-level brain processing allow us in a two-dimensional composition to represent objects from the real world. They explain how we are able to perceive and organise a number of dissimilar shapes in a design and create them into something predictable and recognisable.

Perseverative cognition activity

As we now understand, the greater part of our cognitive processing in daily life occurs without conscious awareness. In addition, our mainly automatic, unconscious perseverative or repetitive cognition operates mostly without our awareness. Perseverative cognition refers to repetitive, usually unconscious, worry or rumination in the form of ideas or images that may either be in anticipation of or continue long after the passing of a stressful event. Worry and rumination are cognitions that often prolong the physiological activation resulting from a stress response. While we are unaware of most perseverative cognition, it can prolong increased activity of our autonomic nervous system even after our conscious worrying has stopped.

Until recently, little attention has been paid to how this unconscious worry and distress can prolong a stress response and cause illnesses related to chronic stress. In everyday life, exasperating but non-life threatening stressors, such as worrying about money or a demanding boss, trigger the release of adrenaline and other stress hormones, which, over time, can have devastating consequences to our health. As Professor of Biological Sciences, Neurology and Neurological Sciences, Robert Sapolsky said:

> *'If you turn on the stress response chronically for purely psychological reasons, you increase your risk of adult onset diabetes and high blood pressure. If you're chronically shutting down the digestive system, there's a bunch of gastrointestinal disorders you're more at risk for as well.'*[11]

Chronic stress-related physiological activity resulting from worry and rumination can last for hours, days, months or even longer. Therefore, we ourselves can make our personally-defined stress events continuously exert effects on our body's systems. Over time, this can lead to deregulation of those systems (higher blood pressure resting levels for example) and ultimately, a psychological and/or physical breakdown. So, just as our intensified cognitions created during stressful events shape the physiological and emotional stress reaction, perseveration of these representations prolongs this physiological and emotional activity, adding to the total time that perceived stressors can have a negative impact on our mental and physical wellbeing. The exact nature of the stressor may be less important than the largely unconscious, repetitive ideas and images about the stressor.

Evidence of perseverative cognition, and the effects that are generated in anticipation of, or following, stressful events, is growing. Since the early 1980s, it has been recognised that severe, constant worry is an essential factor in the onset and maintenance of anxiety and mood disorders.[12] More recently, research has shown that worry, rumination and anticipatory stress are associated with enhanced cardiovascular, endocrinological, immunological and neurovisceral activity. Anxiety in everyday life is associated with increased cardiac activity (in combination with stressful events), which can have adverse effects similar to smoking.[13, 14] Furthermore, worry has been found to predict somatic health complaints like fatigue, neck pain and headaches, and these worry episodes are prolonged when we have difficulties in disengaging our attention from the perceived threatening information. Indeed, it has been suggested that people who suffer from anxiety and dysphoria especially, have trouble with disengaging attention from threatening information.[15-18]

Perseverative cognition, or worry and rumination of stressful events, can also lead to negative affective responses, changes in information processing or an enhanced fear of threat. These processes, which are often occurring unconsciously, interact and enhance each other. Also, worry and rumination associated with increased stress-related physiological activity creates mental exertion with increased negative effect or anxiety. In addition, these chronic stress responses may impair executive functions, such as memory and attention, and are associated with stress-related mental disorders.

It appears that stress hormones impair behaviours mediated by the prefrontal cortex, the area of the brain responsible for executive functioning, suggesting that cognitive inflexibility may be directly caused by neurotransmitter imbalances, including serotonin depletion. Furthermore, the major stress hormone cortisol has been linked with depression.[19] While the underlying mechanisms are not clearly understood, studies have also suggested that chronic stress also causes DNA to age faster. Robert Sapolsky said:

> *'Over time, the ends of your chromosomes fray, and as they fray your DNA stops working as well, and eventually that could wind up doing in the cell... There are now studies showing that chromosomal DNA aging accelerates in young, healthy humans who experience something incredibly psychologically stressful. That's a huge finding.'*[20]

Inflexibility, whether cognitive, emotional or physiological, can be damaging for mental and physical health. Studies indicate that it is possible that the close relationship between cardiovascular disease and psychiatric disorders is attributable to a general state of inflexibility, leading to rumination, worry, obsessions, low heart rate variability and vagal tone, and extended sympathetic arousal. Additionally, inflexibility in any one of these areas can perpetuate it in another. Perseverative cognition, for example, has been shown to cause both extended physiological arousal, and extended or more severe anxiety. Finally, the mostly unconscious perseverative cognitions are associated with higher levels of cognitive inflexibility such as slower reaction times, higher intrusiveness, poorer efforts to inhibit and worsening of mood. It appears that whenever our cognitions become rigid and inflexible, this is a risk factor for health. Together, it clearly suggests that psychological flexibility as demonstrated in metastability, is a key to our psychological health. In fact, metastable dynamics are important for normal brain function.[21] One way to increase and maintain psychological flexibility (and hence physiological health) is the use of somatic exercises – moving our bodies in spontaneous ways or learning to observe without attaching to our cognitive material.[22]

The Zeigarnik Effect

In the context of healthy, ongoing, dynamic, cognitive flexibility, our unconscious cognitive processes have a very helpful and important effect; that is, the ability to remember uncompleted tasks more easily than completed ones. When we begin something and don't finish it, we often have a recurring nagging feeling and thoughts reminding us to finish the task. Or in other words, goals as an object of completion produce motivational tensions.

There is actually a genuine survival reason behind this – without this tension, once we have moved away from a task, we would seldom go back to complete it. Kurt Lewin states that goals, by their very nature, manifest stress or tensions/intentions that create in a person a state of psychological disequilibrium.[23] To re-establish psychological equilibrium, and with it the reduction or elimination of the stress, cognitive flexibility of re-approaching the goal and working on it until realised is necessary. So without closure or completion, we experience an internal tension, stress and preoccupation with the task, whereas completing the task provides closure and a release of the tension.

This observation is now widely known as the Zeigarnik Effect, named after Soviet psychologist, Dr. Bluma Zeigarnik. In experiments, Dr. Zeigarnik found that people tend to remember incomplete or interrupted tasks better than completed ones. If we leave a task incomplete, there is a tendency to experience preservative and intrusive thoughts about that task, as we worry about those things in which we have not achieved closure.[24] It appears that the automatic memory system signals to the conscious mind, which may have moved on to new goals, that the previous activity was left unfinished, in much the same way as we might ruminate and worry about a problem left at work for a whole weekend as it keeps coming back to mind.

This effect is used in academia, work and advertising settings, the idea being that by leaving something incomplete actually makes it more memorable. For example, the phrase, 'Just one more turn,' (meaning as many more turns as it takes to achieve a satisfactory result) is a direct result of the Zeigarnik Effect, since that one more turn is almost always with the intent to complete some problem, quest or upgrade. Another example is an effective speaking technique, which leaves the audience with a question, with something to think about. This not only keeps the topic of discussion alive in the audience but also encourages their remembering the speaker. Further research has found that other factors can moderate the Zeigarnik Effect, such as how motivated people are to do the task, expectancy of level of accomplishment, a better memory, level of task difficulty or the nature of the interruption.[25] Overall however, the Zeigarnik Effect is quite a consistently observed effect, especially when the task is interesting, important and achievable.

When a person falls behind or is unable to find an acceptable solution to a problem, it is as if the non-conscious mind is nagging the conscious mind to take a firm action about the task that is still incomplete. Although these more or less constant thoughts of incomplete task components have the necessary functional operation of helping us to remember to complete or put closure an important stressor, a chronic perseveration if, for whatever reason, the heightened stress response is left empowered and unchecked, can have serious negative psychological, emotional and physiological effects.

Bibliography

1. Ditfurth, H. V. (1980). Der Geist fiel niccth von Himmel. Deutscher Taschenbuch Verlag. Munchen.

2. James, W. (1890). The Principles of Psychology. Henry Holt and Company.

3. Fischer, J., & Whitney, D. (2014). Serial Dependence in Visual Perception. Nature Neuroscience, 17(5), 738-743.

4. Briggs, F., Mangun, G. R., & Usrey, W. M. (2013). Attention Enhances Synaptic Efficacy and the Signal-to-noise Ratio in Neural Circuits. Nature, 499(7459), 476-480.

5. Gardner, J. L., Sun, P., Waggoner, R. A., Ueno, K., Tanaka, K., & Cheng, K. (2005). Contrast Adaptation and Representation in Human Early Visual Cortex. Neuron, 47(4), 607-620.

6. Stanovich, K. E. (2004). Metarepresentation and the Great Cognitive Divide: A Commentary on Henriques' "Psychology Defined". Journal of Clinical Psychology, 60(12), 1263-1266.

7. Purves, D., Brannon, E., Cabeza, R., Huetell, S. A., & LaBar, K. (2013). Principles of Cognitive Neuroscience (2nd ed.). Sinauer Associates.

8. Gregory, R. L. (1997). Knowledge in Perception and Illusion. Philosophical Transactions of the Royal Society of London, Series B: Biological Sciences, 352, 1121-1127.

9. Changizi, M. A., Hsieh, A., Nijhawan, R., Kanai, R., & Shimojo, S. (2008). Perceiving the Present and a Systematization of Illusions. Cognitive Science, 32(3), 459-503.

10. Frith, C., & Dolan, R. J. (1997). Brain Mechanisms Associated with Top-down Processes in Perception. Philosophical Transactions of the Royal Society of London, Series B:Biological

Sciences, 352, 1221-1230.

11. Sapolsky, R. M. (1999). Glucocorticoids, Stress, and their Adverse Neurological Effects: Relevance to Aging. Experimental Gerontology, 34(6), 721-732.

12. Watkins, E. R. (2008). Constructive and Unconstructive Repetitive Thought. Psychological Bulletin, 134(2), 163.

13. Pieper, S., Brosschot, J. F., van der Leeden, R., & Thayer, J. F. (2007). Cardiac Effects of Momentary Assessed Worry Episodes and Stressful Events. Psychosomatic Medicine, 69(9), 901-909.

14. Brosschot, J. F., Van Dijk, E., & Thayer, J. F. (2007). Daily Worry is related to Low Heart Rate Variability During Waking and the Subsequent Nocturnal Sleep Period. International Journal of Psychophysiology, 63(1), 39-47.

15. Fox, E., Russo, R., Bowles, R., & Dutton, K. (2001). Do Threatening Stimuli Draw or Hold Visual Attention in Subclinical Anxiety? Journal of Experimental Psychology: General, 130(4), 681.

16. Fox, E., Russo, R., & Dutton, K. (2002). Attentional Bias for Threat: Evidence for Delayed Disengagement from Emotional Faces. Cognition & Emotion, 16(3), 355-379.

17. Goeleven, E., De Raedt, R., Baert, S., & Koster, E. H. (2006). Deficient Inhibition of Emotional Information in Depression. Journal of Affective Disorders, 93(1), 149-157.

18. Koster, E. H., Crombez, G., Verschuere, B., Van Damme, S., & Wiersema, J. R. (2006). Components of Attentional Bias to Threat in High Trait Anxiety: Facilitated Engagement, Impaired Disengagement, and Attentional Avoidance. Behaviour Research and Therapy, 44(12), 1757-1771.

19. Retrieved from http://www.webmd.com/

depression/features/stress-depression

20. Retrieved from http://news.stanford.edu/
    news/2007/march7/sapolskysr-030707.html

21. Hellyer, P. J., Scott, G., Shanahan, M., Sharp,
    D. J., & Leech, R. (2015). Cognitive Flexibility
    through Metastable Neural Dynamics Is Disrupted
    by Damage to the Structural Connectome. The
    Journal of Neuroscience, 35(24), 9050 –9063.

22. Whiting, D. L., Simpson, G. K., Mcleod, H. J.,
    Deane, F. P. & Ciarrochi, J. (2012). Acceptance
    and Commitment Therapy (ACT) for Psychological
    Adjustment after Traumatic Brain Injury: Reporting
    the Protocol for a Randomised Controlled Trial.
    Brain Impairment, 13(3), 360-376.

23. Lewin, K. (Cartwright, D. Ed.) (1951). Field Theory
    in Social Science: Selected Theoretical Papers.
    Harpers.

24. Baumeister, R. F., & Bushman, B. J. (2008).
    Social Psychology and Human Nature. Thomson
    Wadsworth.

25. Reeve, J., Cole, S. G., & Olson, B. C. (1986).
    Adding Excitement to Intrinsic Motivation
    Research. Journal of Social Behavior &
    Personality, 1, 349-363.

22

Organisms as Coherent Embedded Systems

'The organism as a whole is its continually changing structure which determines its own actions on itself and its world.'

Reid

'Humans can never separate themselves from the environment and never achieve a static perfection without forfeiting organic balance.'

L.L. White

All sentient beings are inseparable from nature and should only be understood as a part of the whole. The interrelationship between organisms and their environment is an oscillating co-arising with an equilibrium between two sets of processes; that is, the organism with its hierarchy of needs and the broader ambiance in which it is a part. Organisation of the organism is the integrated differentiation of an ordered system of hierarchy, and within the hierarchy there is one dominant process, called the organising process. The organism adapts to the wider system which sustains and nourishes it and eventually there is a gradual mutual embedding between the organism and its environment.

All life consists of inseparability and dynamic interactions. As explained in meta-stability, with meaningful information exchange in living things, dualities are bi-stable, and in general multi-stable coordination dynamics confers many advantages on living things, in particular multi-functionality. If any aspect of the duality becomes out of balance and develops too far, it binds the system, perhaps irrevocably. For example, as Kelso so beautifully writes:

> '*Metastable coordination dynamics also rationalises William James's (1890) beautiful metaphor of the stream of consciousness as the flight of a bird whose life journey consists of 'perchings' (viewed here as phase gathering, integrative tendencies) and 'flights' (phase scattering, segregative tendencies). Both tendencies appear to be crucial: the former to summon and create thoughts, the latter to release individual brain areas to participate in other acts of cognition, emotion and action, the two 'forces' that drive coordination dynamics deal fundamentally with meaningful information exchange in living things. One force is the strength of coupling between the elements; this allows information to be distributed to all participating elements and is a key to integrative, collective action. The other is the ability of individual elements to express their autonomy and thereby minimize the influence of others. Self-organisation in the metastable regime is the interplay of both. This is the architecture of mind—metastable mind.'*[1]

In living, organisms can never maintain perfect symmetry. As the Buddha taught, co-arising is universal and is often called a process which consists in the development and transformation of patterns. Even though changes cannot always be foreseen, it doesn't mean that they are arbitrary. However, concepts of permanence cannot be an aspect of this system. The Buddha taught that there is no universal preconceived beginning or end, and nothing material is permanent with a constant identity. Life is unity in diversity and form is the recognisable continuity of a process, for if there were no patterns, our mind could not make sense of world. Indeed, there is an underlying formative process present in all phenomena and underlying all dualisms, known by the Buddha through his grand insight of emptiness (sunyata) or pure experience – the transcending of all absolute dualisms. By understanding pure experience we can understand our true nature or situation, and overcome ignorance.

Life's web and rhythm

All life on earth exists within a web of vibrations, and rhythm is fundamental to all forms of life. Natural rhythms guide all that we do – our very existence, our behaviours are embedded in the web of rhythm and vibration in the environment in which we live. There are profound rhythms, like the diurnal or natural daily rhythms (sunrise and sunset, seasonal, lunar and solar cycles, electromagnetic field (EMF) oscillations) of our planet that we experience, and there are our own internal rhythms (our breathing and heartbeat, for example), which are constant reminders of life's pulsing rhythm that moves within and around us. Life has evolved amidst these natural rhythms and they have been embedded into many of our basic biological responses. One compelling answer to explain these universal phenomena is provided by thermodynamics. According to biochemist Mae Wan Ho:

'Practically all living processes are organised in cycles. The organism is thick with biological rhythms ranging from periods of split seconds for electrical activities of brain cells to seconds such as the heart-beat and respiration, to periods which are circadian and circannual. But no one has ever

*been able to explain why that should be. The
answer is provided by thermodynamics. It turns
out that symmetrically coupled cycles are the key
to both the conservation of coherent energy and
compensation (or cancelling out) of entropy within
the system so that living organisation is maintained
[…]. The way to think about it is that as one cycle
of activity is running down, it is charging up a
second cycle, so that the role can be reversed later.
Similarly, as disorder is created in some part of the
system, a kind of super-order appears in elsewhere,
which can restore order to the first part.'[2]*

Much of our basic daily-life activities are co-arising
around these rhythms. New research is demonstrating
that rhythmical behaviours can be quite complex and have
positive functional advantages for the organism, including
spatial and temporal organisation, prediction of events,
energy efficiency and precision of control. In fact, rhythm
impacts on the communication of the bio-information
that governs many bodily functions, such as the
interconnectedness of mind and emotion, brain and heart
rhythms, the relationships between electroencephalogram
(EEG) rhythms and cognition, as well rhythmic pulsation
dynamics in genetic circuits, which is essential for the
temporal organisation of cellular stress response, signalling
and development.

The rhythms of our breath, heartbeat and brain are
intimately related to our emotions, thoughts and mindset
states. One example is the complex interaction of the
brainstem and higher brain centres connecting the limbic
system and cortical structures, which creates a basic
link between our breathing and our emotions. The quiet
rhythmic breathing of meditation is well known for its
calming effect. Both simple and complex bodily rhythms
are widespread in physiology and these two typical
rhythms – one regular and one irregular – do not usually

exist in isolation. Rather, they have complex interactions among themselves.

Since the 1920s, when physiologists discovered brain waves (alpha, delta, theta and so on), these rhythms (rhythmic electrical currents measurable on the surface of the scalp by means of EEG) were believed to be correlated with various mental states, such as calmness, alertness and deep sleep. These rhythms were also found to vary with perceptual or cognitive events, for example, the phase and amplitude of your brain waves could change if you saw or heard something, if you increased your concentration by focusing on a specific input, or if you shifted your attention. The brain wave categories were largely used as a tool for indexing mental experience. A correlating view is that our subjective experience of the world is that of a 'stream' of consciousness, yet this is a misconception.

However, for the brain, experience is not continuous stream or flow but quantised. According to Gregory Hickok, a Professor of Cognitive Science:

> *'We actually perceive the world in rhythmic pulses rather than as a continuous flow....Rhythms in the environment, such as those in music or speech, can draw neural oscillations into their tempo, effectively synchronizing the brain's rhythms with those of the world around us [...]. We should talk of the rhythm of thought, of perception, of consciousness. Conceptualizing our mental experience this way is not only more accurate, but it also situates our mind within the broader context of the daily, monthly and yearly rhythms that dominate our lives.'[3]*

So, brain waves are not just correlated to mental states but actually help shape our perception, movement, memory – and even consciousness itself. Hickok believes that the brain interacts with the world in rhythmic pulses, perhaps even discrete time chunks. These rhythms correlate with electrical rhythms of the brain and this is how our brain focuses attention.

External inputs are perceived by the brain according to specific rhythmic pulses. Our ability to detect a subtle event, like a slight change in an auditory scene, oscillates over time, cycling between better and worse perceptual sensitivity several times a second. So within its interconnected tissue, the configuration of neural activity is ever-changing, and with those variations the brain is constantly able to realise functional equivalence – the accomplishment of a consistent cognitive state even though the configurations of neural activities are ever-changing. One classic example of this is the cocktail party situation. In a room crowded with partygoers, as you concentrate or focus your attention on your partner's conversation – one particular acoustic stream – your brain synchronises its rhythm to the rhythm of his or her voice, enhancing the perceptibility of that pathway while suppressing others with their own, different rhythms.[4,5]

Bodily rhythms that interact with the external environment represent an essential element in whether we have healthy or unhealthy bodily functions. For instance, our circadian rhythm can be easily disturbed by jetlag or the time of exposure to bright light,[6] and the phase shifting of menstrual cycles can be affected by visible light stimulation.[7] Therefore, it is quite reasonable to say that within the body's framework of dynamic interactions of multiple rhythms, health can be interpreted as a harmony among these rhythms, while disease as a form of discord. Hence, the disruption of normal rhythms and the emergence of abnormal rhythms have been called 'dynamical diseases', or the abnormal condition of physiological rhythms in space and time. This lack of synchrony among internal processes may generate new dynamic patterns that can damage the system's overall dynamic stability. An emerging discipline of 'dynamic diseases' is based on detecting deviations from the dynamics of healthy biological rhythms.

Circadian rhythm

Circadian rhythms signal and affect every aspect of our life. For example, they govern when we wake up, sleep, are active and how much energy we have. They influence how we socialise and how we feel. Circadian rhythms are as predictable as clockwork – our body clock. Our circadian rhythm regulates our biological cycles, recurring at approximately 24-hour intervals. There are patterns of brain wave activity, hormone production, cell regeneration and other biological activities linked by the light-dark cycle over a 24-hour period.

The physiological basis of our biological 'clocks' are groupings of interacting molecules in cells throughout the body. Within the brain, and more specifically located in the hypothalamus just above the optic nerves, lies a group of about 20,000 nerve cells called the suprachiasmatic nucleus (SCN),[8] which coordinates all these body 'clocks' so that they are in synchronisation. The 'clocks' are governed in part by our genetic makeup. In 2006, a protein essential to directing our circadian rhythms was discovered and named CLOCK. Typical in a homeostatic system, functional balance is created by a metabolic protein called SIRT1, which senses energy use in cells and counterbalances CLOCK. Any disequilibrium in the CLOCK-SIRT1 balance was found to lead to sleep disruption and also increased hunger.

In addition, while it has long been known about the significant role light has in governing our circadian rhythms, until recently it wasn't sure how different properties of light, such as colour and brightness, contributed to its governing. Tim Brown, a neuroscientist at the University of Manchester, has discovered that it is the colour of a sunset that our bodies use to regulate the internal clock.[9] When there is less light, such as at night, the SCN directs our sleep-wake cycle by signalling the brain to produce more melatonin, a hormone that makes us sleepy.

There is a now considerable body of evidence supporting the idea that disruption of circadian rhythms is detrimental to the wellbeing of humans and animals. Abnormal circadian rhythms have been linked to various sleep disorders, such as insomnia as well as with obesity, diabetes, depression, bipolar disorder and seasonal affective disorder (SAD).[10] Circadian rhythm disorders can be caused by many factors and some are created by the way in which we live in our modern society.

Shift work sleep disorder – This sleep disorder affects people who frequently rotate shifts or work at night. Work schedules conflict with the body's natural circadian rhythm and some individuals have difficulty adjusting to the change. Shift work disorder is identified by a constant or recurrent pattern of sleep interruption that results in insomnia or excessive sleepiness. There is a growing body of epidemiological evidence that shift work and the associated interference with sleep/wake cycles, light exposure and meal times increases the risk of developing chronic diseases, including cardiovascular disease, diabetes and possibly some cancers.

Jetlag or Rapid Time Zone Syndrome Change – This syndrome results from a conflict between the pattern of sleep and wakefulness between the internal biological clock and that of a new time zone. It is often difficult to adjust and function optimally in the new time zone especially farther away from the point of origin. Recent studies suggest that repeated bouts of jetlag may cause harm to the temporal lobe, an area of the brain important to memory. Eastward travel is more difficult than westward travel because it is easier to delay sleep than to advance sleep.

Delayed Sleep Phase Syndrome (DSPS) – Changes in routine such as staying up late is a circadian rhythm disorder most common in 'night owl' tendencies of going to sleep later – often 2 a.m. or later. If an earlier wake-up time is required, this can lead to daytime sleepiness and impaired work or school performance. These individuals are often perceived as lazy, unmotivated or poor performers who are chronically tardy for morning obligations, while they are often most alert, productive and creative late at night. This is a disorder of sleep timing.

Advanced Sleep Phase Syndrome (ASPD) – This is a disorder in which a person goes to sleep earlier and wakes earlier than desired. ASPD results in symptoms of evening sleepiness, going to bed earlier (for example, between 6 p.m. and 9 p.m.), and waking up earlier than desired (for example, between 1 a.m. and 5 a.m.).

Lunar phases

While the cause is still unclear, there appears to be a link between changes to sleep patterns and lunar phases, especially at the time of the full moon. Apparently, sleep might be delayed by an average of 25 minutes around the time of the full moon, and sleepers have been found to spend an average of 30 additional minutes in REM sleep. Also, sleep duration is often shortened by an average of 20 minutes around the time of the full moon. Measurements of EEG activity showed a 30% decrease in delta waves, a brain wave that indicates deep sleep.

The sleepers slept out of direct exposure to moonlight, which eliminated illumination as a possible cause of sleep disruption or changes to sleep patterns.[11]

These syndromes can have significant problems for our health, but we can minimise their effect and prevent them. For example, the choices we make about our sleep environments and sleep habits can make a significant difference. Limiting night-time exposure to artificial light and increasing exposure to daytime sunlight can shift sleep-wake cycles to earlier times – even for those people who stay up very late. Also, being careful about alcohol consumption close to bedtime, sticking to regular sleep and wake times, making sure the bedroom is dark and free of electronic gadgets can all help to reinforce our healthy sleep schedule.[12] Again, the physical consequences of our behaviours needs to be respected for our overall health.

Seasonal Affective Disorder (SAD)

SAD is a form of depression that is related to changes in the seasons. Sufferers usually begin to feel unwell in the autumn, with symptoms continuing through the winter months until late spring. It can be a significant source of distress, particularly for those who live in especially temperate or boreal regions. It is estimated that SAD affects between 10% and 20% of the Northern latitude population and is more reported in women than in men.[10] Symptoms of SAD typically manifest around the age of twenty years old, and can include weight gain, increased sleep, decreased activity and loss of interest in sex. Such changes resemble physical and behavioural changes that occur in other mammals in response to seasonal decrease of sunlight. Now viewed as a complex disorder resulting from a combination of factors, there appears to be several biologic mechanisms underlying SAD, including retinal sensitivity to light, vulnerability to stress, neurotransmitter dysfunction, genetic variations affecting circadian rhythms, and reduced serotonin levels. However, the primary cause appears to be the delay or advance of the circadian phase.[13]

Humans, and similarly many other mammals, have neural circuits that detect changes in day length and use this information to control the timing of seasonal behaviour. A central component of these circuits is the circadian pacemaker. The circadian pacemaker, in the SCN of the hypothalamus regulates seasonal changes in behaviour by transmitting a signal of day length to other sites in the organism.[14] Neurons in the SCN increase their firing rate abruptly at dawn, and decrease it abruptly at dusk. During the course of the year, the SCN tracks the changing times of dawn and dusk via the retinohypothalamic tract and makes adjustments in the timing of transitions between its periods of high and low neuronal firing. In this way, even relatively minor seasonal changes in day length is sufficient to create changes in the duration of the diurnal period of SCN neuron firing, resulting in the duration of nocturnal melatonin secretion longer in winter than in summer.

The human life-cycle

'A broad definition of life history includes not only the traditional foci such as age-related fecundity and mortality rates, but also the entire sequence of behavorial, physiological, and morphological changes that an organism passes through during its development from conception to death.'

Shea[15]

Figure 22.1 *The ages of man. Birth ➔ Baby/Infant ➔ Toddler ➔ Child ➔ Teenager/Adolescent ➔ Mature adult ➔ Senior ➔ Death*

A life-cycle is defined as the developmental stages that occur during an organism's lifetime. All living things have a life-cycle that includes being born, childhood, developing into an adult and eventually dying. As we grow and enter different phases in our lives, we go through various challenges and hopefully conquer milestones unique to that phase and create a life history. As human beings we are very much interrelated with our socio-economic environment, therefore not only the individual but the family unit has its own stages of development, or life-cycle, as does one's employment, housing, finances, physicality, relationships and education. A person's behaviour, psychological, emotional and physical possibilities and expressions are substantially determined by the challenges of each developmental phase. A person's life is significantly shaped by the tasks and opportunities embedded within their developmental life-cycles.

The biological imperative of movement

Research into natural movement patterns reveals that there appears to be, 'biological imperatives to movement,' built into our bodily system. One such study, published in 2009, found that people tend to move in complementary intervals.[16] After a period of inactivity, people would start moving, and once they had moved about or exercised, they would become inactive for a period. The intervals of movement and inactivity were more consistent in younger people than older ones.

> *'In essence, the young people's bodies seemed to be somehow remembering and responding to what that body had just been doing, whether sitting or moving, and then calculating a new, appropriate response – moving or sitting. In doing so, [...] the body created a healthy, dynamic circadian pattern.'*[16]

Another study looked at the movement pattern of mice, as an animal model equivalent to a young adult or aging senior in human terms. When running wheels were provided, the younger mice exercised a lot, developing marked peaks and valleys of activity. As in the human study, the older mice were less consistent in their activity patterns. The researchers, Dr. Scheer and his colleagues, found that once the ability to exercise (running wheels) was removed, the patterns of the younger mice became more like that of the older ones:

> *'Exercise seems to make the body better able to judge when and how much more it should be moving and when it should be at rest. By prompting the release of a wide variety of biochemicals in the body and brain...exercise almost certainly affects the body's internal clock mechanisms and therefore its circadian rhythms, especially those related to activity.*[17]

This suggests that exercise has a far greater impact on our daily movement patterns than our age alone.

The body as an embedded organism
Creatures of the atmosphere

In the Buddha's psychology we see the body as an embedded organism, with effects constantly co-arising with its interaction and interconnectedness with the forces of nature, including the weather. While no satisfactory agreement has been reached as to how the weather causes, for example, joint pain, there are plausible theories. One leading theory points to changes in air pressure. Barometric pressure is the weight of the atmosphere that surrounds us. If you imagine the tissues surrounding the joints to be like a balloon, high barometric pressure that pushes against the body from the outside will keep tissues from expanding. Barometric pressure often drops before bad weather sets in. This lower air pressure pushes less against the body, allowing tissues to expand – and those expanded tissues can put pressure on the joint. Proponents of the idea use a balloon in a barometric chamber as a simulator to show that when the pressure outside drops, the air in the balloon expands. If the same happened in the area around an arthritic joint, the expansion or swelling could irritate the nerves, causing pain. As rheumatologist David Borenstein explains, '*When there's less pressure, we expand.*' Ultimately, we are embedded creatures that can be affected by atmospheric pressure.

And creatures sensitive to temperature

Hot temperatures

There are two ways in which our body copes with heat – by perspiring and by breathing. Not only high temperatures, but humidity presents a crucial adaptive factor. If there is very high temperature and high humidity, the body will be sweating but the sweat won't dry on the skin. Therefore, the body is not able to cool down as effectively in high humidity. If the temperature remains elevated overnight, the body becomes overwhelmed because it doesn't get the respite that it needs. And in that instance, our body systems that enable it to adapt to heat get confused by the external temperature parameters and stop functioning properly.

If a person is exposed to heat for a very long time, the first thing that shuts down is the ability to sweat. Once somebody stops perspiring and loses that cooling effect, they become very hot and in short order can move from heat exhaustion to heat stroke. Heat rash and muscle cramps are early signs of being overwhelmed by heat. If those aren't addressed, such an unbalanced situation can lead to more severe symptoms.

Cramping of muscles can occur for a number of different issues, including electrolytes not reaching the muscles. The skin turning red and dry is an indicator that heat is impacting a body. Eventually, heat also begins to affect the brain, causing confusion and even the loss of consciousness. As the body temperature increases very rapidly, the central nervous system and circulatory system are impacted. When heat exposure has been prolonged over the threshold, a broad impact on many organ systems, such as kidneys, is usually experienced. People with the highest risk factor for severe heat-related problems are urban dwellers, especially the elderly and very young. Obese people are at an increased risk as are those who on certain medications. And people who are exercising or working physically in the heat, even if they don't meet these criteria, can be at risk as well.

Cold temperatures

Likewise, the human body is not adapted for extremely cold temperatures. Most of us live in temperate and tropical climates, where the temperature rarely drops below freezing. But the human body does have several defences to try and boost our core temperature when we get cold. Our muscles shiver and our teeth chatter, our hairs rise and our flesh forms goosebumps – an evolutionary holdover from the times when our ancestors were covered in fur. The hypothalamus stimulates these reactions to keep the body's vital organs warm until the person can find warmth and shelter.

Keeping the vital core organs warm is the body's priority – even sacrificing the extremities if needed be. The body directs its warm blood close to the core, thereby constricting blood supply to the outer regions. In the very cold, with blood flow reduced, this effect can lead to frostbite, beginning in the fingers and toes, but as tissue freezes and ruptures, damage can extend along the limbs. While fat – the perfect insulator – does not transfer heat very well and, therefore keeps it inside the body, humans, with no fur and relatively little fat, can't adapt well to very cold environments. So again we can clearly see how our inter-relatedness with the natural environment affects our body's physiology.

Smells can make you feel and act differently

Our sense of smell (that is, our olfactory receptors – two small odour-detecting patches made up of about five or six million yellowish cells located high up in the nasal passages) can recognise thousands of different smells, and is directly connected to the limbic system. The limbic system is a set of evolutionarily primitive brain structures located on top of the brainstem and buried under the cortex.[18] These structures are involved in many of our emotions and motivations, for example, fear, anger and sexual arousal. When our smell receptors are stimulated, these sensations are relayed to the cortex, where the cognitive or representation recognition occurs, but only after the deepest limbic parts of our brains have been stimulated. So by the time we correctly recognise a particular scent as, say, lavender, the scent has already activated the limbic system, triggering an emotional reaction.

Our apperception of smell consists not only of the sensation of the odours themselves but also often evoke a memory of past experiences and emotions associated with these smells. So although a smell can evoke strong mood effects, many of our olfactory likes and dislikes are associated with our expectations about an odour, rather than the direct effects of exposure to it. Often, whether a scent is considered pleasant or not is an idiosyncratic matter, depending on specific memories and associations. Some people have positive responses to odours generally regarded as unpleasant (such as chlorine and body perspiration), while some scents usually perceived as pleasant (such as flowers) may be disliked.[19] These discrepancies have been explained by past experiences and memories associated with the particular scents.

Nevertheless, despite individual peculiarities, some significant generalisations about smell preference have been made. For example, people tend to give higher pleasantness ratings to smells that they can identify correctly, including the use of an appropriate colour, for example, the colour red with the smell of cherry. There are some fragrances that appear to be universally perceived as pleasant, such as vanilla, a long-standing example of a pleasant odour used in psychological experiments. Studies using placebos (odourless sprays), have found that while the thought of pleasant fragrances can make us a bit more calm, or cheerful, experiencing the actual smell can also have significant positive effects on our mood and sense of wellbeing.[20] This has been found in all age groups. Researchers have also found differences in olfactory cortical neuron activity in the left and right hemispheres of the brain. It seems that positive emotions are predominantly processed by the left hemisphere of the brain, while negative emotions are more often processed by the right hemisphere.

When we experience a different mood caused by smells, this can also affect our perceptions of other people. Beauty can be in the 'nose' of the beholder. For example, people smelling pleasant fragrances tended to give higher attractiveness ratings to average-looking people in photographs. However, at the extreme ends of the scale, if a person is rated as being very beautiful or unattractive, then fragrance does not affect how the person is perceived.[21] Unpleasant smells can have the opposite affect our perceptions and evaluations. In a similar study, people exposed to an unpleasant odour not only gave lower ratings to photographs of many individuals, but also judged paintings adversely.

Therefore, we need to be mindful of how odours can affect our judgement and behaviour, as was demonstrated by an experiment in a Las Vegas casino. Here, a slot machine, when perfumed with a pleasant aroma, had the amount of money gambled on it increased by over 45%. In addition, a widely reported consumer test of shampoos found that a shampoo ranked last on general performance in an initial test, was ranked first in a subsequent test after its fragrance was changed to a more pleasant one. In the second test, even though only the fragrance had been changed, the shampoo was then described in positive terms as easier to rinse out, foaming better and leaving the hair glossier.[22, 23] So again we see that automatic, biologically based likes and dislikes are often conditioned by past experiences and memory associations, which can significantly affect not only our mood but also our behaviours.

Organ cross-talk and interactions

Important in the cognitive processes and the enmeshing of the body and its environment, the co-arising principle is again critical in the interactions between the unified coherent body systems. Once we remove the primary focus of control away from our conscious cognitive processes, especially when represented as a 'self', the astounding myriad of ways that non-conscious and automatic physical processes coordinate for and manage our existence becomes evident. In fact, our unified body systems operate on functional, automatic mode every moment of our life. When we wake up, get sleepy, are fatigued, hungry or thirsty, all is responded to by the coherent and wide system operation of our body. There isn't an organ in the human body that operates in isolation.

Physical, electrical, chemical, biological, psychological and social phenomena interact through different levels of the body's organisation, requiring different levels of response. The interactions between these different levels are so complex that they can't be reduced to a single level. In a biological system, a change in one part of the body's system will affect the dynamic behaviour of the whole organism. Living systems are necessarily a whole of a diversified complexity that nevertheless coheres into a singular being. For example, body and brain mutually interact and condition each other. In fact, the unity of our conscious experience and our state of health depends on the complete coherence of brain and body. This is obvious when we recognise that the brain is indeed an integral part of the body.

Unfortunately, many people do not conceive of the body as a whole, and instead still think of using a Cartesian partition between mind and brain, and brain and body. Some basic physical interactions include the nervous system (sympathetic, parasympathetic) and its interactions with every single organ including musculoskeletal control. Many physiological and behavioural functions (such as the control of walking, balance, posture, eye movements, blood pressure, fight/flight responses and other sensorimotor functions) depend on the merging within the nervous system of information from different bodily regions. The nervous system is a dynamic platform exchanging information from between one part of the body and another, permitting different (perhaps disparate) organs to influence systems. This happens in both healthy and unhealthy physical processes, processing that can be significantly influenced by hormones.

The liver is often called the most unselfish organ, because almost everything that it does (gluconeogenesis, metabolising waste products, for example) is done for the benefit of the body as a whole. Likewise, the kidneys share a very close role with the heart through the cardiovascular system. An example is provided by Andrew Davenport in his article, 'The Brain and the Kidney – Organ Cross Talk and Interactions',[24] in which he describes how the kidney and the brain play major roles in maintaining normal homeostasis of the extracellular fluid, and as such, regulate intracellular volume by controlling sodium and water balance. Acute and chronic kidney damage affects not only sodium and water homeostasis, but also the accumulation of uremic toxins; it impairs higher cerebral functions and the ability of the brain to adapt to extracellular changes.

It is vital to look at the body as an inter-connected dependent co-arising unit, instead of individual parts. If someone with a lowered adrenal output is given supplemental (prescription) thyroid hormones, then he or she will typically develop many side effects, such as heart arrhythmias, or nervousness.[25] This is because the adrenal glands are further stressed by the additional thyroid – they simply cannot keep up with the increased metabolic activity. In addition, both neurotransmitters serotonin and dopamine are made through a methylation pathway. Research has shown that the pituitary gland needs serotonin and dopamine in order to release the appropriate hormone signals.

There is a physiological hierarchy of needs, much like Maslow's Hierarchy of Needs in psychology.[26] An important example of this is that when the body is attempting to cope with a stress situation, it will create more cortisol and sacrifice the sex hormones. Pregnenolone being a precursor hormone to both cortisol and the sex hormones, your body will use this molecule to first make cortisol (in reaction to the stress), resulting in a lower level of sex hormones. As cortisol, a steroid hormone, is essential to the functioning of the body (you'll die within a couple of hours without it), your body prioritises the synthesis of this hormone. Therefore, the adrenal fatigue of a chronic stress reaction may show up first as a decreased level of sex hormones, leading to a state of sympathetic nervous system dominance, also known as the 'fight or flight' mode.

Unfortunately, with our ever-stressful, fast-paced modern lifestyles, our bodies are using cortisol almost constantly, which can have extensive negative effects on our health. In the whole-body process, mediated by hormones and the immune system, cortisol is just one of the many factors of complex mechanisms that can lead to specific physiological damage associated with chronic stress.[27]

Physicians are beginning to clearly recognise how the human body consists of cooperating integrated systems that work together as one unit. In an important article about the interactions between reproductive, gastrointestinal and urinary tracts, scholars list ten major organ systems of the body which function as interacting systems, with the final product of this cooperative being one unit – the body.[28] Each system depends on the others, either directly or indirectly, to keep the body functioning normally.

An exquisite feature of the living system is its acute sensitivity to weak signals. For example, the retina can detect single photons, and the presence of just a few molecules of pheromones in the air is sufficient to attract male insects to their mates. Similarly, the extreme sensitivity of the human organism applies to all systems; no part has to be pushed or pulled into action, nor be subjected to mechanical regulation and control. Instead, the coordinated action of all the parts depends on rapid intercommunication between the different organs and tissues that comprise the body. The organism is a system of, 'Excitable media,'[29, 30] or excitable cells and tissues poised to respond specifically and disproportionately (nonlinearly) to weak signals, amplifying them into macroscopic action.

Specific body systems

Circulatory System – transports nutrients and gasses to cells and tissues throughout body.

Organs and tissues: heart, blood vessels, blood.

Lymphatic System – transports lymph towards the heart, plays a crucial role in immune system.

Organs and tissues: lymph nodes and vessels, thymus, spleen.

Digestive System – breaks down large molecules into smaller ones to provide energy for the body.

Primary organs and tissues: mouth, stomach, intestines, rectum.

Accessory organs and tissues: teeth, tongue, liver, pancreas.

Endocrine System – helps to maintain growth and homeostasis within the body.

Organs and tissues: pituitary gland, pineal gland, hypothalamus, ovaries, testes, thyroid gland.

Integumentary System – protects the internal structures of the body from damage, prevents dehydration, stores fat and produces vitamins and hormones.

Organs and tissues: skin, nails, hair, sweat glands.

Muscular System – enables movement of the body.

Organs and tissues: muscles.

Nervous System – monitors and coordinates internal organ function and responds to changes in the external environment.

Organs and tissues: brain, spinal cord, nerves.

Reproductive System – enables the production of offspring through sexual reproduction.

Male organs and tissues: testes, scrotum, penis, vas deferens, prostate.

Female organs and tissues: ovaries, uterus, vagina, mammary glands.

Respiratory System – provides the body with oxygen via gas exchange between air from the outside environment and gases in the blood.

Organs and tissues: lungs, nose, trachea, bronchi.

Skeletal System – supports and protects the body while giving it shape and form.

Organs and tissues: bones, joints, ligaments, cartilage.

Urinary/Excretory System – removes wastes and maintains water balance in the body.

Organs and tissues: kidneys, urinary bladder, urethra, ureter.

Homeostasis

'The highly developed living being is an open system having many relations to its surroundings – in the respiratory and alimentary tracts and through surface receptors, neuromuscular organs and bony levers. Changes in the surroundings excite reactions in this system, or affect it directly, so that internal disturbances of the system are produced. Such disturbances are normally kept within narrow limits, because automatic adjustments within the system are brought into action, and thereby wide oscillations are prevented and the internal conditions are held fairly constant.'

Walter B. Cannon[31]

I n his book, *The Wisdom of the Body*,[32] Walter Cannon coined the term 'homeostasis' to describe how the human body automatically maintains steady levels of temperature and other vital conditions such as the water, salt, sugar, protein, fat, calcium and oxygen contents of the blood. Homeostasis is the automatic and coherent response of our body to maintain optimal health via a relatively constant internal environment balance. For example, it maintains our body temperature within a certain range as well as a stable flow of blood through the body to provide optimal nourishment and oxygen to the cells whilst removing toxins. Furthermore:

> *'The brain also has a remarkable tendency to maintain its chemical constancy due in part to a functional barrier between the blood and the brain tissue which prevents all but a few chemicals from entering the brain proper. The barrier appears to function to protect the brain against the myriad chemical fluctuations reflected in the blood,'* and, *'is probably necessary in order for the brain to carry on its intricate functions as a receiver, processor, and transmitter of signals (information) with itself and the rest of the nervous system.'*[33]

Every cell, organ and system in the body relies on a stable environment to function.

The regulative processes in every organism tend to be restorative. Both physical and psychological stress cause physical imbalance. Whether from excessive cold, psychological distress or an injury, our continuing wellbeing depends on the ability of internal systems to quickly appraise, react and adjust to imbalances and recombine homeostasis. This system of accommodation and maintenance is incredibly complex and sensitive. To quote at length Sandi Busch from her informative article, 'What Does Homeostatic Balance Mean?':

> *'The body uses different processes to maintain homeostasis. Receptors throughout the body sense changes in the internal and external environment and send messages to the brain; it responds by telling the appropriate organs to restore equilibrium. Hormones are often used to signal the changes that must be made to restore balance, but the body also uses other mechanisms.'*[35]

To further illustrate the complexity of this system, Busch goes on to explain,

> *'...Envision a "loop" of information, in which an imbalance causes a response to correct the imbalance, the resulting change is sensed by the body and that in turn causes another response. In that way, information is continuously looped and adjustments are constantly made. When any feedback mechanism does not work properly, or when the systems are overwhelmed by constant stress, the imbalance causes illness or disease, such as dehydration and diabetes. Every system in the body contributes to homeostasis. ...The control of blood sugar is a great illustration of homeostasis. The amount of glucose (sugar) must be maintained within strict limits in the blood. When you eat candy, blood sugar goes up (a stress), the pancreas senses the change and immediately secretes insulin to remove the excess sugar. As the sugar level drops, the pancreas receives negative feedback and secretes glucagon to increase blood sugar. The continuous loop through the pancreas ensures the correct balance of blood sugar.'*[35]

INSULIN AND GLUCAGON
regulate blood glucose levels

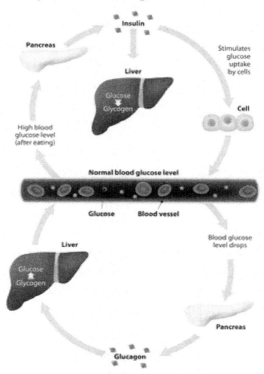

Figure 22.2 *Regulation of blood sugar.*

Thousands of biochemical reactions occur every day that are interrelated to maximise the wellbeing and minimise the destabilisation of our body. An imbalance in the homeostatic processes can lead to disease or even death. The set point of a single variable is fine-tuned by the frequent control of multiple systems. Extremely complex, these biological processes function in amazing relational, coordinated, maintenance and repairing aspects of a living system's integrated network.

The chemical basis of behaviour
Metabolism

Metabolism describes all chemical reactions involved in maintaining the living state of the cells and hence the organism. The human body must get the nourishment and energy it needs from ingested food and drink. Our metabolic processes convert the sugars, fats and proteins from the food into energy forms that our cells can use to needed to power everything we do. The metabolic process involve two kinds of activities that go on at the same time – the building up and the breaking down of energy stores and body tissues to generate more fuel for bodily functions:

Anabolism – The building and storing metabolic processes that supports the growth of new cells, the maintenance of body tissues, and the storage of energy for future use. During anabolism, small molecules are changed into larger, more complex molecules of carbohydrate, protein, and fat.

Catabolism – Comprises those processes that breakdown molecules to release the energy required for all activity in the cells. The (mostly) large carbohydrate and fat molecules are broken down into smaller molecules that can be further catalysed to generate energy for consumption in anabolic processes, heat the body and fuel muscles to contract and the body to move. The waste products released in the process of catabolism are removed from the body through the skin, kidneys, lungs and intestines.

Metabolism is a vital, complicated and constant chemical process; if it stops, then we die. The thousands of concurrent metabolic reactions are coordinated with other body functions to keep our cells healthy and working.

Specific proteins and several hormones of the endocrine system are involved in controlling the rate and direction of metabolism. The thyroid gland releases thyroxine, a hormone which has a key role in determining how fast or slow the chemical reactions of metabolism proceed in a person's body. The hormones of the thyroid gland have a general stimulating effect on metabolic rate. Another gland, the pancreas, releases the hormone insulin to regulate blood sugar levels, for example, after a eating a meal, the pancreas senses the increased level of blood sugar and releases insulin, which signals cells to increase their anabolic activities. Generally, the metabolism works effectively and automatically. But occasionally a metabolic disorder can cause serious medical problems:

Hypothyroidism – The under-functioning of the thyroid gland, resulting in reduced production of the thyroid hormones can consequently a depressed metabolic rate, making one feel tired, sluggish and gain weight.

Hyperthyroidism – The over-functioning of the thyroid gland, causing an increase in metabolic rate, so that the heart may race and you may feel jittery, irritabile and have trouble falling asleep. Severe anxiety and sometimes psychotic behaviour may be caused by hyperthyroidism.

Type 1 diabetes – The pancreas doesn't produce and secrete enough insulin, so blood sugar levels are erratic. Symptoms of this disease include excessive thirst and urination, hunger and weight loss. Over the long term, the disease can cause kidney problems, pain due to nerve damage, blindness, and heart and blood vessel disease.

Type 2 diabetes – This arises if the body can't respond normally to insulin requirements. The symptoms of this disorder are similar to those of type 1 diabetes.

Metabolism is closely linked to nutrition and the availability of nutrients. Food provides a variety of substances that are essential for the building, upkeep, and repair of body tissues, and for the efficient functioning of the body. Essential nutrients that we must acquire from our diet include:

Carbohydrates – Supplied in three forms: starch, sugar, and cellulose (fibre). Starches and sugars are the major and essential sources of energy for humans. Fibre contributes bulk to the diet. Body tissues depend on glucose for all activities. Carbohydrates and sugars yield glucose by digestion or metabolism.

Proteins – The main tissue builders in the body. Proteins are essential to (amongst other things) healthy cell structure, functions, haemoglobin formation to carry oxygen, enzymes to carry out vital reactions, and reproduction. Proteins are also vital in supplying nitrogen for DNA and RNA genetic material and energy production.

Fats – Concentrated sources of energy. They release twice the energy as either carbohydrates or proteins on a weight-by-weight basis. The functions of fats include helping to form the cellular structure, forming a protective cushion and insulation around vital organs helps absorb fat-soluble vitamins and provide reserve storage for energy.

Minerals – These do not contribute directly to energy needs but are important as body regulators and play a role in metabolic pathways of the body. More than 50 elements are found in the human body.

Vitamins – Vitamins play an important role in body chemistry generally, several being necessary for the activation of important enzymes (co-enzymes). Deficiency in thiamine, for example, causes disturbances in sleep, loss of appetite, lethargy and fatigue, while severe niacin deficiency is associated with similar symptoms and, in addition, impairment in memory, orientation and intellectual functioning generally (chronic brain syndrome).

Other important chemicals interacting with brain functions include:

Oxygen – All tissues of the human body depends upon a continuous supply of oxygen for normal functioning. In some tissues tolerance to reduced oxygen availability is low with irreversible changes occurring within a few minutes of oxygen deprivation. The giddiness and loss of critical ability, self-criticism and judgement seen in the test pilot with an inadequate accessory supply of oxygen at high altitudes are changes resulting from a small degree of hypoxia. In complete and sudden oxygen deprivation profound changes occur in mental functioning, which soon lead to irreversible changes and death within a very brief period.

Glucose – Normal brain function is dependent upon an adequate and continuous supply of glucose; slight hypoglycaemia from an overdose of insulin causes irritability, shows poor judgment and changes in mood. More profound hypoglycaemia results, within minutes, in loss of consciousness, deep coma and death.

Exercise physiology

In the past, strenuous physical activity was typically a way of life. People lived in an environment in which physical activities like walking, running, lifting, carrying, pushing, pulling, climbing and so on were necessary for accomplishing many everyday tasks throughout the year. But, with the advent of the sophisticated application of technology like automobiles, telephones, television, elevators, trains and washing machines, the amount of physical activity carried out on a daily basis per person has been greatly reduced. Instead, strenuous exercise has become reserved for planned leisure activities and sporting pursuits. The body, however, still responds to the physical stress in the same way as it always has. Robert Gerszten, Director of Translational Research in the cardiology division at Massachusetts General Hospital explained that, *'[...] how these effects occur is not entirely clear. Exercise physiology is surprisingly very poorly understood.'*[36]

Progressively, research is beginning to unravel the biochemical reactions that occur when a body participates in strenuous activity. Listed below are some of the known hormones and other signalling molecules that are released when a person exercises.

Blood chemistry

Regular exercise offers important benefits for our wellbeing, partly through altering blood chemistry. Firstly, exercise alters the body's physiology by increasing of the oxygen-carrying capacity of blood. This means an increased production of red blood cells and associated oxygen-carrying proteins (haemoglobin, myoglobin). In addition, the number of mitochondria (or energy-producing organelles of cells) will increase to handle the higher demand for energy. Blood sugar levels fluctuate as glucose is catabolised for energy. Next, the body will trigger a chain of chemical reactions to break down stored energy in the muscles, liver and adipose tissue. The release of the stored sugar will elevate glucose levels until they are depleted through activity. This helps to normalise our glucose, insulin and leptin levels by optimising insulin/leptin receptor sensitivity.

Brain chemicals

When performing (primarily) aerobic exercises (those requiring increased oxygen consumption), researchers at the Oregon Health and Science University found that increased stimulation of brain regions that are involved in memory function and an increase in the production of a neurotransmitter known as Brain-Derived Neurotrophic Factor (BDNF), which plays an important role in memory.[37] BDNF rewires memory circuits so they work better, thereby benefitting overall brain health. As BDNF levels increase, the growth rate of neurons in the hippocampus (thought to be the centre of emotion, memory and autonomic nervous system) increases as well. The increased production of BDNF is also thought to aid focus during sustained exercise, helping individuals to stay on-task and not get distracted by the world around them. *'When you exercise and move around, you are using more brain cells,'* says Dr. Ratey, who is also the author of *Spark: The Revolutionary New Science of Exercise and the Brain*, *'Using more brain cells turns on genes to make more BDNF.'*[38]

There are several other chemicals that are released by exercise, which can affect your mood, outlook and physical comfort level. These chemicals aid the brain in interpreting and transferring signals to and from the body, reducing pain and elevating moods naturally.

Hormones

When you move, your muscles release hormones. Some interesting hormones relating to physical activity include:

Irisin, or the 'Exercise Hormone' – Exercise causes this hormone to break off into your bloodstream and circulate throughout your body, hence its nickname of the 'exercise hormone.' The validity of irisin has generated controversy among scientists. However, 'Data unequivocally demonstrate that human irisin exists,' said study researcher Bruce M. Spiegelman, a Professor of Cell Biology and Medicine at Harvard Medical School.39 While the paper definitively confirms that irisin circulates and is altered with exercise in humans, the benefits are still unclear.

Testosterone – The primary male sex hormone secreted in the testicles that powers sex drive and fuels bones, hair and muscle growth. Following strenuous exercise, levels of testosterone rise for between fifteen minutes and one hour depending on age, fitness level and intensity of the exercise. The body uses circulating testosterone to build muscle mass.[40]

Oestrogen – Determines whether carbohydrates or fat fuel the body during an intense exercise session. Women tend to burn fat for fuel, while men tend to burn carbohydrates, because women have higher oestrogen levels.

Peptide YY/Ghrelin – A vigorous 60-minute workout on a treadmill affects the release of these two key appetite hormones. Ghrelin is the only hormone known to stimulate appetite (peptide YY is an appetite suppressant). While researchers aren't entirely sure how it happens, exercise does increase levels of peptide YY, which may make you less hungry after a workout. They found that the treadmill session (aerobic exercise) caused ghrelin levels to drop and peptide YY levels to rise, indicating the hormones were suppressing appetite.[41]

Endorphins – These block pain and cause feelings of exhilaration and happiness, allowing a person to power through any discomfort caused by exercising. Endorphins are produced by the hypothalamus and the pituitary gland during painful or stressful situations as well as during periods of excitement, including exercise, as a response to the physical stress of sustained physical activity. This results in enabling the body to exercise for longer periods without becoming fatigued or sore.

Serotonin – Responsible for happiness, restful sleep and a healthy appetite. Levels of this neurotransmitter will increase with regular exercise. Serotonin works with endorphins to make physical work a pleasurable activity. In addition, more serotonin means more energy and clearer thinking. Associated with mood, appetite and libido, individuals with high levels of serotonin tend to be happier and more upbeat compared with people with low serotonin levels.

Dopamine – A pleasure chemical. Low dopamine levels can lead to lack of motivation, fatigue, addictive behaviour, mood swings and memory loss. Some people who are low in dopamine compensate with unwholesome behaviours to get their dopamine boost. This can include abuse of caffeine, alcohol, sugar, drugs, shopping, video games, sex, power or gambling. Exercising can increase the amount of dopamine in certain regions of the brain, promoting positive wellbeing and even countering negative mental states. It's been shown that meditation can also increase dopamine levels, improving focus and concentration.[19] Hobbies of all kinds – knitting, quilting, sewing, drawing, photography, woodworking, home repair – bring the brain into a meditative state. These activities increase dopamine, ward off depression and protect against brain aging.

Growth factors – that work with satellite cells to help stimulate and regulate production of more muscle. Growth factors like hepatocyte, fibroblast and insulin send signals to the satellite cells to move to an area of damaged muscle following exercise to regulate reparative growth of muscle mass growth.[42]

The microbiome and its multiple roles: the gut-brain axis

All vertebrates have a symbiotic relationship with what is called gut microbiota.[43, 44] Surprisingly, cell by cell, we are mostly made up of bacteria. It is estimated that there are up to 100 times more bacteria than human cells in the human body, and most of them live in our gut. Biologists now believe that much of our wellbeing depends on microbial activity. At birth, the gut (our digestive tract or a portion thereof, especially the intestine or stomach) is sterile, but over time our gut develops a diverse and distinct variety of bacterial species, determined by genetics as well as by which bacteria live in us and those around us. In a human adult, the gut bacteria can weigh as much as five pounds, and they make up an organ of sorts, whose functions are only now being uncovered.

The Human Microbiome Project, coordinated by the US National Institutes of Health (NIH),[45, 46] estimates that a normal adult's gut consists of 100 trillion microbes. Collectively they are known as the microbiome. According to the NIH, the microbiome interacts with and influences organ systems throughout the body, including neural development, brain chemistry and a wide range of other phenomena, such as emotional behaviour, pain perception and stress responses. For example, the brain can have a strong influence on the microbiome – mild cognitive stress reactions can change the microbial balance from beneficial to disease-causing bacteria, making us more vulnerable to infections and triggering a cascade of molecular reactions that feed back to the central nervous system. Although research into how the microbiome affects psychological wellbeing in humans is still relatively new, gastroenterologist Premysl Bercik, MD says, *'[...] data suggest that bacteria can have profound effects on behavior and brain biochemistry, probably through multiple pathways.'*[47]

For example, there is evidence of bacterial translocation (or 'leaky gut') being associated with approximately 35% of people with depression.[48] Our digestive system is normally surrounded by an impermeable wall of cells. However, certain behaviours and medical conditions can compromise this wall, allowing toxic substances and bacteria to enter our bloodstream. While there is not yet a lot known about this syndrome, it is generally recognised by physicians to exist. There are numerous possible causes of this condition including the regular use of painkillers or antibiotics; infections (such as HIV); autoimmune disorders; alcohol abuse; inflammatory bowel disease; other inflammatory disorders; gluten hypersensitivity; severe food allergies; radiation therapy; psychological stress or exhaustion.

Demonstrating the significance of the microbiome gut-brain axis, Bercik and colleagues reported having completely changed the behaviour of a species of mice by giving them a mixture of antibiotics that significantly changed the composition of their gut bacteria.[48] The mice changed from being normally timid and shy, to bold and adventurous. Bercik went on to report that the antibiotic mixture also boosted levels of a BDNF in the hippocampus. When the antibiotic mixture was stopped, the animals soon reverted to their usual, timid behaviour, and their brain biochemistry also returned to as it was prior to treatment.

The ecosystem of the microbiome is also intimately entwined with our immune, endocrine and nervous systems. Furthermore, it is crucially linked to the brain – our diet and gut bacteria influence our behaviour, thoughts and mood: '*Scientists are increasingly convinced that the vast assemblage of microfauna in our intestines may have a major impact on our state of mind.*'[49] Not only does the microbiome affect brain biochemistry, stress responses and behaviour, it also produces many neurochemicals that the brain uses to regulate basic physiological processes as well as mental processes such as learning, memory and mood. For example, Dr. Siri Carpenter estimates that gut bacteria manufacture about 95% of the body's supply of serotonin, which influences both mood and gastrointestinal (GI) activity.[48] Similarly, Lyte, proposes a neurochemical, 'Delivery system' by which gut bacteria, such as probiotics, can send messages to the brain.[50]

Gut bacteria both produce and respond to the same neuro-chemicals – such as gamma-aminobutyric acid (GABA), serotonin, norepinephrine, dopamine, acetylcholine and melatonin – that the brain uses to regulate mood and cognitive processes. Such neurochemicals probably allow the brain to tune its behaviour to the feedback it receives from the mass of bacteria in the gut. Recognising that communication between the brain and the gut is bidirectional also points to the possibility that keeping anxiety and depression under control, may improve inflammation in the gut, and vice versa: treating inflammation in the gut may improve mood by altering brain biochemistry.[51,52] The microbiome is often referred to as the 'second brain', as it is the only organ to have its own independent nervous system – an intricate network of 100 million neurons embedded in the gut wall, which can continue to function even when the primary neural conduit between it and the brain, the vagus nerve, is severed. With the microbiome's multifaceted ability to communicate with the brain, along with its immune function, *'It's almost unthinkable that the gut is not playing a critical role in mind states.'*[48]

Dr. Katrin Andreasson, Professor of Neurology at University of Stanford, has been investigating the role of microglia and the brain's immune cells in Alzheimer's disease. Her work suggests that the prodromal stage of Alzheimer's disease involves an inflammatory response; a particular receptor, EP2, may predispose individuals to developing the condition.[53] In mouse models of Alzheimer'sdisease, EP2 increases inflammation, suppresses microglial function and allows the protein amyloid to build up. Inhibiting EP2 restores healthy microglial function. In the mouse model, removing the EP2 receptor decreased inflammation and the amount of amyloid present, and restored memory. Inflammation can be kept down in other ways that might help prevent or delay Alzheimer's, such as a healthy diet low in sugars and fats, exercising and getting enough sleep help.[48]

Research has confirmed that the microbes common to the human gut can affect our thoughts and feelings. For example, in adequate amounts, probiotics are thought to be fundamental in improving digestion and immune responses. One study found that compared with individuals who received a placebo intervention; participants who received a multispecies probiotics intervention demonstrated significantly reduced ruminative thoughts.

> *'Even if preliminary, these results provide the first evidence that the intake of probiotics may help reduce negative thoughts associated with sad mood. As such, our findings shed an interesting new light on the potential of probiotics to serve as adjuvant or preventive therapy for depression.'*[54]

The research into understanding the role of the microbiome in relation to human emotions and behaviours has become very compelling. Exploring functions and mechanisms of the human body as part of a whole, interdependent, dynamic system is far more accurate than trying to understand it as comprised of individual independent systems.

Epigenetics: a new insight to biology

Another fascinating and important new branch in biology is epigenetics, or the study of changes in gene activity which are not caused by changes in the DNA sequence. Environmental influences, including nutrition, stress, and emotions can modify genes without changing the sequence of nucleotides (A, T, C, and G – the four-letter alphabet of DNA).

The epigenome (chemical compounds that modify, or mark, the genome in a way that tells it what to do, where to do it, and when to do it) refers to the overall state of a cell, and works as an interface between the environment and the genome. So at its most basic, epigenetics is the study of chemical mechanisms that modify gene activity (turning genes on and off, like a light switch or switching genes to operate in a detrimental way) but does involve any alteration to the genetic code; instead, they affect how cells 'read' the genes. However, the changes can still be passed down to at least one successive generation.[55]

As an example, epigenetics studies the reason why a skin cell looks different from a brain cell or a muscle cell. All three cells contain the same DNA, but their genes are turned 'on' or 'off' differently, which creates the different cell types. So in other words, epigenetics studies the factors that cause the body's genes to turn off or turn on by exploring the effects of the physical, social and electromagnetic environment on our cells' actions. Preetha Anand suspects that only 5–10% of all cancer cases can be attributed to genetic defects, whereas the remaining 90–95% have their roots in environmentally-induced epigenetic alterations.[56] What we eat, where we live, who we interact with, when we sleep, how we exercise, even aging – all of these factors can cause chemical modifications in our genome. As biochemist Mae Wan Ho stated:

> '*As regards implications for social policies, we already have a great deal of knowledge on how social deprivation, psychological stress, and environmental toxins can have dire effects on us and our still unborn children and grandchildren while social enrichment, caring environments and cognitive and physical exercises, and stress reducing mind-body techniques can have beneficial effects on infants, children and adults alike. The implications on the appropriate interventions for health, education and social wellbeing are clear.*'[57]

So, while it seems we cannot control approximately 30% of our genetic makeup, we can control about 70%.

The study of epigenetics proves that there is a strong correlation between our life environment and our health, not only in our generation, but in the lives of future generations. It was previously thought that an embryo's epigenome was completely new, basically created from scratch, but this isn't completely true. Some epigenetic changes do pass from generation to generation (epigenetic inheritance). Early in an embryo's development, most signals come from within cells or from neighbouring cells. As cells grow and divide, they faithfully copy epigenetic tags along with the DNA. This is especially important during embryonic development, as past experiences inform future choices. A cell must first know that it is an eye cell before it can decide whether to become part of the lens or the cornea. The epigenome enables cells to remember their past experiences long after the signals fade away. The mother's nutrition is important at this stage in the development of the foetus. Other types of signals, such as stress hormones, can also travel from mother to foetus. In infancy, a wider range of environmental factors begin to shape the epigenome. Social interactions, physical activity, diet and other inputs generate signals that travel from cell to cell throughout the body.

Signals from within the body continue to play an important role for many processes, including physical growth, development and learning, throughout our lifetime. Environmental signals allow cells to respond dynamically to the outside world while internal signals direct body maintenance, such as replenishing blood cells and skin, and repairing damaged tissues and organs. During these processes the cell's experiences are transferred to the epigenome, where they shut down and/or activate specific sets of genes.

Examples of inherited epigenetic changes have been shown by experiments with rat models, which were exposed to a crop fungicide that can cause susceptibility to cancer. Epigenetic defects were transferred to the offspring through gene changes.[57] Similarly, research has shown that when mice are given cocaine, the memory problems they develop are passed on to three generations of descendants because of epigenetic changes.[55] Through these and other studies, scientists are rethinking the way in which organisms have evolved and how traits are passed on from parent to child.

Psychoneuroimmunology

'The mind and body are dependent on each other the way two sheaves stand up by leaning against each other.'

Samyutta Nikaya (2.14)

Psychoneuroimmunology (PNI) studies the complex and intimate communications, interactions and regulation among our psychological processes, behaviours, central nervous system (CNS), immune system and the endocrine system. A pioneer of this growing branch of research, Dr. Robert Ader states, *'Its [PNI] central premise is that homeostasis is an integrated process involving interactions among behavior and the nervous, endocrine, and immune systems.'*[58] PNI is increasingly showing how changes in a person's mental or emotional state can modify the molecular profile of his or her immune or hormonal system, and thus affect the whole body.[59] Neuroscientist Candace Pert, credited with discovering the opiate receptor, demonstrated in her research that emotions regulate what you experience as reality. We all know the experience of the world and even our 'self' seems better when one is emotionally feeling good.[27,2]

Contemporary imaging machines have been employed to study the link between pain and the processing of pain by the body.[60] The pain experience is complex and involves sensory, cognitive and emotional components, which depend on bi-directional communication with the spinal cord. One study provided evidence that explicitly presented pain-related words lead to activations within regions of the brain's pain matrix (comprising parts of brainstem, hypothalamus, thalamus, amigdala and areas of the cerebral cortex). It showed that pain-related verbal stimuli create non-specific responses, induced by the affective quality of stimuli, but also according to the attention afforded to the tasks. When tasks involved imagination, the specificity of pain-related words is reflected in the activation of regions associated with the cognitive dimension of pain, such as the dorsolateral prefrontal cortex (DLPFC) and the inferior patietal gyri (or IPG). The findings suggest that the perception of pain-related words changes the central nervous processing that is associated with the cognitive dimension of pain. These changes may alter the processing of acute and chronic pain sensations through associative learning, as the basis for verbal priming effects.[61]

The effectiveness of music in pain reduction has been demonstrated over a wide diversity of clinical populations.[60] Whilst there has been extensive research showing that music-induced analgesia can reduce stress, depression and distress in people with acute and chronic pain, neuroscientist Christine Dobek's research showed observable changes in neural function in the entire CNS in response to changes in pain perception related to music analgesia. [60] Different responses to music stimuli were found within regions known for descending modulation, and familiar classical music had a unique effect on neural activity in these regions compared with unpleasant music, reverse music and no music. Dr. Dobek's study confirmed that the emotional attractiveness of music affects neural activity in the brainstem and spinal cord. Music-induced analgesia seems to work by evoking a rewarding response in the brain that activates the descending analgesia system, indicating therefore that music is processed in various areas distributed throughout the brain including limbic areas, cortical regions and reward-related mesolimbic circuits. Dopamine mediates the mesocortical and mesolimbic circuits to (potentially) trigger opoid release in the nucleus accumbens (NAc) whilst listening to music. When a pleasurable experience, music can have a positive affective impact on an individual.

The stress phenomenon

An important focus of PNI is the complexity of the stress phenomenon and its potentially harmful influence on the body. In fact, any belief that there isn't an intimate interaction between physical and psychological stressors is a misconception. The stress response typically expresses itself in two main ways. Firstly, the endocrine pathway causes the secretion of several stress hormones, including corticotropin-releasing hormone (CRH), adrenocorticotropic hormone (ACTH) and cortisol.[62] It is well known that cortisol has a potent and wide-ranging effect on many organs. After being secreted, cortisol is distributed throughout the body via the bloodstream. While a single, brief, episodic spike in cortisol levels does not create a problem, issues may arise if levels are elevated repeatedly or over a prolonged period of time; unchecked either because r of continued exposure to aggravating conditions or a lack of effective intervention to minimise the reactions.[62] If left unchecked, these chemicals can devastate the body's homeostatic balance because they can change the surface receptors present on cells, which then only allows a very specific peptide or chemical, that was perhaps never intended to bind to the cell, to do so, thereby altering the cell's chemistry or affecting gene expression. Secondly, the autonomic pathway (which involves the activation of the sympathetic nervous system that stimulates the adrenal gland to secrete adrenaline) may be affected. Adrenaline, like cortisol, has a large number of effects on several body systems, one example being that persistent adrenal surges can damage blood vessels and arteries, raising blood pressure and increasing the risk of heart attacks or strokes.

Chronic stress

The brain and bodily systems can't differentiate between an actual and an imaginary threat. The physiological changes that follow a perceived stress event (and hence the response), if not quickly stabilised in the short term, can have a high price if it becomes chronic. Chronic stress not only results from long-term, repeated exposure to a specific stressor, but can also be caused by negative emotional ruminations about the past. Even perseverative toxic thoughts and emotions create stress reactions that can wreak havoc on homeostatic imbalances in one's mind and body.[63] Various studies have demonstrated that the operational capacity and functioning of the brain is lower in stressed than in non-stressed animals.[64] In addition, it has been found that in response to long-term stress responses, the branching dendrites, where much of the brain's information and memories are stored, decrease in size and in volume.[65] Researchers speculate that this is why some people have perseverative, or difficulty, in inhibiting the long-term stress response and also why many chronically stressed people suppose they have a poor memory.[65]

Another way of describing this condition is provided by the Gestalt Therapy proponents. If the organism's needs or sensibilities remain in an unfinished, unresolved situation, in the Perls/Goodman theory, the organism will keep on trying to resolve the unresolved contact, either through action or rumination, especially if the motivating drive is deemed essential and the organism is very young. Instead of giving up on its needs, the organism will take emergency measures delay any unfavourable resolution or consolation. Too much time spent putting the organic needs on hold can turn the unresolved situation (original stress situation) into a chronic stress emergency making not only musculo-skeletal rigidity and other physiological reactions in the organism but also a reduction in the overall energy available for making new contact and spontaneous creative adjustment. If the organism's needs continue to go unmet, the chronic emergency becomes the new normal and eventually passes out of awareness, although still withdrawing energy and lessening the quality of awareness and contact with the internal as well as external environment.

Chronic stress, by causing a negative mind-body interaction, is considered a significant risk factor for many disease processes because the response weakens the immune system's ability to fight infection. The negative effect on the immune system owing to repeated activation of the stress response eventually takes its toll on the body. Prolonged stress contributes to high blood pressure, promotes the formation of artery-clogging atherosclerotic plaques, infection and pain, as well as causing brain changes that may contribute to anxiety, depression and addiction.[66] Chronic stress may also contribute to obesity, both through direct mechanisms (causing people to eat more) or indirectly (decreasing sleep and exercise) and numerous other problems.[67] Therefore reducing chronic can boost the immune system, enhance wellbeing and reduce overall morbidity and mortality risk.

As more of the information about the interactions between our bodily systems is being elucidated, a bidirectional interacting set of processes (immune system interacting with the nervous system), each regulating the other for healthy or unhealthy results, is becoming clear. Summarised in Appendix 1 are the numerous specific effects that stress has on the body, as reported by the American Psychological Association.[66]

The placebo effect on stress

To further appreciate the two-way process between the relationship of mind and body, the placebo phenomenon must be acknowledged. The placebo effect is a curious aspect of healing. A placebo is a sugar pill or other non-active prescription, which lets the patient believe that he or she is being treated medically, and while it is difficult to measure, some physicians believe that up to one-third of all patients improve after taking a placebo. In fact, there is wide consensus as to the helpfulness of the placebo effect as medical and surgical treatment, as well as controlled short-term clinical trials of antidepressants.

Some studies suggest that the placebo effect triggers an increase in the body's production of endorphins, one of the body's natural pain relievers.[68] Also, reported in a study by Helen S. Mayberg and colleagues, there is an increased metabolism in the posterior cingulated, which is probably an early indicator of the brain's compensatory capacity in response to a placebo response.[69] This increase in metabolism is comparable to that measured in the posterior cingulate midway through a twelve-week course of interpersonal psychotherapy.[70] As the basic concept of PNI hypothesises that the mind and body are inseparable, it seems logical that the power of suggestion will have an effect either way.

Expectation seems to play a potent role in the placebo effect. Researchers believe there is a relationship between how strongly a person expects the placebo to have an effect and whether or not results occur. The stronger the feeling, the more likely it is that a person will experience positive results. Likewise, if people expect to have negative side effects such as headaches, nausea or drowsiness, there is a greater chance of those reactions happening.[80]

Scientists have recorded brain activity in response to receiving a placebo and have shown that, for example, when participants are told they have taken a stimulant, their pulse rate speeds up, blood pressure increases and reaction times improve. The placebo effect appears to be part of a human potential to be relieved by something for which there is no apparent medical basis just by reacting positively to a 'healer'. Since, the brain seems to respond to an imagined scene much as it would to something it actually sees, a placebo may help the brain go back and remember a time before current physical or psychological symptoms and produce certain physical chemical changes. This is called Remembered Wellness.[81]

When directed in a constructive path, the positive placebo is an illustration of the therapeutic potential of the mind-body relationship. With a wholesome mindset, a person can enhance the immune function and improve his or her mind-body condition. The Buddha tells us that with a wholesome, serene mindset, happiness will follow, *'If a man speaks or acts with a pure mind, happiness follows him, like a shadow that never leaves him.'*

The immune system: neuroimmunology

Neuroimmunology describes the study of the interrelationship between the nervous and immune systems. A discovery made by a team of researchers from the University of Virginia (UVA), *'may call for a reassessment of basic assumptions in neuroimmunology.'*[82] They found a direct link between the brain and the immune system via lymphatic vessels that were not previously known to exist. As blood vessels carry blood around the body, lymphatic vessels carry immune cells throughout the body.

It's becoming increasingly clear that our brain, our immune system and our gut microbes are intricately linked. Autism, for instance, may be associated with gastrointestinal problems and a potential over-reaction in the immune system. Jonathan Kipnis, a professor at UVA's Department of Neurosciences and the director of UVA's Centre for Brain Immunology, reported:

> 'Moreover, neurological diseases like multiple sclerosis and Alzheimer's have long been linked to changes in immune system function, and autoimmune diseases of the gut, like Crohn's disease, correlate with psychiatric illness.'[82]

It hasn't always been clear how such connections arise, but now both a gut-brain axis and a link between the immune system and brain have been more clearly shown. Kipnis emphasised the importance of this discovery:

> 'We believe that for every neurological disease that has an immune component to it, these vessels may play a major role. Hard to imagine that these vessels would not be involved in a [neurological] disease with an immune component...In Alzheimer's [for example], there are accumulations of big protein chunks in the brain. We think they may be accumulating in the brain because they're not being efficiently removed by these vessels.' And, 'Careful studies have shown that the brain does interact with the peripheral immune system, albeit in unique ways. Immune cells do, somehow, circulate through the brain, and antigens – which would normally stoke an immune response – do drain from the brain into the lymph nodes.'[82]

The immune system as an ecological system

Professor Alfred I. Tauber has cogently proposed that contrary to what is popularly thought about the immune system (that it operates solely in the defensive role of immunity against pathogens, allergens or toxins), it does, in fact, operate and cooperate with so-called 'foreign' visitors to the body. Tauber states that from an ecological perspective, we, as individual organisms, actually live in a community of others that contribute to our welfare.[83] So when we think about our immune system in a larger context, it should include how our internal and the external environments sense and act upon each other and allow a free exchange between our 'host' environment and the external environment.

There is a growing body of evidence that the immune system isn't a passive system just waiting to react to outside threats, but a highly proactive system that changes in response to external cues, such as from the physical environment and social behaviour. Psychologist Robert Ader echoed the same belief when he stated:

> *'Together, behavioral, neural, endocrine, and immune processes of adaptation constitute an integrated network of defences and, insofar as immuno-regulatory processes are concerned, the assumption of an autonomous immune system is no longer tenable. It is not possible to obtain a full understanding of immune regulatory processes without considering the organism and the internal and external environment in which immune responses take place.'[84]*

In short, our immune system uses many different pathways to communicate with and activate numerous interactions between our bodies and the external environment. The immune system possesses 'cognitive' functions too, in that it 'knows' how to recognise healthy versus harmful visitors, and it has a certain intentionality, or volition, to react in the appropriate way to nullify any dangerous substances.

From the point of view of the immune system (in the larger context of our whole organism), there is no isolated, circumscribed, static, rigidly self-defined identity designated as 'the self'. Accordingly, 'self/non-self' separation recedes as a governing principle, even with immunity, when it is appreciated as both outer-directed against the deleterious and inner-directed in an on-going communicative system of internal homeostasis. From this dual perspective, immune function falls on a continuum of reactivity, where the character of the immune object is determined by the context in which it appears, not by its character as other *per se*. Tauber asserts that more simplistic models have too often obscured this cardinal lesson and writes, '*The "me" (or "I") serves as the variable linguistic label of a function of possessive identity, which in the translation of Freud's das Ich has been forever called (inaccurately) "the ego"*.'[85]

Neurobiology

'The mind is the basis for everything.

Everything is created by my mind, and is ruled by my mind.

When I speak or act with impure thoughts, suffering follows me

As the wheel of the cart follows the hoof of the ox.

The mind is the basis for everything.

Everything is created by my mind, and is ruled by my mind.

When I speak or act with a clear awareness, happiness stays with me.

Like my own shadow, it is unshakeable.'

Dhammapada 1-2

As the Buddha pointed out, if we're looking for happiness or fulfilment, the place to look for it is inside. While there is a continuing heated debate in neurobiology about the relationship between thoughts and the brain, Rick Hanson, Ph.D., a psychologist, wrote an insightful article called, 'Mind Changing Brain Changing Mind' (www.rickhanson.net). In this, he summarises several important, accepted facts, which provide the basis for understanding the biological processes that accompany meditation; and the importance for a disciplined Bhavana or mind-culture practitioner to attain wholesome results on the journey for mental purification. Recognising how our thoughts influence the structure of our brain, and *vice versa*, as well as how our cognitive construction of a 'self' are only a creation of our neural networks, is very instructive and can support us on our journey to Enlightenment.

Research in the field of neuroplasticity is beginning to clarify the circular, interdependent relationship between the brain and the mind. It has been found that changes in behaviour, environment, neural processes, thinking and emotions – as well as changes resulting from bodily injury – bring about significant changes in neural pathways and synapses. The citta, or mind, also alters both the brain's physical structure and functional organisation – as your brain physically changes your mind changes, and as your mind changes, your brain changes. In his article, Hanson defines mind as being, *'The flow of information through the nervous system, most of which is forever unconscious'*.

When some of those neurons make connections and become more sensitive to stimulation, this networking builds structure in the brain and those changes become stable. As the synaptic connections strengthen in response to the increased activity and new synapses form, then that specific region of the brain becomes increasingly more active, receives increased blood flow, more glucose, more oxygen, and grows.

Through meditation and other concentrated thought processes, we can use our mind to build neural structures and increase particular regions of the brain's mass. This increase in our brain's specific cortical layers can be highly beneficial in developing our ability to hold onto positive, wholesome and skilful mental states. The more we practice, the stronger the integration and coherence that develops within the brain.

Within the vast networks of the brain, the anterior cingulate cortex (ACC) has been found to be the area that manages what is called 'effortful attention', or paying attention in a deliberate way. For example, when we practise the four foundations of mindfulness, we use the ACC; performing metta (compassion meditation), where we integrate our thoughts and feelings together, stimulates the ACC and, therefore, strengthens it by firing and wiring those particular neural networks. The region can also increase in mass depending on the amount it's used through meditation. Meditation also strengthens another region of the brain called the insula, which supports us in our ability to become more empathic with others.[87]

Research has indicated that the deep, non-conscious structure of the brain is actually the most significantly active when thoughts surface. When you observe your thoughts, you can see the outer signs of neural activity by watching them emerge, display and then disperse.

Interestingly, after a thought but just before a new thought forms, there's an 'empty' quiet moment, where structure hasn't yet congealed. This can be a productive meditation practice of staying with the empty moment and even trying to expand it. Increasing the time spent in that quiet space, before any neural assemblies take form, is an instructive process along the path to Awakening.

Once a representation has formed and become fully established in our mind – an image, an emotion, a view, a thought – then that representation is captured. The representation can quickly become identified as a subject and as an aspect of our 'self'. Once we identify with the image, it becomes difficult to un-identify with. So while these identified aspects of 'self' arise as impermanent mental objects, they easily can become stable patterns of neural and mental activity because we treasure, hence, strengthen those particular patterns above any others. Nevertheless, even these images related to 'self' are just neural patterns of the mind in the brain, not qualitatively different from other neural patterns that may be triggering us to run or breathe or eat. Even though these patterns exist, they're impermanent, dependently arisen and mere constructions of our brain's cognitive apparatus. Yet the neural activity of 'self' construction is very powerful because through our subject-object separation, we continually claim ownership of experiences, claim agency of actions, and claim identification with both internal states and external objects (like our new car or sports team). But actually, executive functions such as organising and planning, or agency action, can operate without any 'self' present. In fact, for most of the time a 'self' is irrelevant to our functioning in the world and how we are feeling.

While the 'self' seems real and substantial, it helps our non-identification practice to remember that it is only evolving and impermanent patterns in the mind and brain. The 'self' exists in the way that memory allows it to exist, and like all physical biological processes, memories are transient, illusionary, and it therefore is foolish to cling to them. To quote Hanson:

> 'Whatever of self there is in the brain, it is compounded and distributed, not coherent and unified; it is variable and transient, not stable and enduring. In other words, the conventional notion of self is a mythical creature.'

As we grow to understand that the representations of 'self' are only fictional, and what they represent does not substantially exist, we can then start taking our 'self', 'with a pinch of salt' (as the expression goes), that is, not to take ourselves so literally. For us to do that – and this is a revolutionary discovery and very important in our understanding – our minds need to be trained with some long-term disciplined practice. The more we study how our mind and brain are intertwined, the better we can learn how to use the mind to change the brain, which will then support the development of our future mind. Neuropsychology supports the idea that we have the freedom and possibility to condition and create our particular mind states, which are supported by our nurtured brain structures.

After the gradual transformation and ripening to maturation of our habits, latent tendencies, non-identification with the subjective ownership of experience, calming and stabilising our physiology and behaviour in our life patterns, we no longer respond immaturely or egotistically to our desires and aversions. This doesn't mean that we become emotionless and detached automatons, but rather that we develop the perspective and ability to remain stable, balanced and unsusceptible to the quirky ups and downs of our immature, selfish emotions. Even for the most accomplished meditation practitioner, strong emotions can arise, but when they do they are observed with the acceptance and objectivity of mindfulness and the stability of equanimity. Emotions may have an impact, but it is only momentarily, before the stability of calm and dispassion evaporate them away.

Through the transformative process, there becomes a greater awareness and respect for our body, serenity of the emotions, increased kindness of the heart, flexible and realistic attitudes. More genuine human relationships grow out of a deeper awareness of our affinity with the web of life and there is a relinquishing of the Great Poisons of greed, anger and ignorance. We learn not only how to proceed anew, but also, importantly, what we can do without. Through a clearer understanding and acceptance of our shortcomings and the extent of our unwholesome tendencies, we learn an ever-greater sense of humility that the path to regaining our original mind state will take time, personal effort and commitment to the journey.

In the end, an Arahant can be described with two words: simple and stable. For they have come to value their present moment, their elementary life experiences; life as it is, not as a construction of what it should be. The cravings, identifications and 'self' enhancements are no longer potent forces in one's life. Instead, in the simplicity of everyday existence, we can actively participate in the creation of our now; carefully, with creativity, sensitivity and forethought, we enact our actions to interact wholesomely in the medium of life. We are artists and life becomes our art form. We act and respond and modify as the forms created through our interactions with life are constantly changing. We and our medium of interaction grow and transform, by degrees, as a result of our learning using insightful awareness in all aspects our life.

Body electric

Our body is capable of generating electricity, and this ability is actually a key part of our achieving health. In fact, everything we do is controlled and enabled by electrical signals running through our bodies. Electricity allows our nervous system to send signals to our brain. These signals are actually electrical charges that deliver nearly instantaneous communication. The messages conducted via electrical signals in our body are responsible for controlling the rhythm of our heartbeat, the movement of blood around our body, and much more. Our biological clock even uses electrical activity in order to help keep our circadian rhythms in order. We are electrical beings. Since much relies on electrical signals, any breakdown in our body's electrical system is a real problem. For example, when you get an electric shock, it interrupts the normal operation of the system, like a power surge. But how, exactly, does this electrical activity take place?

We can generate electricity since our bodies are huge masses of atoms, with protons positive charge, neutrons neutral charge and electrons negative charge, and there is a flow of electrons. When we say the nervous system sending 'signals' to the brain, or synapses 'firing,' and so on, what we're talking about is electricity carrying nearly instantaneous messages between point A and point B. The crucial signals that tell our heart to speed up when we're in danger come from a mass of cells in our heart called the sinoatrial node, or SA node. It is located in the right atrium, and controls the rhythm of our heartbeat and the movement of blood from the heart to every other part of our body. It's our body's natural pacemaker, and it uses electrical signals to set the pace.

But our pulse isn't the only thing that relies on electrical impulses. Almost all of our cells are capable of generating electricity. Negativity is the natural resting state of your cells. It's related to a slight imbalance between potassium and sodium ions inside and outside the cell, and this imbalance sets the stage for your electrical capacity. It's also how the SA node tells your heart muscles to contract, how your eyes tell your brain that what they just read is the word 'brain', and how you are comprehending this article at all. Your brain is the hub of your nervous system. It is made up of 100 billion nerve cells. Each cell is connected to around 10,000 others. So the total number of connections in your brain is about 1000 trillion. Your brain is comprised of a tight network of nerve cells, all interacting with one another and generating an overall electrical field. This electric field is detectable with standard medical equipment like an electroencephalogram (EEG). We can generate only between 10 and 100 millivolts.

Not only your brain, but our entire body has an electric field. Anywhere there's a nerve cell, there's electricity and it's concentrated the greatest around your head because that's where the bulk of your nerve cells are. Any time you've felt the shock of static electricity, or used a touch-sensitive screen, you've understood that you have an electric field. Being an electric field, all those overlying electric vibration patterns that comprise your brain waves are governed by the same equations governing the electromagnetic spectrum, light, particles and everything else in the universe. Your thoughts are formed in this electric field. The measurable perturbations and disturbances in the brain's overall electric field are your actual thoughts racing through your mind. The thoughts you are thinking of, the words your mind is processing, are all electrical impulses that can be measured if you had a few wires hooked up between your head and a machine.

So thoughts are energy, the same as everything else.

Since we are conscious, we can choose what part of the noise around us to be affected by, and how we in turn would like to affect it. Some even hypothesise that the higher the frequency of our thought/brain wave vibration/rhythm, the higher our consciousness. For example, stuck, immobile low-frequency thought vibrations create depression, while active, dynamic faster brain vibration patterns create happiness and engagement with the world. From this hypothesis, our level of our mind's vibration/rhythm is how we create our reality and how it may continue to be.

The electrodynamics of health

> 'Most of the fields surrounding the cells and us are invisible, but their effects are not. It is time to look for them as this regards our understanding about ourselves.'

Dr. Daniel Fels

> 'There is a strong evidence that EMFs and radio/microwave frequencies are associated with accelerated aging (enhanced cell death and cancer) and moods, depression, suicide, anger, rage and violence, primarily through alteration of cellular calcium ions and the melatonin/serotonin balance.'

Dr. Neil Cherry of Lincoln University, New Zealand

The human body as a complex energetic system

Science now confirms that in addition to biochemical processes, the body is suffused by a quantum electrodynamics field, interacting on many levels of subtle energy, patterns and significance. Our bodies are networks of complex energy fields that interact with the physical and cellular systems, and as with the physical systems, the quantum electrodynamics fields are powerfully affected by emotions, thoughts, nutrition and environmental factors. There is a hierarchy of subtle energy systems that coordinate electrophysiological and hormonal functions as well as cellular structure within the body. In this model, consciousness is an energetic form that is closely related to the cellular expression of the physical body and continually influencing health or illness. In turn, disease states may arise when energy systems are out of balance, therefore any rebalancing, reorganising, and resetting of the body's energy fields helps regulate cellular physiology and restore optimal functioning.

As indicated by Pokorný, a fundamentally disturbed electrodynamics field characterises cancer cells:

> *'Mitochondrial dysfunction (that develops before the appearance of the cancer malignant properties) and diminished power and coherence of the electrodynamics field may be the most pronounced differences between the healthy and the cancer cells in the clinical phase.'*[88]

Furthermore, Pokorný asserts that high-capacity information transfer between the body organs and the brain may be mediated by the electromagnetic field. In general, the human bio-energy field is proposed to have a magnetic structure, which directs atomic particles to their correct function in the body and controls all information transfer or communication between cells and organs. This is the body's master control system; it ultimately determines our chemistry, metabolism and cell structure. And if our body's field pattern and cellular instructions are wrong, then the result is often ill health. Whilst there are numerous reports stating that electromagnetic fields are too weak to cause burns but are linked to cancers and other illnesses, such as leukaemia.[89, 90] These hypotheses are often dismissed because of a presumed absence of 'possible biological mechanisms' to account for the illnesses. Pokorný's model, however, represents a valuable source to understand the sensitivity of organisms to weak electromagnetic fields, and much more: that the electromagnetic processes in living cells, the interaction inside and among cells is mediated by an electrodynamics field and supports the development of a non-linear quantum theory for biological systems.

Organisms are thought to be excitable, open, non-equilibrated energy systems, which can produce exaggerated, large effects, even under the slightest provocation. All living processes are highly dynamic and unpredictable and it is impossible to forecast with certainty how the system will develop. This unpredictability (also defined in physics as non-linearity of a system) is perfectly described in the 'butterfly effect', in which it is said that a proverbial butterfly flapping its wings in the Amazon rainforest could affect the weather in New York. Living processes must have an overall stability to be dynamic systems – ever changing to meet and adjust to new internal and external environmental demands and swinging between different quasi-periodic states. But, at the same time, these processes are not at all random. The healthy heartbeat, the electrical activities of the brain, the nervous system, all exhibit chaotic dynamical behaviour, characterised in physics by an extreme sensitivity to the initial conditions, and when modified, even slightly, they cause unpredictable changes in the system, as indicated by Chaos theory.[91]

Yet the hypothesis of the existence and functionality of electrodynamics fields is not new. In the 1930s, American biologist Harold Saxton Burr[92] proposed that all living organisms are moulded and controlled by electrodynamics. Then, in the beginning of the 1950s, a researcher named Becker[89] showed that all organisms' bodies have a Direct Current (DC) field, and that electric currents produced throughout the body are involved in controlling growth and regeneration. These fields are in addition to the accepted knowledge of the electrical activities of the brain and heart. Becker further proposed in the 1960s that an electrical communication system exists within all living things. As the body uses electromagnetic signals of different frequencies and to different extents to intercommunicate, it would be surprising if external electromagnetic fields did not have an effect. It is becomingly increasingly evident that electrodynamics and electric currents are involved in intercommunication throughout the body and that weak magnetic fields are generated as a result.[89]

Effects of electromagnetic fields on the body

Recently, there has been an increase in radiofrequency (RF) exposure from wireless devices as well as reports of hypersensitivity and diseases related to electromagnetic field (EMF) and RF exposure. In fact, the American Academy of Environmental Medicine (AAEM) has documented numerous studies showing this exposure has adverse effects on health with diseases such as cancer, neurological diseases, reproductive disorders, immune dysfunctions and electromagnetic hypersensitivity because these new, yet pervasive and powerful devices invariably interfere with the electromagnetic signals that support and organise life.[93]

It is well known that long-range EMF or RF forces can act over large distances to set a biological system oscillating in phase with the frequency of the electromagnetic field. Even passive resonant circuits can imprint potentially long-lasting effects of a frequency imprint into water and biological systems. RF exposure causing changes associated with degenerative neurological diseases such as Alzheimer's, Parkinson's and Amyotrophic Lateral Sclerosis (ALS) has been reported. Epidemiological studies of RF exposure occurring non-locally have reported neurological and cognitive disorders such as headaches, dizziness, tremors, decreased memory and attention, autonomic nervous system dysfunction, decreased reaction times, sleep disturbances and visual disruption. Pulsed electromagnetic frequencies (EMF) have been shown to consistently provoke neurological symptoms in subjects, while exposure to continuous frequencies did not. From such a perspective, it seems increasingly clear that a quantum physics model is necessary to fully understand and appreciate how and why EMF and RF fields are harmful to living beings. These interactions can have long-range effects which cannot be shielded, are non-linear and by their quantum nature have uncertainty. Once a specific threshold of intensity has been exceeded, it is the frequency that triggers a reaction. All molecules radiate their own identifying energy patterns, spreading their own specific energy signature (wobble or vibration).

Specific frequencies of electromagnetic radiation regulate DNA, RNA and protein synthesis (assemble), alter protein shape and function and control gene regulation, cell division, cell differentiation, hormones secretion, nerve growth and function. The signalling speed required to make this happen is faster than is possible via a bio-chemical mechanism and in fact seems to require electromagnetic (or faster) speeds. Electromagnetic or acoustic vibrations can create a constructive interference or 'harmonic resonance' in atoms. Focused energy waves interact with atoms and the atom absorbs energy and starts to vibrate faster as a result. Kidney stones have been treated by doctors with constructive interference mechanics.

Thoughts, the mind's energy, directly influence how the brain controls the body: they represent an incredibly powerful form of energy that can activate or inhibit the function of a cell's proteins via constructive or destructive interference.

> 'Every cell in our body has a characteristic vibration. When these cells vibrate at a certain rate and in a certain pattern, the body functions well and the person feels good. When they vibrate at a different rate and pattern, the body functions less well and the person feels not so good [...] every thought is a pattern of energy characterized by a certain vibratory rate and pattern [...] the vibratory pattern of the thought and its consequent emotion are experienced throughout the entire body, by each cell, and this vibratory influence triggers the release of certain kinds of neuropeptides which flood through the body [...] thus thoughts are patterns of energy which influence the functions of the whole body.'[59]

Many cognitive theories have been developed to try to explain the mind-body connection involved in emotional processing, how emotions are experienced by our body and labelled by our brain, as essentially, they are evolutionary processes necessary for the human species' survival.[94] Most of these cognitive models agree with the assumption that emotional processing is strongly embodied and tied to both physiological and psychological mechanisms. Our conscious mind experiences the chemical communication signals between cells as emotions. If positive thinking and emotions are good for you, imagine what negative thinking can do.

Electromagnetic radiation effects on people from everyday electronics

Despite differences in study results, ELF-MF and radio frequency electromagnetic fields do seem to influence our circadian rhythms. Numerous studies have reported changes in sleep patterns, and melatonin and cortisol secretion after exposure to these fields. It is likely that some individuals are more sensitive to electromagnetic fields than others, based on genetic background or current health status. Indeed, magnetic fields have been found to significantly affect cardiac function, as well as many other body systems and problems.[95]

Different types of magnetic fields may have different effects on, say, the cardiac rhythm. This sensitivity extends to all external fields, including their interactions with each other and with the body. There is a wealth of evidence to support the claim that the everyday technologies we use today emit electromagnetic radiation that can penetrate our body, affecting our health and disturbing our environments.[96] General or public use of EMFs for personal use should be limited to low strength ELFs or high frequency EMFs that do not create heating. For years now, research has linked EM radiation to serious diseases like cancer, Alzheimer's, Parkinson's and others. For example, after an extensive review of more than 2,000 such studies, the National Institute of Environmental Health Sciences concluded[97] that EMFs, '*should be regarded as possible carcinogens*.' Even the Environmental Protection Agency now cautions to, '*limit your exposure*.'[98]

Why is radiation dangerous?

Our bodies use electromagnetic fields to function properly – every cell in the body may have its own EMF. Researcher and author Robert Becker wrote in his book, *The Body Electric*[99] that our cells actually communicate with each other via bioelectrical signals and electromagnetic fields. These natural EMFs help regulate important biochemical processes of all kinds. Maintaining balance in those cellular electromagnetic fields is crucial to our physical health. Unfortunately, as previously explained, our body can also be influenced by the powerful artificial EM radiation around us. Magnetic radiation (which is part of any EMF), can easily penetrate the body, so if you are near a powerful EMF, electromagnetic radiation will flow both around and inside you.

Dr. Becker states that the body's electrical signals can easily be affected by *ambient* radio waves, microwaves and other forms of electromagnetic radiation and that powerful, artificial EMFs can change the frequency of the body's electrical fields, distorting the balance and alter its communications, causing physical, mental and emotional chaos. Even when we leave that strong electromagnetic field environment, our body's systems tend to store electromagnetic radiations within the cells as electromagnetic oscillations. These oscillations can remain inside us, continuing over time to affect our body's most important processes.

The healthy human body resonates at around ten hertz. Frequencies above that can create biological stress, tissue damage and serious health problems.[100] The electromagnetic fields posing the most risk are those that are very strong, very near the body, or of high frequency. Mobile phones, for example, have powerful EMFs (often in the microwave range), and as they are typically held close to the head or kept close to the body, have attracted much attention for being a potential risk to our health.

In addition, numerous studies conducted worldwide have shown that overexposure to EMFs can lead to weakened immunities, lowered resistance to bacterial and viral infections and cancer. While hotly debated, a 2007 report, the BioInitiative Report, concluded that the existing standards for public safety are completely inadequate to protect your health.[101] The report included studies demonstrating that electromagnetic fields:

- Affect gene and protein expression (transcriptomic and proteomic research);
- Have genotoxic effects – RFR and ELF DNA damage;
- Induce stress response (stress proteins);
- Affect immune function;
- Affect neurological activity and behaviour;
- Cause childhood cancers (leukaemia);
- Impact melatonin production (links in laboratory and cell studies); promote breast cancer and Alzheimer's Disease melatonin.

Furthermore, other well-known studies[102] have linked EMFs with:

- Enzyme changes that affect DNA and cell growth, possibly resulting in cancer, birth defects and foetal abnormalities;
- Changes in metabolism and increased cell growth;
- Gene expression changes, which can result in cancer;
- Increased production of stress proteins within cells, linked to Alzheimer's disease;
- Chronic stress;

- Neuro-hormonal changes;
- Electro-smog disturbing the growth of cells and the information flow between cells.

Some studies are also investigating the role of radiofrequency radiations in the modification of our natural metabolic balance. For example, research is being conducted into the possibility of a connection existing between different types of health risks, such as some neurodegenerative diseases or cancer, and the radiation emitted by ordinary wireless devices.[103] Accordingly, a recent study published in *Electromagnetic Biology and Medicine*,[104] reported the results from a series of experimental studies aimed at discovering the effects of low-intensity radiofrequency radiation in the metabolism of living cells. In particular, oxidative stress was observed, which represents, '*An imbalance between the production of reactive oxygen species (ROS) and antioxidant defense.*'[105] Reactive oxygen species are a product of metabolic processes when the cells are under metabolic stress or aggressive environments, such as may result from exposure to radiofrequency radiation.[104] Oxidative stress mechanisms are known as a key-factor in the onset of cancer. Therefore, the assertion can be made that radiofrequency radiation poses a risk as a possible carcinogenic factor. The researchers go on to highlight the need for a precautionary approach in using wireless technologies, such as cell phones and wireless internet.[104] Indeed, in 2011, the International Agency for Research on Cancer classified radiofrequency radiation as a possible carcinogen for humans.[106]

Bibliography

1.   Kelso, J. A. S. (2008). An Essay on Understanding the Mind. Ecological Psychology: A Publication of the International Society for Ecological Psychology, 20(2), 180–208.

2.   Ho, M. W., & Knight, D. P. (1998). The Acupuncture System and the Liquid Crystalline Collagen Fibers of the Connective Tissues. The American Journal of Chinese Medicine, 26, 251-263.

3.   For the full article, please see: http://www.nytimes.com/2015/05/10/opinion/sunday/its-not-a-stream-of-consciousness.html

4.   Hari, R., & Kujala, M. V. (2009). Brain Basis of Human Social Interaction: From Concepts to Brain Imaging. Physiological Reviews, 89(2), 453-479.

5.   AI & Society. (2012). Special issue: Witnessed Presence. Journal for Knowledge, Culture and Communication, 27(1).

6.   Choy, M., & Salbu, R. L. (2011). Jet Lag: Current and Potential Therapies. Pharmacy & Therapeutics, 36(4): 221-224, 231.

7.   Johnsson, A. (2008). Light, Circadian and Circannual Rhythms. In: E. Bjertness (Ed.), Solar Radiation and Human Health. Oslo: The Norwegian Academy of Science and Letters, 57-75.

8.   Retrieved from http://www.livescience.com/13123-circadian-rhythms-obesity-diabetes-nih.html

9.   Brown, T. M., & Piggins, H. D. (2007). Electrophysiology of the Suprachiasmatic Circadian Clock. Progress in Neurobiology, 82(5), 229-255.

10. Wirz-Justice, A. (2006). Biological Rhythm Disturbances in Mood Disorders. International Clinical Psychopharmacology, 21 (suppl 1):S11–S15

11. Retrieved from http://www.scientificamerican.com/article/it-must-be-the-moon-tired/

12. Retrieved from https://sleepfoundation.org/sleep-tools-tips/healthy-sleep-tips/page/0/1

13. Retrieved from http://flipper.diff.org/app/items/5338

14. Retrieved from http://learn.genetics.utah.edu/content/inheritance/clockgenes/

15. Shea, B. T. (1990). Dynamic Morphology: Growth, Life History, and Ecology in Primate Evolution. In: DeRousseau, C. J. (Ed.), Primate life history and evolution, 325-52. Wiley-Liss.

16. Hu, K., Van Someren, E. J., Shea, S. A., & Scheer, F. A. (2009). Reduction of Scale Invariance of Activity Fluctuations with Aging and Alzheimer's Disease: Involvement of the Circadian Pacemaker. Proceedings of the National Academy of Sciences, 106(8), 2490-2494.

17. Gu, C., Coomans, C. P., Hu, K., Scheer, F. A., Stanley, H. E., & Meijer, J. H. (2015). Lack of Exercise Leads to Significant and Reversible Loss of Scale Invariance in Both Aged and Young Mice. Proc Natl Acad Sci U S A, 112(8), 2320-4.

18. Retrieved from http://my-ms.org/anatomy_brain_part2.htm

19. Retrieved from http://www.sirc.org/publik/smell_emotion.html

20. Nimmermark, S. (2004). Odour Influence on Well-being and Health with Specific Focus on Animal Production Emissions. Ann Agric Environ Med, 11, 163–173.

21. Retrieved from http://www.sirc.org/publik/smell_emotion.html

22. Hirsch, A. R. (1995). Effects of Ambient Odors on Slot-machine Usage in a LasVegas Casino. Psychology & Marketing, 12(7), 585-594.

23. Retrieved from http://www.sirc.org/publik/smell.pdf

24. Davenport, A. (2008). The Brain and the Kidney–organ Cross Talk and Interactions. Blood purification, 26(6), 526-536.

25. B.L.J. Treadwell, B. L. J., Savage, O., Sever, E. D., & Copeman, W. S. C. (1963). Pituitary-Adrenal Function during Corticosteroid Therapy. The Lancet, 281(7277), 355–358.

26. Maslow, A. H. (1943). A Theory of Human Motivation. Psychological review, 50(4), 370.

27. Chrousos, G. P., & Gold, P. W. (1998). A Healthy Body in a Healthy Mind – and vice versa – the Damaging Power of Uncontrollable Stress. The Journal of Clinical Endocrinology and Metabolism, 83(6), 1842-1845.

28. Winnard, K. P., Dmitrieva, N., & Berkley, K. J. (2006). Cross-organ Interactions Between Reproductive, Gastrointestinal, and Urinary Tracts: Modulation by Estrous Stage and Involvement of the Hypogastric Nerve. American Journal of Physiology-Regulatory, Integrative and Comparative Physiology, 291(6), R1592-R1601.

29. Goodwin, B. C. (1994). How the Leopard Changed its Spots: The Evolution of Complexity. Princeton University Press.

30. Goodwin, B.C. (1995). Biological Rhythms and Biocommunication. In: Biocommunication, S327 Living Processes, pp.183-230, Open University Press, Milton Keynes.

31. Cannon, W. B. (1929). Organization for Physiological Homeostasis. Physiological Reviews, 9(3), 399-431.

32. Cannon, W. B. (1932). The Wisdom of the Body. W W Norton & Co.

33. Read full article at: http://psychology.jrank.org/ human-behavior/pages/cmxyrsmolo/chemical-bases-brain-changes.html

34. Retrieved from http://www.biology-online.org/9/6_ homeostatic_mechanisms.htm

35. Read full article at: http://www.livestrong.com/ article/77571-homeostatic-balance-mean/

36. Lewis, G. D., Farrell, L., Wood, M. J., Martinovic, M., Arany, Z., Rowe, G. C., & Gerszten, R. E. (2010). Metabolic Signatures of Exercise in Human Plasma. Science Translational Medicine, 2(33), 33ra37-33ra37.

37. Yamada, K., & Nabeshima, T. (2003). Brain-derived Neurotrophic Factor/TrkB Signaling in Memory Processes. Journal of Pharmaceutical Sciences, 91(4), 267-70.

38. For the full article, please visit: http://www.health. harvard.edu/press_releases/regular-exercise-releases-brain-chemicals-key-for-memory-concentration-and-mental-sharpness

39. Jedrychowski, M. P., Wrann, C. D., Paulo, J. A., Gerber, K. K., Szpyt, J., Robinson, M. M., & Spiegelman, B. M. (2015). Detection and Quantitation of Circulating Human Irisin by Tandem Mass Spectrometry. Cell Metabolism, 22(4), 734-740.

40. Mooradian, A. D., Morley, J. E., & Korenman, S.G. (1987). Biological Actions of Androgens. Endocrine Reviews, 8(1), 1–28.

41. Broom, D. R., Batterham, R. L., King, J. A., & Stensel, D. J. (2009). The Influence of Resistance and Aerobic Exercise on Hunger, Circulating Levels of Acylated Ghrelin and Peptide YY in Healthy Males. American Journal of Physiology - Regulatory, Integrative and Comparative Physiology, 296(1), R29-35.

42. Rudnicki, M. A., & Charge, S. B. (2004). Cellular and Molecular Regulation of Muscle Regeneration. Physiological Reviews, 84(1), 209-38.

43. Institute of Medicine (US) Forum on Microbial Threats. (2006). Ending the War Metaphor: The Changing Agenda for Unraveling the Host-Microbe Relationship: Workshop Summary. 1: Microbial Communities of the Gut. Washington (DC): National Academies Press (US), available from: http://www.ncbi.nlm.nih.gov/books/ NBK57074/

44. Kostic, A. D., Howitt, M. R., & Garrett, W. S. (2013). Exploring Host–microbiota Interactions in Animal Models and Humans. Genes & Development, 27(7), 701–718.

45. NIH Human Microbiome Project: http://hmpdacc. org/

46. Turnbaugh, P. J., Ley, R. E., Hamady, M., Fraser-Liggett, C., Knight, R., & Gordon, J. I. (2007). The Human Microbiome Project: Exploring the Microbial Part of Ourselves in a Changing World. Nature, 449(7164), 804–810.

47. Bercik, P., Denou, E., Collins, J., Jackson, W., Lu, J., Jury, J., & Collins, S. M. (2011). The Intestinal Microbiota Affect Central Levels of Brain-derived Neurotropic Factor and Behavior in Mice. Gastroenterology, 141(2), 599-609.

48. Carpenter, S. (2012). That Gut Feeling. American Psychological Association, 43(8), 50. Retrieved from http://www.apa.org/monitor/2012/09/gut-feeling.aspx

49. Full article available at http://www. scientificamerican.com/article/mental-health-may-depend-on-creatures-in-the-gut/

50. Lyte, M. (2011). Probiotics Function Mechanistically as Delivery Vehicles for Neuroactive Compounds: Microbial Endocrinology in the Design and Use of Probiotics. Bioessays, 33(8), 574-581.

51. Fehér, J., Kovács, I., & Balacco, G. C. (2011). [Article in Hungarian] Role of Gastrointestinal Inflammations in the Development and Treatment of Depression. Orvosi Hetilap, 152(37), 1477-85.

52. Sonnenburg, J., & Sonnenburg, E. (2015). The Good Gut: Taking Control of Your Weight, Your Mood and Your Long-Term Health. Penguin Press.

53. Stanford Medicine News Centre. (2014). Blocking Receptor in Brain's Immune Cells Counters Alzheimer's in Mice, Study Finds. Retrieved from http://med.stanford.edu/news/all-news/2014/12/blocking-receptor-in-brains-immune-cells-counters-alzheimers.html

54. Steenbergen, L., Sellaro, R., van Hemert, S., Bosch, J. A., & Colzato, L. S. (2015). A Randomized Controlled Trial to Test the Effect of Multispecies Probiotics on Cognitive Reactivity to Sad Mood. Brain, Behavior, and Immunity, 48, 258-264.

55. Retrieved from http://learn.genetics.utah.edu/content/epigenetics/

56. Anand, P., Kunnumakara, A. B., Sundaram, C., Harikumar, K. B., Tharakan, S. T., Lai, O. S., & Aggarwal, B. B. (2008). Cancer is a Preventable Disease that Requires Major Lifestyle Changes. Pharmaceutical Research, 25(9), 2097-2116.

57. Ho, M. W. (2014). Evolution by Natural Genetic Engineering. Institute of Science in Society, full article available at http://www.i-sis.org.uk/Evolution_by_Natural_Genetic_Engineering.php

58. Freeman, D. L. W. (2009). Mosby's Complementary & Alternative Medicine: A Research-Based Approach (Third edition). pp. 82-83. Mosby Elsevier.

59. Pert, C. (1997). Molecules of Emotion: The Science between Mind-body Medicine. Scribner.

60. Dobek, C. E. (2013). Effects of Music on the Pain Response in the Central Nervous System using Functional Magnetic Resonance Imaging. A thesis submitted to the Centre for Neuroscience Studies, Queen's University, Kingston, Ontario, Canada. Retrieved from https://qspace.library. queensu.ca/bitstream/1974/8083/1/Dobek_ Christine_E_201306_Msc.pdf

61. Richter, M., Eck, J., Straube, T., & Miltner, W. H. R. (2010). Do Words Hurt? Brain Activation During the Processing of Pain-related Words. Pain, 148, 198-205.

62. Institute of Medicine (US) Committee on Health and Behavior: Research, Practice, and Policy. Health and Behavior: The Interplay of Biological, Behavioral, and Societal Influences. Washington (DC): National Academies Press (US); 2001. 2, Biobehavioral Factors in Health and Disease. Available from: http://www.ncbi.nlm.nih.gov/ books/NBK43737/

63. Frandsen, K. J., Hafen, B. Q., Hafen, B. Q., Karren, K. J., & Smith, N. L. (2001). Mind/Body Health: The Effects of Attitudes, Emotions and Relationships (Second Edition). Benjamin Cummings.

64. McEwen, B. S., & Gianaros, P. J. (2010). Central Role of the Brain in Stress and Adaptation: Links to Socioeconomic Status, Health, and Disease. Annals of the New York Academy of Sciences, 1186, 190–222.

65. Radley, J. J., Sisti, H. M., Hao, J., Rocher, A. B., McCall, T., Hof, P. R., & Morrison, J. H. (2005). Corrigendum to "Chronic Behavioral Stress Induces Apical Dendritic Reorganization in Pyramidal Neurons of the Medial Prefrontal Cortex". Neuroscience, 103(3), 805.

66. Retrieved from http://www.apa.org/helpcenter/stress-body.aspx

67. Retrieved from http://www.health.harvard.edu/staying-healthy/understanding-the-stress-response

68. Retrieved from http://www.cancer.org/treatment/treatmentsandsideeffects/treatmenttypes/placebo-effect

69. Mayberg, H. S., Silva, J. A., Brannan, S. K., Tekell, J. L., Mahurin, R. K., McGinnis, S., & Jerabek, P. A. (2002). The Functional Neuroanatomy of the Placebo Effect. American Journal of Psychiatry, 159(5), 728-37.

70. Mayberg, H. S. (2003) Modulating Dysfunctional Limbic-cortical Circuits in Depression: Towards Development of Brain-based Algorithms for Diagnosis and Optimised Treatment. British Medical Bulletin, 65: 193–207.

71. Retrieved from Pain Management Health Center, http://www.webmd.com/pain-management/what-is-the-placebo-effect

72. Benson, H. (1995). Placebo Effect and Remembered Wellness. Mind/Body Med, 1, 44-45.

73. Louveau, A., Smirnov, I., Keyes, T. J., Eccles, J. D., Rouhani, S. J., Peske, J. D., & Kipnis, J. (2015). Structural and Functional Features of Central Nervous System Lymphatic Vessels. Nature, 523(7560), 337-41.

74. Tauber, A. I. (2008). The Immune System and Its Ecology. Philosophy of Science, 75(2), 224-245.

75. Ader, R. (Ed.), 2007. Psychoneuroimmunology. (Fourth ed.). Academic Press, San Diego.

76. Tauber, A. I. (2012). From the Immune Self to Moral Agency. AVANT III, 1/2012. Retrieved from www.avant.edu.pl/en

77. https://www.rickhanson.net/mind-changing-brain-changing-mind/

78. Tang, Y. Y., Lu, Q., Feng, H., Tang, R., & Posner, M. I. (2015). Short-term Meditation Increases Blood Flow in Anterior Cingulate Cortex and Insula. Frontiers in Psychology, 26(6), 212.

79. Pokorný, J. (2011). Electrodynamic Activity of Healthy and Cancer Cells. Journal of Physics: Conference Series , 329(1), 012007.

80. Institute of Science in Society. ISIS miniseries "Fields of Influence". Retrieved from http://www.i-sis.org.uk/FOI4.php

81. Pokorný, J., Pokorný, J., & Kobilková, J. (2013). Postulates on Electromagnetic Activity in Biological Systems and Cancer. Integr Biol (Camb), 5(12):1439-46.

82. Cambel, A. B. (1993). Applied Chaos Theory-A paradigm for Complexity. Academic Press, Inc.

83. Institute of Science in Society. Life is Water Electric. Retrieved from http://www.i-sis.org.uk/Life_is_Water_Electric.php

84. Electromagnetic and Radiofrequency Fields Effect on Human Health. American Academy of Environmental Medicine. Retrieved from https://www.aaemonline.org/emf_rf_position.php

85. Plutchik, R. (1984). Emotions: A General Psycho-evolutionary Theory. In: Approaches to Emotion. (Klaus R. Scherer, Paul Ekman, Eds.). Psychology Press, Taylor & Francis Group.

86. European Commission. (2007). Scientific Committee on Emerging and Newly Identified Health Risks: Possible effects of Electromagnetic Fields (EMF) on Human Health. Retrieved from http://ec.europa.eu/health/ph_risk/committees/04_scenihr/docs/scenihr_o_007.pdf

87. NIH National Cancer Institute. Electromagnetic Fields and Cancer. Retrieved from http://www.cancer.gov/about-cancer/causes-prevention/risk/radiation/magnetic-fields-fact-sheet

88. Ahlbom, I. C., Cardis, E., Green, A., et al. (2001). Review of the Epidemiologic Literature on EMF and Health. Environmental Health Perspectives, 109(Suppl 6), 911-933.

89. United States Environmental Protection Agency. Radiation Health Effects. Retrieved from http://www.epa.gov/radiation/radiation-health-effects

90. Becker, R., & Selden, G. (1998). The Body Electric: Electromagnetism and the Foundation of Life. Harper Collins.

91. Karinen, A., Heinävaara, S., Nylund, R., & Leszczynski, D. (2008). Mobile Phone Radiation Might Alter Protein Expression in Human Skin. BMC Genomics, 9(77).

92. BioInitiative Working Group. Sage, C., & Carpenter, D. (Eds.). (2007). BioInitiative Report: A Rationale for a Biologically-based Public Exposure Standard for Electromagnetic Fields (ELF and RF). Retrieved from http://www.bioinitiative.org/

93. SafeSpace. What is EMF? Retrieved from http://www.safespaceprotection.com/harmful-effects-electromagnetic-fields.aspx

94. Metabolic Imbalance Caused by Radiation from Wireless Devices Linked to Many Health Risks. News Medical. Available at http://www.news-medical.net/news/20150725/Metabolic-imbalance-caused-by-radiation-from-wireless-devices-linked-to-many-health-risks.aspx

95. Yakymenko, I., Tsybulin, O., Sidorik, E., Henshel, D., Kyrylenko, O., & Kyrylenko, S. (2015). Oxidative Mechanisms of Biological Activity of Low-intensity Radiofrequency Radiation. Electromagnetic Biology and Medicine, (0), 1-16.

96. Rahman, T., Hosen, I., Islam, M. M. T., & Shekhar, H. U. (2012). Oxidative Stress and Human Health. Advances in Bioscience and Biotechnology, 3, 997-1019.

97. World Health Organisation. (2014). Electromagnetic Fields and Public Health: Mobile Phones. Fact sheet 193. Retrieved from http://www.who.int/mediacentre/factsheets/fs193/en/

23

Happiness

The concepts of happiness and wellbeing play a central role in Buddhism. Nibbana is a worthwhile goal to pursue because through a mental and emotional transformation, it represents the highest happiness – as well as the end of suffering. True happiness, contentment and harmony come from a liberated mind. The dispositions that are a driving force of suffering are precisely those unwholesome mental states that lie at the heart of all our non-beneficial behaviours – conflicts, dissensions, rivalry and warfare. Whilst these unwholesome tendencies dominate our mental lives, we are incapable of becoming really happy.

In the suttas, there is a constant positive reference to the delight and happiness created in the various stages of meditation. These refined levels of pleasure are in contrast to the suffering we experience along with the flagrant, sense-based pleasures. This provides an early incentive for continuing the practice of meditation; once we understand that meditation provides serenity and happiness and, in some cases, rapture, it is much easier to persevere with our practice, especially in the early stages of our journey.

We recognise that in practising sīla (behavioural discipline) and mental culture with an accompanying voluntary simplicity of lifestyle, we find a new freedom and happiness. We start to understand that the stress, anxiety, worry, fear and many of the other sufferings of life are actually part and parcel of the existence that we are pursuing when we are not following the Path. We soon discover that much of the modern world is a commercial enterprise which creates stress for all by seducing us into craving more and more sensual objects. We soon understand too that a proper scale of values is very important in terms of our happiness in life. Progress in material satisfaction alone is not enough for wholesome happiness. With this understanding, we become content with a simpler life because we know that it leads to a happier life. That action is a mark of progress on the path to inner freedom.

The Buddha named four kinds of lay happiness: the happiness of possession (of such things as health, wealth, longevity, partner and children); the enjoyment of such possessions; freedom from debt; and a blameless moral and spiritual life. However, even with such an ideal life, a more sublime and higher happiness and security can only be found in the transformation of our minds and the reinforcement of this by consistent practice. So the wise lay person, whilst still wisely participant in this world, reduces involvement with the modern ways of life as the way to seek happiness. Rather, a wise person trains the mind and actions.

While the economic environment of society influences a person's character, it doesn't determine the character. In all situations, a person can always exercise free will and take responsibility, acting according to his or her own conscience irrespective of the overriding social structure. Free will, as psychologist Victor Frankl said, is, 'the last of human freedoms – to choose one's attitude in any

given set of circumstances, to choose one's own way.'[1]
While the Buddha understood and supported our need
for economic and environmental security, he also saw
the dangers and insecurity of seeking our happiness only
through material wealth and reputation.

Buddhism does not teach that happiness is wrong or
that you should try to eliminate it from your life. What it
does say is that inferior sense-based pleasures should
not be allowed to become the basis of unskilful mental
activities, especially craving and grasping. Pleasure
in and of itself is neither skilful nor unskilful; it is our
attitude towards pleasure that is either skilful or unskilful.
The skilled person does not allow the pleasurable to
take hold of the mind. This is an idea that the Buddha
used in describing his own experience on the path to
Enlightenment. We must have a healthy and wholesome
attitude toward pleasure. Do not run after pleasure.
There can be no grasping or clinging. All physical
pleasures are relative and transitory, and therefore
ultimately unsatisfactory. They are not the absolute and
unconditioned happiness of nibbana.

Achievement for the layperson

For some people beginning to practise Buddhism, doubt
can be a major obstacle to overcome. That is, the
doubt that as a layperson, one cannot advance very far
toward achieving Enlightenment. However, this doesn't
necessarily have to be the case. Indeed, Siddhartha
himself stated that he was not a unique saviour – this is
far above what people can aspire to become themselves.
Instead, he claimed to be just a man who had realised an
extraordinary Truth – nibbana. Buddhism is concerned with
how anyone can follow a definite path of mental culture
and development to realise that same consciousness.

In his own lifetime, Siddhartha witnessed many of his followers reach Enlightenment. After his death, and down through the centuries, thousands more have experienced the awakened state – and not only monks. Buddhism is a teaching that explains how realisation can be acquired in one's life – here and now.

Bhikkhu Bodhi says that many of the Buddha's followers who attained the first three stages of Awakening, from stream-entry through to non-returning, were indeed laypeople.[2] Schopen, however, goes a step further and lists evidence from the suttas, *'that lay people can achieve the fourth fruit – arahantship.'*[3] Throughout history, people from all walks of life (including among them labourers and people of the lowest castes), have joined the Buddhist community. Many people have claimed to have attained Right Knowledge through their practice. The Buddha's purpose was to teach the dhamma for the uplifting and liberation of all beings from ignorance and suffering. In aspiring to declare the dhamma to all, the Buddha saw the world as a single group, not as an artificially stratified society divided by race, religion and status.

While it is true that generosity, moral virtues and other topics are commonly taught to laypeople in Buddhism, there are also many instances in the suttas in which they have received the same profound discourses as the monastics. For example, in the Nagara Sutta, the Buddha, after expounding on insight into dependent arising and the eight-factor path, concluded by declaring that this 'ancient path' (the Noble Eight-factor Path) discovered and travelled by the Buddha has been explained to the monks, the nuns, and the male and female lay followers. He affirmed that, *'This holy life has become successful and prosperous, widespread, popular, reached the masses, well proclaimed amongst devas and humans.'* The

Buddha himself never once said that arahanthood could be attained only by the renunciant. So, as is often the case with goal achievement, much of how successful we are depends on our Right Intention and Effort; the Buddha exhorted all to begin diligently, and today.

Cultivation of the attachments

People often find the words 'detachment' and 'nonattachment' confusing in the practice of meditation in Buddhism, because it may seem as though a Buddhist is a person who has no concern or no emotional involvement with the world or the environment; or secondly, it can appear that the meditator has no concern or involvement with his mental content. But this is not what the Buddha taught. The nonattachment described in Buddhism is not a kind of selfish flight from the world; rather, it is a necessary retreat for the development of an insightful introspective practice. The intensity of the withdrawal, of course, depends on the extent of commitment to the Eight-factor Path (take, for example, the usual difference between the monk and a layperson). Secondly, to counter the negative mental conditioning of the past, nonattachment to unwholesome states is necessary, just as a proactive, wholesome, mental purification process from beginning to end is necessary. Therefore, constant monitoring, effort, and intervention in one's mental arena are needed to reach nibbana.

One mental state tends to lead to another, and to yet another, in accordance with the simile of the relay chariots, but none of them is to be grasped *per se*. One grasps neither purification of virtue nor purification of the mind; one does not grasp purification of view, or even purification by knowledge and vision. Leaving them all behind, there comes the final 'let go' to attain that perfect extinction without clinging – nibbana. This is the subtlest necessity in this dhamma.

Bhikkhu K. Ñänananda explains the necessity of nonattachment to precepts as one makes progress along the path to Enlightenment:

> 'Accordingly, what we have here are so many scaffoldings for the up-building of meditation and knowledge. Probably due to the lack of understanding of this deep method, some Buddhists take up concepts in a spirit of dogmatic adherence. That attitude of determined clinging on is like clinging on to the scaffoldings to live on them or after arriving to the far shore with a raft, taking the raft out of the water and carrying it as one travels on land. Ultimately, the motivation for this is a deep insecurity based on ignorance.'[4]

Since meditation is an introspective process, there can be no successful higher meditation without some nonattachment to the objects of the senses. So with this progressive introspection moving toward more subtle meditative mental states, it is natural that one should become more detached from the world of sense objects. Gradually, thoughts are channelled from broad to more subtle levels, and they are let go through non-identification. Concepts serve only as scaffolding for the systematic development of meditation and knowledge. In the context of the path of practice, the identification of one thing is for the purpose of abandoning another. There is an attitude of detachment in this course of practice. Based on this maxim, the Buddha outlines the way in which he guides one towards nibbana.

> 'Letting go of them all and grasping not one,
>
> That peaceful one, leaning on none,
>
> Would hanker no more for existence.'

The Buddha's final stage of teaching is to let go, dis-identify and transcend even the wonderful experience of the purest samadhi states of mind with pure experience.

Cure for suffering

Life is a continuous process giving each of us the opportunity to mature spiritually. In fact, you, the reader, have been taking advantage of a great gift, the teachings of the Buddha, to help guide yourself in your journey. With the Buddha's Awakening, he discovered a remedy for suffering. The culmination of his long spiritual journey gave him insight into the nature of dependent origination and emptiness. The Buddha then understood that our cognitive manifestations are relative, constructed and impermanent. He also saw that dukkha (the pre-enlightened cognitive experience) can be attenuated and eventually eliminated through practice of the Eight-factor Path, and the reorientation and correct understanding of our cognitive world.

The Enlightenment proposed by the Buddha is unlike any other form of salvation. Before the Buddha, there was no articulated non-substantial way to exit the world of saṃsāra and suffering. The Buddha revealed the Middle Way between a life of sensate pleasure and a life of practicing extreme asceticism. The Buddha's teachings lead to compassion, equanimity and insight. They are also resonant with what modern cognitive science and physics can now tell us about how our bodies and the physical environment work and interact. Buddhist ideas offer an alternative sense of our existence, away from an emphasis on monotheistic and Cartesian duality, which is both plausible and liberating.

Upon achieving a true understanding of the nature of reality, one attains Enlightenment and extinguishes the fuel – the desires and cravings – for the fire of continuity (the cycle of rebirth). The insight of Enlightenment allows the letting go of the subject-object duality, something which otherwise creates dukkha, through ignorance. Enlightenment replaces that duality with an understanding that our existence is the world of experience as we create it. Or in other words, dukkha is based on our own constructions of our 'world' and our clinging to the illusions we construct – our pre-enlightened experience. We come to understand that our structuring and seeking for understanding of sensory inputs through the operation of the five khandhas also depends on our cognitive processes. In moving from initial to secondary characteristics and then creating abstract categories of the original undifferentiated sensory information, we name them not on the basis of some inherent, independent qualities, but by the way we perceive, categorise and differentiate between them. Our world is subjectively constructed, or as Thomas Kuhn stated,

> *'There is, I think, no theory independent way to reconstruct phrases like "really there"; the notion of a match between the ontology of a theory and its "real" counterpart in nature now seems to be illusive in principle.'[5]*

What our cognitive apparatus typically creates, or imagines, is dualism, most notably of a subject-object split. Achieving the goal of nibbana is to realise that this view of the external world is not true – the world does not exist in the way that we construct it as subject and object. A consequence of this is that the ontological status of the 'I' is dependent. Enlightenment is a cognitive reorientation. It is not ontology but epistemology. There is no ontological ealm of emptiness out there, a stratum existing above nd beyond the conventional world. Nibbana has no ategorised features, no differentiation of colour, taste, odour, sound, or form, so we don't realise that it's right here. When we stop creating the world, we stop imputing the feeling of solidity that creates a notion of separation. But that doesn't mean that we shut off the senses in any way. It's pointless to try to find peace through nullifying or erasing the sensory world. Peace comes as we progress on our journey; we shed the veneer, the films of confusion, of opinion, of judgment that come with our conditioning so that we can finally discern things as they really are. At that moment, dukkha ceases. There is knowing. There is liberation.

Reorientation of the mind

To achieve the radical reorientation of mind that the Buddha teaches can be difficult. Nobody can act for us, and we have to work diligently. Diligence does not mean obsession, and so it differs greatly from the extreme asceticism that the Buddha eventually gave up. Following the Middle Way requires patience and determination, but not torturing oneself. To support this radical change in thinking, we have to alter our state of mind from tense, excited and confused to supple, tranquil and clear. Nibbana cannot be experienced so long as the mind is engaged in creating fictions and treating the illusory as real.

The Second Noble Truth informs us how we create suffering, enabling us to know that we can stop doing so. Some people think it creates a paradox to have intention on our spiritual path and yet to also seek Enlightenment. This should not be a concern, however, for we must prepare the ground for our Enlightenment. If we follow the Eight-factor Path, we purify our minds in preparing ourselves for the insight with which we will be able to understand and experience nirodha.

So, as the Buddha counselled, not only do we need to be diligent in our practice, we also need to reject self-defeating attitudes that can distract us from the path toward Enlightenment. Such thoughts as, 'It's too difficult,' 'I don't have the time,' 'This takes many lifetimes,' or, 'In modern society, it's impossible to achieve,' are all Mara's distractions and discouragements to keep us enmeshed in samsāra.

Yet we can progress toward Enlightenment and achieve it in this life. To progress, we need to purify our minds and generate thoughts that have wholesome attributes like joyfulness, contentment and compassion, which are spiritually 'light' in nature. We should avoid thinking and acting in unwholesome ways out of anger, greed or selfishness. We need to lift ourselves up in the gradual process that ultimately leads toward awakening. We need to follow the Eight-factor Path gratefully and with eager anticipation of the time when we will leave our rafts on the shore because we no longer need the teachings. Not only do we need to practice meditative exercises to transform the cognitive apparatus, but also to act with compassion toward ourselves and to others.

While the Buddha's teaching is deep and profound, it isn't mysterious. He constantly encouraged his students to question him, because Enlightenment is gained through insight, not blind faith. The Buddha was a human being, not a god, and Buddhists do not worship him. Instead, we use recollections of the Buddha and images of him as inspiration to continue with diligence on the path to enlightenment. The Buddha taught how to correctly understand this life. Through his instruction, he points the way for us. The Buddha provided a map to help us avoid the many perilous traps that our minds can conjure. The Buddha's defeat of Mara highlighted the importance

Chapter Twenty-three

of equanimity, and with equanimity our meditation can be pleasant and rewarding. This is why the members of the Buddha's Sangha were all reported to have smiling faces. Their journey to nibbana was a path of joy, wisdom and compassion, and ours can be too. The Buddha's teachings can be realised by each one of us in this very life – they provide a message for all. Shortly before his death, the Buddha told his followers, 'When I am gone, my teachings shall be your master and guide,' and just before he died, he added, 'Indeed, bhikkhus, I declare this to you: It is in the nature of all formations to dissolve. Attain perfection through diligence.'[6] The Buddha still calls and guides us to take the journey of liberation.

The message of the Buddha is a message of happiness. His achievement is that of one of the most penetrating of intelligences. His boundless love and benevolence go out to all sentient beings. His life and his teachings have greatly influenced the world. May all sentient beings eliminate their negative attitudes, open up innate wisdom, cultivate purity and virtues, and travel well on the path to Enlightenment.

Bibliography

1. Frankl, V. E. (1985). Man's search for meaning. Simon and Schuster.

2. Bodhi, B. (1984). The Noble Eightfold Path-- The Way to the End of Suffering. The Wheel Publication.

3. Schopen, G. (1997). Bones, stones, and Buddhist monks: collected papers on the archaeology, epigraphy, and texts of monastic Buddhism in India (Vol. 2). University of Hawaii Press.

4. Nibbana: The Mind Stilled, Sermon 4 p. 65 Nanananda (2003). Nibbana - The Mind Stilled (Vol.1) (PDF). Dharma Grantha Mudrana Bharaya. pp. IX. ISBN 955-8832-02-2.

5. Kuhn, T. S. (2012). The structure of scientific revolutions. University of Chicago Press.

6. Translated from the Pali by Sister Vajira & Francis Story. (1998). Maha-parinibbana Sutta: Last Days of the Buddha. DN 16. PTS: D ii 72, chapters 1-6.

24

The World without a 'Self'

'The process whereby our thoughts generate actions, which touch others, which touch still others, and thus a vast web of conscious minds together weave the fabric of their reality, forever creating new ways of seeing and being.'

L. Gabora[1]

The Buddha's Annatta doctrine of 'no-self' is now strongly supported by correlations found within modern psychology and biology. The results strongly support the validity of the Buddha's teachings as a psychological doctrine that has revolutionary personal and social ramifications when accepted. We have seen that while much of Western psychology emphasises the 'self' as a primary and rational shaper of human thoughts, decisions and emotions. In fact, the conscious apparatus is only the gatekeeper between the profound automatic and non-conscious physical forces acting in concert within the body and interacting with the surrounding environment.

The concept of 'self' needs to be kept in perspective. Based on knowledge attained through Enlightenment, the 'self' is correctly understood as a conceptual construction or autobiographical fiction created by an advanced cognitive apparatus. The consequences of identifying with, clinging to and having a conviction in the representation of a 'self' are detrimental not only to the psychological and physical wellbeing of the individual but also to the social interactions between individuals and between people and the rest of the world.

If an Enlightened perspective – including the Buddha's doctrines of impermanence, 'no-self' and dis-ease – were to became more prevalent and prominent in human thinking, then it is likely that, the world would be a much kinder, ecological, safe, harmonious, cultured, spontaneous and happier place. Through proper training and diligence it is possible for humans to develop cognitive experiences and insightful perspectives that lead ultimately to a more mature mind, one that is not dominated by egoism and ignorance.

The path to maturity is not mystical or esoteric but, in fact supported by the results of scientific research in biology and psychology. Both lifestyle and intellectual guidelines can be found on the path, which will help us to develop our life in a way that offers happiness through a wholesome and skilful relationship with both our being and the external environment. As the artificial subject-object boundary between the fictional 'self' and our living environment is reduced, we become more aware and sensitive to the interdependency and interactive nature of life and appreciate different perspectives.

This transformation centres on the new state and conditions of citta (mind/heart). We remember that the Buddha considered citta as the core of personality, the focus of purpose, activity, continuity and emotionality – the agent. For the Buddha it is not a soul (attti), but an empirical, functional being. Its functions are similar to what has become called the ego in psychodynamic psychology. The person knows, via citta, that one exists – it usually gets given a label and he or she can observe their own mind, train it, critique it and carry on a dialogue with it.

Involved primarily in the momentary conscious contents and processes, citta also includes all layers of the cognitive system. In following the Eightfold Path, not only the conscious state is changed, but the whole personality. As a result of the transformed citta, there is an open, active and energetic frame of mind. The transformed citta becomes free from obsessions and biases and is therefore calm and constant. Consequently, the accessible state of the deep unchanging refuge (original mind), unperturbed by desires and sustained by correct insight, is always available. As expressed in the simile of the deep ocean, in this mind there is a clear distinction between the unstable, rapidly changing surface (or foreground) and the deep, unchanging depth (or background).

While someone's feelings remain as they always have, what is different after transformation is that the person no longer reacts, fixates, craves and becomes attached; the mature personality foundation is firm, consistent yet responsive and flexible, it is not motivated by whims and passing emotions. That is not to imply that neither passivity nor motivation should be part of our emotions. On the contrary, dhamma-practice doesn't eradicate personality even though it reduces our identification to it – it doesn't make a person an impersonal android. We know that no human being can live without motivating factors (which are often labelled as needs). In fact, the suttas assume that all sentient beings, and in our case human beings, have the personal needs of air, food, clothes, shelter, occupation and community, yet the follower of the Buddha is also described as 'wanting little' (S I 63).[2]

The mature personality, who has developed insight and dispelled the ignorance of the belief in a static, substantial self, becomes free from the emotions and desires created by egoism and attachment. A new type of health is created through the 'right understanding' of the conditions of life. One's emotions are fully known and controlled and motivated by understanding, friendliness, kindness and compassion.

As Kalupahana explains:

> 'In the context of the five aggregates (khandhas), the Buddha was not reluctant to speak of "I" or "myself" or even of the "self." Without admitting to a "ghost in the machine" or a transcendental apperception, the Buddha was willing to recognize the feeling of individuality, of self. It is a feeling that can contract and expand depending on the context. It does not represent a static entity to which everything belongs. [...] There seems to be no justification for assuming the Buddha encouraged the annihilation of this feeling of self. Indeed, the reality of feelings and emotions that occur in the stream of experience are relevant to an explanation of harmonious life.'[3]

We can clearly see that as much as the Buddha emphasised the elimination of egotism, he did not intend the annihilation or depersonalisation of what modern psychology labels the empirical 'self', or the individual experiences. The terms 'I' and 'self' are pragmatic linguistic conventions, which reflect the living experience that all conscious beings have. The idea of 'no-self' doesn't mean that we don't exist or that we are robots with no volition to act in the world – we are constantly changing beings, always in flux. Giving it a fixed name and identity is just a convention that humans derived to enable us to talk about it. The whole idea of 'self' is a fiction or a narrative.

The problem is that as soon as we attach labels and concepts onto something, our egos start objectifying it, conclusively establishing and creating fantastic stories to make something static and permanent out of it. And that's where our point of illusion and suffering begins. Actually, the 'I' refers to an illusory epiphenomenon, a useful abbreviation standing for a myriad of identifications, schemas and the many biochemical and electrical transactions taking place between them. We come to regard our 'I' as real, this is the reference that culture and society gives to the level of complexity in the physical system underlying it, and so, as the Buddha discovered, we are conditioned to construct notions using high-level abstractions.

In the Buddha's psychology, the intrusion of the 'self' into the field of sense perception begins with the construction of the notions of 'I' (subject) and 'mine' (object). Therefore 'self' originates at the stage of sensation and this duality is maintained until it is fully crystallised and sustained by ourselves at the conceptual level. We don't recognise this is abnormal, however, because the subject-object relationship is the foundation of cognition. So what starts as a complex, conditionally arisen physiological process, develops into the duality concept of subject and object, 'I' and 'mine'. The concept of 'I' forms the matrix of the complex cognitive process and serves as a convenient symbolic device, just as the concept of 'self' a cognitive construction.

As David J. Kalupahana states:

> '...This selectivity in consciousness accounts for the possibility and, therefore, the ability on the part of the human being to choose, think and act, and these represent the core of selfhood or personality in the Buddha's doctrine.'³

All of Buddhist interventions aim at reclaiming the purified citta, or the original mind. When this transformation of citta (or purification) is complete, nibbana is attained. The especially difficult hindrances to overcome on the way to purification are our misconceptions about the world and ourselves; our clinging, unwholesome and compulsive habits; our laziness or being too busy to follow the path; doubt, desires and emotions, fears and worries; and lifestyle behaviours contrary to the five precepts, or the ten paramis.

But, after diligent application of the programme, these obstacles can be overcome and a healthy mind developed, which is able to know the world 'as it really is.' In the reduction and then final elimination of the distractions and diversions of the 'self' belief, practitioners become much more centred and aware of the sensitivity and coherence of one's body. Physical, cognitive and emotional activities are all aspects of the interaction of subtle energies within the unified body, rather than the objectified body, in which the body and mind are separate and distinct through the subject-object split of dualism. The physical system we call our body is a field on which different physical and mental forces interact and influence each other. Also, the living body organises itself, adjusting habitual movements, actions and instruments to fit within the conditions of its external environment. No distinction should be made between the living body and the environment and our conceptual systems are grounded in a relative historical contingency (living cultural and physical memory) and the embodied bodily experience.

The small, egotistical mind is continuously grasping and fixating activity with focused attention, while the expansive, freed mind is the background of whole awareness. Bhavana practice ultimately reveals awareness as a unified field, in which strict dualistic divisions between subject and object, mind and body, an inner and outer world, and the unconscious versus conscious mental states are dispensed with. Believing in the dualistic separation as objective reality and failing to recognise the ground of original awareness is ignorance.

As we develop serenity and equanimity, and appreciate our peaceful 'refuge' of the background quiet, our subtle autonomic body processes become healthier and bright. Our bodies are 're-wired'. We can more easily sense and ease any fixations and contractions in our body whenever we suffer, experience stress or imbalance. As we become more sensitive to this field of awareness, then we have a more reliable guide for health. By lessening and losing the fixated 'self' image, we become more aware of the body's internal speech as well as sensitive to the effects of interactions with our external surroundings.

Pre-enlightenment 'self' identities, decisions, perspectives and 'self' priorities are usually crude, biased, out dated, 'self'-reinforcing, based on confused and conflicting interests and are often obsessive, sense-based and inflexible. Cultivating new insights and intentions supported by the Buddha's teachings has a transformative effect on the structure of the mind. There is a sensitivity and dynamic system of intelligence that is continually processing information through which brain/heart functions play a part. Information is energetic – thoughts, impulses, feelings, reactions – all are in continual flux. Through our awareness and effort, wise generosity and trust can be fostered. As a result, new psychological tendencies and mental habits can be established: they mould our lives by generating a continuous flow of causation, reactions and responses, triggering further responses and finally becoming part of who we are. Our schemas become shaped by what we focus on and cognitively nurture.

Through neuroplasticity, epigenetics and other physically based learning interactions, we literally change who we are and what to invest in our mind. In understanding this principle of cause and effect, the key to joy and compassion, lifelong clarity and stability can be found. We initiate and foster our healing responses that allow us to give up what harms us, and to begin to nurture what is good and enriching. There is nothing clearer and more essential to learn in order to live life well.

Belief in a static, substantial 'self' is an illusion. The 'self' is only a constantly changing narrative, an abstraction, a crafty construction. Without 'self' interference, bliss arises, is experienced, and then, without clinging, it disappears, like the mist of a summer's morning. This bliss results from certain conditions experienced by living through the refinement process. Bliss is created by freeing the mind of obsessions, a natural state where the pressure of thinking, of worrying, of attaching is released. The natural, blissful feeling of refining one's mind also has positive bodily results. When the mind is relaxed in a natural feeling of happiness, there is no stress, there is no debate in the mind, it's empty of representations – just aware in the moment, existing coherently with a relaxed and positively stimulated body.

Through the Buddha's teachings, our state of mind is reconditioned and purified leading to an optimal state of mind and body. The reconditioning is created by a change of interaction of the mind with itself and with the environment. There is the truth of mutual conditioning or interdependence, stating that all phenomena arise dependently on others, so our mind awareness only specifically manifests in terms of the conditions that we have established through our daily norm. All is interconnected. This is the core of conditionality, and implies that the good we have done will lay down a residue of brightness and support a wholesome effect on our mind and the body, verifying the existential pragmatic rational in doing the wholesome and avoiding the unwholesome.

The Buddha's Eightfold Path is a clear, valid psychological programme that leads us out of inflicting stress and worry on ourselves and others and finding our original pure mind. Right View helps us to recognise this Truth. For example, through cultivation, the Five Precepts, life can be lived free from regret and with a clear heart. Loss of 'self'-preoccupation allows personal encounters with others without a selfish motive of needing to acquire something, material or abstract. However, if the non-dual experience and re-orientation does not go deep enough, the danger of selfish tendencies manifesting remains, and so does any inclination to selfishly manipulate others. As long as there is an identity with 'self', the restraint provided by the guidelines of ethical behaviour is needed. Any negativity that is expressed – talking aggressively to people, taking objects that belong to other people, harming other creatures, not being responsible for my actions by lying – accumulates not only in social relationships, but perhaps more importantly in the mind. If the five precepts or ten paramis are maintained, then interactions with the environment is instead very positive because unwholesome, toxic personal interactions do not arise, and so people do not react in aversive, defensive or angry ways.

Therefore, the interdependence, the relationship of 'my-self' with 'my-self 'and also with my environment is being constantly conditioned and knowing that, with proper mature, non-selfish, egotistical behaviours, life can be lived freely, without regret and with a content heart and mind. When these become established as our natural qualities, we are at ease, calm and fully authentic in the sense of being open to life, not alienated. This is our natural existence, our Eden – when we know our original mind. However, these qualities become buried, hidden by abusive or deluded behaviour and these behaviours are acquired through dispositions that give more value to subject-object separation, alienation, egotism and the three defilements of greed, hate and ignorance, rather than wholesomeness, inclusion, kindness and maturity. Through the Buddha's psychological programme and other similar interventions, we can regain that capacity of non-separation. To do so, we have to re-model the mind not only through the immediate ethical choices we make, but on a deeper level too. The hindrances and the defilements that we have continually created in our life also need to be adjusted. Our transformation is confirmed through our action. To regain our original mind, insight meditation of observing ourselves and doing wholesome actions reconditions our negative states of mind.

To regain our original mind, the path leads to the mature development of our mental states. So instead of keeping worry, stress and anger in our mind, we remove those conditions that create the negativity and harmful thoughts. We then see the world in a different way, without defilements. Meditation, in its peaceful states, instructs us in how to avoid getting caught up in the influxes and consequent stress. One very important basis of suffering is the influx of sensuality. We are often encouraged and can easily believe that everything, including ourselves, is only a sensory object. We easily respond to the constant sense inputs with either craving or aversion. Even if we achieve our desires, we can't retain the pleasant experiences and nor can we avoid unpleasant ones – our desires are always changing. Meditative training brings psychological support in terms of factors of awareness, which help us to understand that sensual influxes always change until eventually we maintain equanimity in the tempest of life. An agile yet calm mind is experienced, and as a result we come to know about our innate balance (or homeostasis) and wellbeing. Even when carrying our perhaps stressful livelihood, with a mind secure in equanimity, our mind remains balanced and will not become rigidly fixated. That's the way the path works; problems are teachers to our cultivation of serenity. A sense of direction and purpose guides every journey, so that one travels faithfully through to its end. The Buddha's journey reveals for us our fullest potential as human beings. When we meditate and find a balanced parasympathetic bodily state, energy is restored to the whole system and we can feel positive and enriched. When we become balanced, we experience the healing that allows us to also act to the world in a kind, intelligent manner.

Humans and nature: we are one

There are direct implications for ecological ethics throughout the Buddha's teachings. There is a holism. The Buddha emphasised the interdependence of human and non-human life, the importance of the ecosystem and of natural processes. By rejecting the concept of a substantial 'self', and comprehension of the interdependency of all phenomena, the importance of the distinction we usually make between ourselves and other living beings lessens. Such an attitude views the world as a vast interdependent field, in which no life form, no matter how insignificant it may seem, is an outsider. There is a state of connectedness and interdependence of all phenomena.

The significant realisation that there is no independent 'self' – that the perception of 'self', of 'me', of 'mine' is only an egotistical representation, therefore leads every person to inter-dependently co-exist. Undercutting the usual ignorant anthropomorphic view of the validity of the successful domination and control of the environment by humans, naturalist Aldo Leopold claimed that, '*The biotic (life factor) mechanism is so complex that its working may never be fully understood.*'[4]. There is a deeper ecology that recognises the inherent worth of other beings aside from their utility. Another writer who expressed a similar deep view of ecology was R.G.H. Siu:

> '*The term Ecology, as used locally, does not have the connotation of the "environment" as used in America. There is no separation of man and his environment; rather there is a fusion of man and his environment. Ecology represents the study of the ecological entity as a whole. When a given ecological complex appears unfavourable from the standpoint of man, for example, he does not have a prior claim to adjustment on the part of the other elements of the complex. The others have just as much "right" to demand modification of his behaviour as he has on theirs. All are one in Nature. There is an appreciation of this Oneness and the delicate interrelationships of its diffusions.*'[5]

So humans are not an isolated island in a sea of existence, but rather their being is shared ultimately with all. This becomes a clear and apparent relationship with all existence through the Buddha's teaching of anatta.

Bibliography

1.   Gabora, L. & Aerts, D. (2005). Distilling the Essence of an Evolutionary Process and Implications for a Formal Description of Culture. In: Proceedings of the Center for Human Evolution Workshop #4: Cultural Evolution (W. Kistler, Ed.). Foundation for the Future, Seattle WA.

2.   de Silva, L. (2013). One Foot in the World: Buddhist Approaches to Present-day Problems. Access to Insight (Legacy edition). Retrieved from http://www.accesstoinsight.org/lib/authors/desilva/wheel337.html

3.   Kalupahana, D. J. (1987). The Principles of Buddhist Psychology. SUNY Series in Buddhist Studies. State University of New York Press.

4.   Leopold, A. (1979). Some Fundamentals of Conservation in the Southwest. Environmental Ethics, 1(2), 131-141.

5.   5 Siu, R. G. H. (2001). The Land of Keikitran and Eleevan. Hats off Books.

25

Closing Thoughts

A key aim of writing this book has been to show how the Buddha's teaching of 'no-self' has support and important implications in not only the theory but also practice of modern psychology. As we have seen, recent developments in psychological research have been an embracing and strengthening of the 'self' concept. Since the study of psychology is enmeshed in the Western culture, not only has the importance, independence and superiority of 'self' been enhanced, but also therefore, the dualistic, static and alienated position of humans in regard to the rest of existence. There is a desire to escape inner conflict through harmony in static form but this is not possible. Unwittingly, with an aggrandisement of the 'self' comes inherent anxiety and depression. For with the continual propping up of an abstraction that is by its nature impermanent, ever prone to change, challenge and elimination, one is constantly insecure, anxious and unstable. However, the difficulty goes beyond the making real an ideal, an abstraction but with a belief in the substantiality, permanence of the abstraction, there is the ignorance that it needs to be satisfied through the basic senses. Happiness becomes equated with a satisfaction of experiencing the 'self' – consuming, clinging to what the 'self' identifies as 'likes' and averting what it 'dislikes'.

Whilst in the biological, evolutionary sense this has an advantage, when it comes to the 'self' it can proliferate into the absurdity of the glorification of narcissism.

So while modern psychology is more and more coming to formulate the 'self' as an on-going narrative, a construction, and abstraction, there hasn't been the next logical shift to that which the Buddha offered over two thousand years ago – that is, the idea that there is no substantial 'self'. Once that shift occurs, there is an important and dramatic alteration is a person's personality configuration. As has been described frequently, the angst or anguish often associated with the belief and inflation of the 'self' disappears with the insight of the illusionary nature of 'self', with the attendant bliss and liberation. As a person's state of mind changes, so does their interaction with other people, living beings and the world. In following the Buddha's path to reclaim the 'original mind', we progressively become less susceptible to emotional swings; become more calm, realistic, kind, cognitively flexible and creative. We respect and nurture our body more as well as better understand the interdependence of all existence. We become more humble knowing that 'my' wants, perception and opinion are based on an inherently narrow subjective view, and that the more we try to satisfy that very small piece of the pie which is the 'I', the more we become alienated from the rest of the world, resulting in increasing loneliness and isolation.

These existential consequences of a belief in a substantial 'self' cannot be 'cured' or ameliorated by making the 'self' stronger, more resilient, more adaptable, more egotistic; nor by making the 'self' more compliant, passive and docile. The out for this existential or distressing human condition is to become wise and understand the illusion of the belief of 'self' as a permanent static entity. Only through the disengaging processes provided by the therapy of the Buddha can we reach the mental states that allow us to see beyond the societal and cultural norms and habits that create for us the immature, conceited perspective that ultimately creates our suffering. The tragedy of this situation is that our culture and history create a conceptual box that imprisons us into believing this is the only reality. We judge and measure our happiness and actions based on our narrow egocentric definition of reality as seen through the schemata of the substantial abstracted notion of 'self'. Leaving us trapped in our own illusions, believing them to be true. We are caught in a bad dream with little possibility of being Awakened.

Yet, it is possible to see the deception or misunderstanding for what it is. The Buddha Awakened, he awoke from the deception like a person understanding the magician's trick and was no longer fooled by appearances. Out of compassion he reflected on what he had learned and decided to teach this to others so they would no longer be deceived also. This is the correct direction for modern psychology. Our future social development is inseparable from our mental development. It is a doctrine based on pragmatics and empirical verification. It is rooted in a holistic perspective which understands the interdependence and hierarchical nature of existence. The Buddha's doctrine recognises the importance of the environmental impact on the body and the need for basic sustaining environmental supports for sentient beings. It advocates a mutually supportive interaction of society and the environment as well as society and human beings. It looks first to the conditions to help create and support wholesome active living, contentment, healthy bodies and purified cognitive states.

As the background of emptiness highlights the foreground of ego activity, the relationship with the body dramatically changes. No longer is the body bullied by the 'self' and created or used in the service of narcissism or hedonistic excess. Rather, the body becomes the home of experience. The body becomes intimately known and respected. It is the all of our existence. It is the foundation of our experience. With the dethroning of the 'self' as the primary mover of our life, the body becomes the clear innovator and generator of most of how and what we experience, feel and do. As a result, our focus changes to being much more grounded in the present, keeping our awareness in control of how we respond the dynamic changing experiences that we have. This is the correct Buddhist relationship between body and awareness. Our mindfulness with equanimity controls our constant interaction with the inner and outer stimulations, while our body is the field force that creates a functional balance attempting to maintain the survival of our organism.

The Buddha gave us pragmatic and functional guidelines to envelop and follow to best serve our being throughout life, and therefore end our suffering. That includes a mature and realistic attitude and appraisal of the travails that living provides and of the final outcome – death. Much of the suffering we experience in our life is created by an inflation of the importance of the 'self' and the subjugation of the body. With the appropriate understanding and attitude toward the factiousness of 'self', a grounding in the body is achieved, the harmful excesses and abuse that is often continuously perpetrated on the body, such as smoking, alcohol or drug abuse, excessive or under-eating, and physically punishing behaviours, ends, and the harmonious state that the body always attempts to create is respected. Within a harmonious body, the emotions and mental state are much better supported to be enlivened, energetic and happy. We can see therefore, that the Buddha's teachings offer a programme that is comprehensive and adaptable to all conditions found on this earth.

May all be well and happy!

Appendix A

Explanation of the effects of stress on the different systems of the human body

Musculoskeletal System

When the body is stressed, muscles tense up. Muscle tension is the body's way of guarding against injury and pain. Chronic stress causes the muscles in the body to be in a more or less constant state of guardedness, which may trigger other reactions of the body and even promote stress-related disorders. For example, both tension-type headache and migraine headache are associated with chronic muscle tension in the area of the shoulders, neck and head.

Respiratory System

Stress can make you breathe harder and more rapidly, which can actually trigger asthma attacks or hyperventilation, even initiating a panic attack.

Cardiovascular System

The heart and blood vessels work together in providing nourishment and oxygen to all tissues of the body. These two elements are also coordinated in the body's response to stress. Acute stress causes an increase in heart rate and stronger contractions of the heart muscle, with the stress hormones – adrenaline, noradrenaline and cortisol – acting as messengers for these effects. In addition, the blood vessels and the heart dilate, enabling an increased volume of blood to be pumped around the body and elevating blood pressure. This is known as the 'fight or flight' response. Once the acute stress episode has passed, the body returns to its normal state. Chronic stress results in a continual increase in heart rate elevated levels of stress hormones and of blood pressure. This can take a toll on the body and increase the risk for heart attack or stroke as well as contribute to inflammation in the circulatory system, particularly in the coronary arteries.

Endocrine System

When the body is stressed, the hypothalamus signals to the autonomic nervous system and the pituitary gland to produce epinephrine and cortisol, sometimes called the 'stress hormones'.

Adrenal Glands

Stress signals from the hypothalamus cause the adrenal cortex to produce cortisol and the adrenal medulla to produce epinephrine. This starts the process that gives your body the energy to run from danger.

Liver

When cortisol and epinephrine are released, the liver produces more glucose, a blood sugar that would give you the energy for 'fight or flight' in an emergency. If the extra energy is not used then the body is able to reabsorb the blood sugar, even if you're stressed again and again. But for some people that extra blood sugar can result in the development of type 2 diabetes.

Gastrointestinal System

Oesophagus

When stressed, you may eat much more or much less than you usually do. If you eat more or different foods, or increase your use of alcohol or tobacco, you can experience heartburn or acid reflux. Stress or exhaustion can also increase the severity of heartburn pain.

Stomach

In stressful situations, the brain becomes more alert to sensations in your stomach. Your stomach can react with 'butterflies', nausea or pain. You may vomit if the stress is severe enough. And, if the stress becomes chronic, the stomach is at increased risk from developing ulcers.

Bowel

Stress can affect digestion and what nutrients your intestines absorb. It can also affect how fast food moves through your body, leading to diarrhoea or constipation.

Nervous System

The nervous system has several divisions: the central nervous system (CNS) comprising the brain and spinal cord, and the peripheral nervous system (PNS), which includes the autonomic and somatic nervous systems. The autonomic nervous system (ANS) has a direct role in physical response to stress and is divided into the sympathetic nervous system (SNS), and the parasympathetic nervous system (PNS). When the body is stressed the body shifts all of its energy resources toward 'fight or flight'. The SNS signals to the adrenal glands to release adrenalin and cortisol. Once the acute crisis is over, the body usually returns to the unstressed state. Chronic stress is detrimental to the body via the effects that continuous activation of the nervous system does to other bodily systems.

Male Reproductive System

In the male anatomy, the autonomic nervous system, produces testosterone and activates the SNS, which stimulates arousal. The excessive amounts of cortisol released when stressed can affect the normal biochemical functioning of the male reproductive system. Chronic stress can affect testosterone production, sperm production and maturation, and even cause erectile dysfunction or impotence.

Female Reproductive System

Menstruation

High levels of stress may be associated with absent or irregular menstrual cycles, more painful periods and changes in the length of cycles.

Premenstrual Syndrome

Stress may make premenstrual symptoms worse or more difficult to cope with Symptoms may include cramping, fluid retention and bloating, negative moods and mood swings.

Menopause

As menopause approaches, hormone levels fluctuate rapidly. These changes are associated with anxiety, mood swings and feelings of distress. Thus menopause can be a stressful in and of itself. Some of the physical changes associated with menopause, especially hot flushes, can be difficult to cope with. Furthermore, emotional distress may cause the physical symptoms to be worse. For example, women who are more anxious may experience an increased number of hot flashes and/or more severe or intense hot flushes.

Appendix B

Special experiences

The Buddha talked about 'special experiences', and they are often reported by people who have meditated. In the suttas, there are six types of super-knowledge – the exercise of psychic powers, the divine ear, the ability to read the minds of others, recollection of past lives, knowledge of the death and rebirth of beings, and knowledge of final liberation. Any of these may only be achieved by highly advanced practitioners of meditation. They occur when the factors are right, and they have no special significance. These experiences are not indicative either of Enlightenment or of progress towards Enlightenment, since they are not necessarily associated with the Right Knowledge that leads to Enlightenment. The correct attitude towards them as they occur is simply to observe them. These experiences are like many others in meditation. The prescribed approach is just be mindful that they are occurring, without attaching any particular significance to them, and let them go when they pass.

CPSIA information can be obtained at www.ICGtesting.com
Printed in the USA
BVOW06s1028170516

448402BV00008B/21/P

9 781909 985193